T0301253

Visual Branding

Visual Branding

A Rhetorical and Historical Analysis

Edward F. McQuarrie

Professor Emeritus, Santa Clara University, USA

Barbara J. Phillips

Rawlco Scholar in Advertising and Professor of Marketing, University of Saskatchewan, Canada

Edward Elgar
PUBLISHING

Cheltenham, UK • Northampton, MA, USA

Published by
Edward Elgar Publishing Limited
The Lypiatts
15 Lansdown Road
Cheltenham
Glos GL50 2JA
UK

Edward Elgar Publishing, Inc.
William Pratt House
9 Dewey Court
Northampton
Massachusetts 01060
USA

A catalogue record for this book
is available from the British Library

Library of Congress Control Number: 2016949928

This book is available electronically in the **Elgar**online
Business subject collection
DOI 10.4337/9781785365423

ISBN 978 1 78536 541 6 (cased)
ISBN 978 1 78536 542 3 (eBook)

Typeset by Servis Filmsetting Ltd, Stockport, Cheshire
Printed and bound by CPI Group (UK) Ltd, Croydon, CR0 4YY

Contents

Figures

Web-archived figures

These figures can be viewed at https://www.e-elgar.com/visual-branding-companion-site.

Tables

Boxes

Acknowledgments

McQuarrie thanks his editor at Edward Elgar Publishing, Alan Sturm, for taking another chance on him before the first wager was complete. He is grateful to Santa Clara University for all its support, financial and otherwise, which made this project possible. He acknowledges how the Web eased his access to old magazines, contemporary brand marks, and all manner of historical data. Technology has speeded up and made more pleasant scholarly efforts that were once hard and grinding. And last, McQuarrie wants to celebrate his past two decades of collaboration with Barb Phillips.

Phillips thanks Ed McQuarrie for a fabulous 20 years of research collaboration. She is also grateful to Rawlco Radio for financially supporting her scholarship, both on radio and on advertising more generally.

Introduction

Today psychology dominates the study of visual branding. But the concepts that underwrite psychological research cast a veil over brands, masking what brands have learned to do. In this book we lift the blindfold by means of rhetorical and historical analyses. Visual branding needs to move beyond purely psychological accounts.

RHETORICAL VERSUS PSYCHOLOGICAL ANALYSIS

Consider the Tide ad in Figure 0.1, next page. Psychology explains that laundry detergent is a low-involvement product: consumers will minimize their investment in deciding which brand to buy. Hence, ads for detergent will only be peripherally attended, and heuristically processed. A consumer may enjoy the pretty colors of the ad for a fleeting moment, and then attach a positive feeling to the Tide brand. The large number of days mentioned in the caption will be heuristically processed as an extreme value, and nudge up consumer perceptions of Tide's effectiveness.[1]

Rhetoricians approach this Tide ad differently. We see a complex visual metaphor that relates Tide to a stained glass window. Such a window will project a beautiful array of colors for centuries, which suggests that Tide can protect colors on clothing for a very long time. Stained glass, along with the Biblical reference ("on the seventh day He rested"), call to mind the authority of scripture and church. The consumer is invited to believe in Tide, to have faith in its capabilities and efficacy.

The historically aware rhetorician also absorbs clues that date this ad to the twenty-first century and not any earlier era. We can easily date the ad by noting that: (1) the brand name and logo appear only on the package; (2) the brand name is emblazoned on a shield which merges into the remainder of the package design; (3) the picture bleeds to the margins of the page; (4) the picture has been constructed in software rather than photographed in a studio; (5) the picture takes over the entire ad, so that words are inscribed on it; and finally (6) by the brevity of the copy and its subservience to the picture. It was not possible to produce such an ad 100 years ago. It was borderline feasible 50 years ago. Today such visually accomplished ads are commonplace.

1

Figure 0.1   Contemporary ad for Tide detergent

The rhetorician sees the consumer as a culturally and historically located creature. Rhetoricians also see consumers as capable: able to draw a wealth of inferences from a picture. And rhetoricians see advertisers and brand managers as clever: able to visually guide the consumer toward favorable inferences about the brand without ever making an explicit verbal claim which could be subjected to criticism, and dismissed as incredible. Finally, the historically minded rhetorician asserts that both consumers' facility and advertisers' ability emerged in history.

ADVERTISING AT THE JUNCTURE OF DISCIPLINES

Scholars in the humanities also claim to know advertising. As we step away from the business disciplines and out of the shadow of psychology, toward aesthetics, design, history, and literature, rhetoric transforms into a familiar and welcome notion, but also grows slippery and indistinct; it becomes a Humpty Dumpty word, one that means whatever the user wants. Humanities scholars need to hear that we will apply classical rhetoric to illumine visual branding.

Classical rhetoric is the original rhetoric of Greece and Rome. One central idea animates classical rhetoric: that in any persuasive situation, there can be found a short list of devices able to accomplish the rhetor's purpose. There are only a few routes to exhort a crowd to war. There are only so many ways to eulogize a dead hero. Only a few gambits can persuade a jury to acquit. That's what Aristotle meant when he defined rhetorical skill as the "ability, in each particular case, to see the available means of persuasion" (Aristotle *Rhetoric* I.1.2, Kennedy 37). The means can be grasped because they are small in number; the list is short.[2]

There is nothing novel about treating advertising as the rhetoric of a consumer society; that point has been tossed about a thousand times. But in most such claims, rhetoric is only a catchphrase, cueing the vague notion that a grab bag of tricks can be found out. Labeling advertising as applied rhetoric sounds grander than stating "today commercial persuasion is one common example of persuasion." Only when we fix the meaning of rhetoric, by specifying classical rhetoric, does the assertion gain traction. From an Aristotelian stance, to claim that there is a rhetoric of visual branding translates to: "there are only six types of brand logos," or "all the pictures that might promote a brand can be grouped into a dozen categories."

To apply classical rhetoric to visual branding violates deeply held tenets of psychology. Psychologists know that an advertisement, when viewed by a consumer, is naught but a stimulus. Like any visual stimulus, it can be arrayed in an N-dimensional conceptual space, where each dimension indexes a property shared to some degree by all visual stimuli.[3] Each dimension or property – how vivid, concrete, or complex the stimulus – permits of infinite gradation. Just as the deep structure of Chomsky's grammar enables us to construct an infinite number of sentences, so also, assumes the psychologist, must there be an infinite variety of persuasive stimuli. Viewed from the standpoint of psychology, only a Cartesian model, a coordinate geometry of infinite gradations, can bring order to this plethora. The psychologist knows that classical rhetoric must be mistaken in its search for distinct types or gambits. Infinite must trump discrete.

Psychology dominates discussions of branding in scholarly journals in marketing, advertising, and consumer research. Rhetorical perspectives remain rare. Today it is difficult for a scholar in the business disciplines to escape the root psychological mindset: stimulus → response. The psychologist knows that to study brand logos, you first construct a set of graphic designs with carefully varied stimulus properties, then expose these logo stimuli to consumers, who respond on rating scales.[4] Statistical analyses of these stimulus–response pairings reveal which logo properties influence which consumer responses. How else to gain knowledge of visual branding?

We'd ask the reader coming from a business discipline to be honest with yourself: does not that experimental and psychological account sound appealing? What other knowledge of brand logos could there be? If not backed up by experiment, and theorized in terms of underlying universals, can any alternative method even claim to give knowledge? Thus does psychology tighten its grip: don't you brand managers want to be scientific?

Historians will respond vigorously: of course there are alternative paths to knowledge! Stimulus and response experiments, however powerful, do not exhaust the possibilities. Although historians cannot perform experiments, we commit no solecism to speak of historical knowledge. Except, alas, that none of the major marketing, advertising, and consumer journals publish much historical work either.[5] We may have knowledge of history, yes; but is this scientific knowledge, knowledge that could yield theoretical advances? Scientific and theoretical knowledge are what the major marketing, advertising, and consumer journals aspire to produce. Longitudinal content analyses – mathematized data examined over time – may appear in these journals; but history, of the kind seen in Marchand's (1985) book, is notable by its absence.

Scientific psychology is as resolutely anti-history as it is anti-rhetoric. Note how we could slip in the statement that "consumers" would rate the logo stimuli. We did not have to be precise, or indicate that we meant "returning veterans attending college on the GI Bill in 1953," or "white, upper-middle-class American students, all aged 20–22 when the research was conducted, whose median SAT score was at the 90th percentile." From a psychological perspective, just as any stimulus can be termed an ad, any member of *Homo sapiens*, in any setting, can be called a consumer. Theoretical knowledge strives to be universal. The goal in psychology is not to study affluent and academically accomplished American college students; it is to produce universal knowledge. And that's why – wait for it – consumer psychologists based in the USA use only smart affluent college students in their experiments.[6] The goal of a scientific psychology is to identify processes which are universal across *Homo sapiens*. Therefore, any convenient supply of *Homo sapiens* will do when conducting an experiment.

Our sarcasm is fueled by bitter experience. Psychological research strives to be timeless.[7] It intends to produce universal and enduring theoretical findings. That makes it okay to use the narrowest sample and the most restricted and artificial stimuli. The protestation by psychologists: we're not studying these students or any one real brand, but universal truths, of which these handy consumers and artificial brands are but instances, on a par with any other instance. Got it? The narrower the sample and more artificial the stimuli, the greater the generalizability of the findings. By studying no particular consumer or brand, general truths, applicable to all consumers and brands, emerge more clearly.[8]

Does that stance leave you shaking your head? Then you may be receptive to this historical and rhetorical analysis of visual branding. You will find no factor analyses of seven-point rating scales here, and no artificial brands. We examine real ads sampled from over a century, real brand logos as these morph over time, and long-term trends in the technological and economic substrate on which brand advertising rests.

A third shortcoming of psychology, as pursued in consumer and social psychological experiments: it is besotted with words. *Logos* dominates *eidos*. If you look over the experiments published in the *Journal of Consumer Research*, the *Journal of Consumer Psychology*, and the *Journal of Advertising* – journals that we've read, reviewed for, and published in for decades – you will chiefly find words manipulated, not imagery. There are exceptions.[9] But the vast majority of psychological studies of consumer persuasion create their experimental designs by varying words in either the instructions or the ad stimulus. The consumer is approached as a careful reader of prose. Would the results generalize to subjects who had not spent the entirety of their young lives studying written instructions in school, and who had not been selected to be above the 90th percentile for scholastic aptitude? Might these research designs reflect the verbal proclivities of the professors who devise them, more than the distinctive features of advertising and branding? Good questions.

There's nothing wrong or trivial about studying verbal persuasion. Outside of advertising and branding, a great deal of everyday persuasion proceeds verbally. But brand advertising is distinguished, among all other persuasive activities today, and as compared to past attempts at persuasion down through the millennia, by its reliance on pictures and graphic design. Everyone knows that advertising accounts for a large chunk of the persuasive activity that occurs each day in America. Not everyone realizes that American print advertising has grown more visual, more pictorial, every decade for the past century.[10] Magazine ads from after 2000 are measurably more pictorial than ads from as recently as the 1980s, which are more visual than those from the 1950s. Not only are pictures bigger, and more intensively crafted, but words occupy less and less of the ad, becoming fewer and fewer in number. Ads from the 1920s read like tomes.

Scholars are free to study whatever they want; but it seems silly when an entire discipline, self-identified as responsible for advancing knowledge of advertising and branding, persists in constructing verbal experiments when the chosen topic provides a privileged and unique opportunity to study pictorial persuasion. Yes, words do persuade. Fine; so study radio commercials, or voter pamphlets, or the pitches of used car salesmen. The opportunity posed by print ads, and the branding that occurs there, is to study how pictures persuade.

Finally, psychology is not the only competitor of rhetoric. The discipline of semiotics also lays claim to visual branding. But rhetoric is not semiotics. Alas, if you are in business, or reading this in a business school, both semiotics and rhetoric may sound equally fusty and obscure. For those interested, we lay out the differences in Box 0.1.

DEFINITIONS AND SCOPE

Visual

Visual branding includes any effort to identify and promote a brand using pictures, visual elements, or visual arrangements. These last two vaguer categories require expansion. Color provides a good example of a visual element. There does not have to be a picture for color to be present and used in branding; visual elements are distinct from pictures. Typeface is another example of a visual element, as are spokes-characters, such as Tony the Tiger for Kellogg's. The configuration of visual and verbal elements in a brand's trademark is an example of a visual arrangement used to brand.

Pictures vary as to content and style. In terms of content, pictures may be more or less representational, and may depict people, scenes, objects, and much else. We will touch on pictorial content in this book, but it is not central to our aims. The problem: there is no short list of pictorial content. That makes pictorial content refractory to rhetorical analysis. There are short lists of pictorial styles and of stylistic devices in pictures; hence, a rhetorical analysis of pictures will gravitate toward a focus on style. Pictorial content is also problematic because it seduces: the tendency is to climb through the pictorial window, to deal with the objects behind, and then quickly move on to the social and cultural matrix from which the ad emerged.[11] This distracts from inquiry into the branding performed by the ad. Ads may be valuable to social and cultural historians, but this book is not a social or cultural history. We study the history of visual branding by means of the stylistic devices deployed in ads.

A final note on scope: television commercials are visual, and more: the pictures move and make sounds, as do web animations and videos. But the history of visual branding in these media is shorter; much shorter, in the case of animated web ads. And sampling is much harder to pull off. The same concerns apply to product packaging.[12] Although visual branding occurs on television and the web and on packaging (and in contests and sponsorships and specialty advertising giveaways), within the limits of a book-length treatment we must stick to print advertising, and the pictures, elements, and arrangements that occur there. And among print media, magazines, more than newspapers or billboards, give access to the fullest panoply of techniques and technological capabilities. In short, we examine visual branding as it has been pursued in magazine advertisements from the beginning of the twentieth century down to the present.

Brand

Ah, but what is a brand? In mundane terms, a brand is a corporate asset, like a patent or other piece of intellectual property.[13] In concrete terms, a brand is an identifier attached to products and services; it names the good offered for sale. A brand is not to be confused with the corporate entity that currently owns it; we collectively label that enterprise and its employees as the advertiser in some contexts, and in others, as brand management. The brand is not its owner.

But none of these definitions take us far. Brands are incorporeal entities that exist independently of their owners and of the goods that they name. Brands exist and are developed primarily in discourse. Brands are cultural things. Although incorporeal by nature, brands, like souls, are multiply embodied. Brands can be made concrete and present as objects, as names, and as visual representations. Brands are complex signs. But none of its representations can ever be "the" brand.

Confused? Sorry, it can't be helped. Brands are special.[14] Brands have analogues, but brands and branding are cultural things unique to late capitalist social arrangements. There were no brands in Renaissance Italy, or

BOX 0.1   SEMIOTICS VERSUS RHETORIC

Rhetoric? Semiotics? What's the difference? Viewed from a mainstream, psychological standpoint, both disciplines sound equally marginal or on the fringe. This box sketches a contrast, the better to position the rhetorical approach to advertising.

Semiotics is much more general than rhetoric. Anything that can function as a sign – anything that can stand for something to somebody – is fair game for semiotics. Neither words nor conventional symbols are necessary for the sign-function to operate. Signs are everywhere. Some semioticians, imperialistic in spirit, would subsume art, language, literature, philosophy, and any other arena where meanings operate, making semiotics the master human science.

Semioticians were among the first to examine how pictures, and visual elements within pictures, could function as signs. If only because linguistics had already secured its position in the universities, semioticians have been wont to study what linguists do not and will not consider: signs not carried by words. Hence, anyone interested in visual branding needs to come to terms with semiotics; it has a historically well-situated claim to supply the fundamental concepts for understanding how visual branding works.

Rhetoric is much less general than semiotics; it could even be described as a derivative, tertiary discipline. The writ of rhetoric is confined to the public address that calls an audience to action. In Greece and Rome, this meant either an appeal to a jury, or a speech exhorting citizens, or a paean coaxing an emotional response. The first two applications survive essentially intact in the contemporary world: we still have juries, and citizens still vote. The paean seldom occurs any longer in traditional form (for example, funeral orations are rare), but has been replaced, and greatly expanded as a share of discourse, in the arena of brand advertising.

All three elements are important for defining the scope of rhetoric. Firstly, private settings are not appropriate venues for rhetoric. The man who applies rhetoric at the family dinner table is a curious sort of humbug. In everyday life we have many occasions to persuade, but rhetoric cannot help us here. Use of rhetoric on family members would be unlawful force. Secondly, rhetoric also presumes an audience: a large number of individuals who bear an arm's-length relationship to the rhetor. When we speak to one person or a few people in private, we may coax, cajole, plead, or implore, but we do not have much opportunity to apply rhetoric. Thirdly, rhetoric is not about explaining, teaching, discussing, conversing, or any of the myriad other uses to which signs can be put. Rhetoric is laser-focused on getting members of an audience at arm's length to do something the rhetor wants them to do. Rhetoric is instrumental communication. It falls a vast distance away from poetry, art, or any other expressive, self-focused use of signs. Rhetoric only applies to motivated sign use. The rhetor is an interested party who attempts to move an audience.

Two things should be clear from the contrast thus far: semiotics is a much more fundamental and general discipline; but rhetoric maps much more tightly onto the advertising enterprise. Accordingly, semiotics suffers from a version of the failing that plagues psychology: because semiotics aspires to embrace all forms of sign use whatsoever, semioticians tend not to study any one domain of sign use in depth.

That baleful urge toward universality drives many semiotic accounts deep down to the micro-operations whereby a sign stands for something, since only these micro-operations are truly universal across all the human contexts in which signs appear. In the visual sphere, this leads to long disquisitions about the meaning of a curved line or a camera angle, and disputes about what rule allowed us to infer "stained glass" from the Tide ad in Figure 0.1. Often the semiotician never makes it up to the level of the whole page, replete with verbal text, pictures, and brand markings tangled together, where the rhetorician plies his trade.

A second vice of semiotics, historically accidental but deeply woven into the fabric of its discourse, is the drive to treat pictures as a language. One sees this particularly in Continental semiotics, where de Saussure, a linguist, was the father of the discipline. This urge leads to loose talk about the grammar of pictures, or the codes in the ad. We depart from semiotics in denying that pictures can be a language. Visual elements conform to nothing so precise as a code. Computers run on code. Humans draw inferences. The advantage of rhetoric is that it steers clear of these commitments and encumbrances, free to be omnivorous about what persuades, and how, subject only to a ruthless pragmatism.

the Roman Empire. There were no brands before capitalism reconfigured the world. Brands are new, as new as the Industrial Revolution and mass markets and media.

A brand is like a nation, which has a flag, a seal, and many other signs, but which is not its flag, or its seal, or any of its representations. A brand is protean, like a symbol, in being able to generate meanings without being tied to any single one. There's nothing novel about symbols, which have existed throughout human history, and maybe before.[15] But brands differ from other symbols, most of which cannot be owned, nor sold, nor bought. Brands are unique to our culture, the culture of late capitalism, when the market rules and so much of everyday life revolves around selling while at work, and buying when not working.

To be a cultural thing means to exist primarily in the minds of the people who participate in the surrounding culture. Cultural things are created and renewed in discourse and practices. Any cultural thing will be manifest in many representations, no one of which exhausts the meaning of that cultural thing, but each instance of which pushes and tugs at the overall gestalt. Brand meaning is fluid, sometimes viscous, sometimes tumbling downslope. Brands aren't like numerals, or signs for mathematical operations; a brand's meaning is loosely bound and malleable. It mutates and drifts; it has a topology, not a shape. A famous example: until the 1950s, Marlboro was a cigarette bought mostly by women.

A brand does not change its name; that's as meaningless as the sentence, "its name was changed to its name." The phonemes stay, but the meaning of those phonemes may change. By contrast, brands do change their visual representations. The same name puts on different clothes. And as clothes make the man, when its visual representation changes, the meaning of the brand may change, drift, or evolve as well. Brands are thrown, as Heidegger might have said: they are historical entities rather than Platonic forms.

The historical and rhetorical challenge is to take the measure of change in brands, and in branding. Few brands endure as radical a makeover as Marlboro; but almost no brand stays frozen in its original visual representation. Think about how Betty Crocker has changed. Quick now: does that sentence refer to the brand or the spokes-character? The phonemes and even the spelling are unchanged; and the corporate ownership (General Mills) has remained constant.[16] But the Betty Crocker who smiles from a package or ad today doesn't look much like the matron who looked out from an ad in the 1920s.[17] Yet, she had that same name. And the brand seeks roughly the same demographic, now as then. It is one brand in history: there has to be some overlap in what that matron meant, to the 1920s lady of the house, and what that dimpled, smiling, younger woman, who looks out from a 2015 picture, means to today's homemaker. And yet, today's female head of household, however invariant her demographic, does not have the same cultural identity, as the woman who shopped for and bought Betty Crocker in 1925.

Of one thing we may be sure. If Betty Crocker, the brand, were still to use the 1920s or 1930s or 1950s image of Betty Crocker the spokes-character in its 2015 visual branding, the brand would acquire a different meaning in the eyes of today's consumer than it now has. But that altered meaning would not be the same meaning as those earlier consumers derived from viewing that exact same image.

Cultural meanings, in technologically advanced late capitalist societies, are inherently unstable. Brands navigate these shifting shoals. An unsmiling older woman, of severe countenance, does not mean the same thing to the American female consumer of 2015, as that image meant when that consumer's grandmother was young. Betty Crocker must be re-imagined, over and over.

Sometimes brands have to change their visual representation to keep their brand meaning steady. Sometimes brands have to change their meaning in order to seize market opportunities or to maintain their market position; then their visual representations must change apace. It may even be that visual representations have to change continually if the brand is to be kept fresh. This dynamic is even more visible in ad executions than in slow-to-change elements such as spokes-character and trademark. But each change in visual representation has the potential to feed back into the brand, and change what the brand means; which is to change the brand, which is only its ensemble of meanings.

You may not be accustomed to reading historical musings about branding. Business journals have no time for such reflections; after all, where's the (psychological) theory? It is radical to view brands as historical creatures. This raises a methodological question. If real brands are historically situated entities, can brands and brandedness be replicated artificially? Can a stimulus prompt, ginned up in the laboratory, and exposed to a college student rather than a purchaser, reproduce what took a firm decades and billions of dollars to forge out in the world? These questions have been avoided for too long, but are crucial for assessing the contribution of psychological research to branding.

Historical phenomena repay historical inquiry: brands need to be studied in the field, and over long periods of time. Our goal is to help the reader see branding afresh by means of rhetorical and historical analyses. We want to unfreeze the knee-jerk understanding of ads as "visual stimuli," "processed," by "consumers." The actions of branding and advertising produce cultural artifacts, the crafted and crafty designs of culturally situated men and women, aimed at a mass of other cultural beings, with the hope of provoking a desired response, which may be far more subtle than "After seeing that ad, I'd now give this brand a 6 on that seven-point scale."

Withal, rhetoricians respect the limits of their discipline. Many human responses do belong to psychology, and are best approached using psychological concepts and theories. The rhetorician doesn't know anything about how to connect the mental responses to the ad occurring at home, to subsequent action in the store. That is an intra-psychic matter. Other human responses belong to anthropology, or sociology, or to other disciplines concerned with the study of cultural things that do not dwell solely within the individual mind. But the designs themselves, these acts of visual branding to which consumers psychologically respond, are not stimuli and do not belong to psychology. Branding is a historically situated rhetorical enterprise whose structures have not yet been glimpsed, and whose divagations have yet to be traced.

The rhetorician sees an advantage to studying brands. We know what the brand sponsor seeks to accomplish: sell goods for profit. No one knows what the purpose of literature is, or whether art has one purpose or many. That uncertainty complicates rhetorical analysis in those spheres. Although a rhetorical analysis of brand advertising will mostly produce findings limited to that sphere, the clarity of purpose in branding may yield new insights into rhetoric itself. Many contemporary attempts to apply classical rhetoric are resuscitations: efforts to port the terminology of Greek and Roman times into the present, and to effect a wholesale carry-over of old knowledge treated as established and perfected. We lack that antiquarian passion. We think rhetoric can be like science, a dynamic discipline which can forge new knowledge when confronted with new problems. The study of branding offers to cash out that promise.

Visual Branding

To switch to the verb shifts the focus of inquiry: how are brands built, improved, expanded, updated, or refurbished? These verbs drawn from the building trades provide a salutary reminder: brands are property. Key to branding is ownership. The rhetorical criterion for branding, more especially visual branding, is captured in the neologism "ownability," which we first encountered while interviewing graphic designers employed by ad agencies.[18] Any picture, visual element, or visual arrangement that can be owned can build a brand; and any change to any of these may potentially remodel the brand.

The United States, beginning over a century ago, has elaborated a system of law and regulation that confers extensive property rights on brands, as have other nations. Put another way, because a brand is like a symbol, the limit on what can belong to the brand is undefined, albeit known to be of considerable extent. The boundary on what can be claimed, on what belongs to the brand, is worked out in the courts, and evolves with case law. Much, much more than the name and trademark may be owned; trade dress is the more comprehensive term. In the Epilogue we review some of the conceptual issues that arise at the boundary of what belongs to a brand.

The main thrust of the book, the historical tale, concerns advertisers discovering how to brand visually. Among the great benefits of looking at old magazine ads – the real thing, held in the hand, even as these crumble and smell of the basement – is to discover how rudimentary, how hit-and-miss, were some of those initial efforts at branding. The fitful, haphazard quality is most apparent in the visuals. By contrast, early copywriters had millennia of experience on which to draw in crafting the verbal spiel.[19] And copywriters had news to share: many of the products were innovations, as exciting to our grandparents as a new iPhone today. There was plenty to say about brands, and the writer of paeans had thousands of years of expertise on which to call.

In 1900, there was no color photography. Typeface had only begun to be liberated from lead type. Color printing of any kind was rare and expensive. There was a long history of art, engraving, and iconography, but these designs had never concerned mere things, material goods, mundane conveniences. Visual persuasion had a history, but only in traditional contexts, to celebrate church, king, and noble.[20] There were few precedents for crafting a visual presentation of a new, mundane object, or of how to vary these presentations so that they could appear month after month and remain fresh while not drifting or veering in signification. And the technology for creating visuals kept changing, becoming more powerful and offering ever more control. The early brand advertisers, they didn't quite know what they were doing. Their efforts at visual branding were tentative and untutored.

Branding developed in history, and advertisers got better at branding as generation of graphic designers succeeded generation, and as more powerful tools became available. For the student of rhetoric, to examine brand advertising in the early 1900s is to be a fly on the wall in ancient Syracuse, watching trial after trial on the agora, as the first Greek rhetoricians assembled their art.[21] To look at ads from the 1950s and 1980s is to sit at the knee of Shakespeare and his cohort, as medieval rhetoricians reshaped their inheritance from the ancient world. And to look at ads from the 2000s is to take a ride on the transcontinental railroad in 1870, astounded and excited, but having no clue that someday freeways would traverse that land. The moral: we have no more reason to believe that visual branding has reached its acme in 2015 than our great-grandparents had to laud the steam locomotive as the pinnacle of transportation technology. Branding is not a settled art.

POSITIONING

This verb, a bit of marketing jargon, refers to how an offering relates to its competitive set; how this book compares to other efforts in the field. There is nothing new about conducting a historical study of advertising; but the position for which we aim is new. Marchand's (1985) book provides a master template for many efforts.[22] He offers a social and cultural history of American advertisers and consumers in the 1920s and 1930s, conceived as a hinge point where the modern forms of both advertising and consuming were set. Marchand writes not so much a history of advertising or advertisements, as a history of the social and cultural values manifest in ads of this era, along with a history of the people who created these ads and of the consumers who made up their audience. As with any social history, Marchand is keenly interested in the class and gender of those who created advertisements, as compared to that of their audience. As with any cultural history, Marchand wants to understand the source of the values to which ads appeal, and how these values came to be introduced and advanced. Marchand represents the mainstream of accounts written by historians. Ads provide Marchand much of his source material, but serve only as a locus for inquiry directed outside those ads, at the era in which they appeared.[23]

Pollay (1985) anchors a different tradition more characteristic of marketing scholarship. He was among the first to produce a content analysis of ads across a lengthy period. Papers in the tradition of Pollay – and these do tend to be journal papers, not books – might better be termed longitudinal content analyses, rather than histories, as that descriptor is used by humanities scholars. In these efforts, the material of interest – in Pollay's case, magazine advertisements – is sampled over time in the same way that a survey researcher samples people across space. A vast number of ads were published over the decades studied; the content analyst by necessity samples a fraction. The goal is a representative sample of material, gathered at equal intervals along a time line, much as a survey researcher tries to canvass neighborhoods from across the city and not focus unduly on respondents in one block or district. Once the ad sample is obtained, coders, typically students, are trained on a set of rules and then put to work to count the elements identified as of interest. For instance, Pollay had coders count elements such as ad size, the proportion devoted to a picture if present, whether the ad used color, and similar mechanical elements.

In longitudinal content analyses, anything defined by a rule can be counted; it might as well be labeled content machining. Once the counts are in hand and keyed to the time line, a trend analysis of any desired degree of statistical sophistication can be performed. That is the strength of content analyses: to quantify change and test its magnitude. The weakness: only things that college students can be trained to count may be analyzed. Most of the social and cultural matters discussed by a historian like Marchand will fall outside that ambit: their subtlety is too great. The eye of an experienced scholar sees much more than can be expressed in mechanical rules. For the historically inclined, content analyses are likely to appear both terribly superficial, and too empty of human agents.[24]

In this book, like Marchand, we rely on our own educated minds to examine the time course of branding in ads. The two of us have been looking at ads, sampled from diverse time periods, for a long time now.[25] But like Pollay, and unlike Marchand, we focus on elements visible in the ads, not on what ads reflect about the social and cultural world beyond. And also unlike Marchand, and departing from standard practice in historical accounts, we do not focus on the people who made these ads. There are few proper names in our account, and no biographical sketches.[26] We focus on the ad documents that survived, which we approach as their audience perforce did: as mass media, broadcast rather than addressed, from no named source other than the brand whose ad this is. We assume – and this is more heroic, and less certain of success – that we can know the purpose of these ads. We believe that all the ads we discuss, from the earliest to the latest, share a single straightforward aim: to brand, to make audiences aware of, interested in, and desirous of the brand, so that the remainder of the marketing effort can bring the consumer to act – to buy. Holding that assumption as our compass, we look at what ads contain, mostly ignoring words, and focusing on what is visible. We study what advertisers show, not what they tell, and how what is shown varies and changes over time. Where Marchand answers "Who?" and Pollay answers "What?" we seek to uncover "How?"

To date, no one has brought a rhetorician's eye to bear on the visual elements of magazine advertising, sampled over a lengthy period.[27] Rhetorical accounts of advertising have been offered, but there is as yet no history of rhetorical devices used in branding, especially not visual devices.[28]

PLAN OF THE BOOK

The chapters in Part I provide a history of visual branding in magazine advertising, in the United States, from before 1900 down to the present. In Chapter 1, we explain the choice of start date, and give a broad brush account of major trends and developments. To highlight change over time, our method is to dip into the ongoing, unending stream of advertising only at intervals: the turn of the century, then the 1920s, the 1950s, the 1980s, and the early 2000s. Picking periods separated by approximately one generation – 25 to 30 years – sharpens the contrast between early, middle, later, and recent efforts at visual branding. The people crafting ads in the 1950s were not the same individuals as those crafting ads in the 1980s or the 1920s.

Throughout, we primarily sample from leading magazines directed at women, such as the *Ladies Home Journal* or *Good Housekeeping*, supported in the early years by examples from competitive publications mostly now forgotten.[29] We stick to a restricted sample of products as well, again with the goal of capturing what changed and what did not. The American economy grew enormously over the period. There were also changes in printing technology and the economics of magazine production, such as the advent of color photography, and a sustained decline in the costs of color reproduction. Entire new product categories, the fruits of technological innovation, came into being. These external factors are acknowledged, but are not our primary concern. We want to know why color photography replaced color illustration, once technological and economic developments permitted. The focus is on what ad designers could do with color photography, and later with computer graphics software, once these tools were in hand.

After the initial broad brush survey, Chapter 2 reproduces and comments upon selected ads from each period. By the close of the chapter, the reader will have seen copious examples of visual branding, early and late, and be able to grasp viscerally and immediately how visual branding has changed over the past century.

Next, the chapters in Part II focus on the brand's trademark or logo, seen in more conventional treatments as the central element in visual branding, but here presented as only one aspect. Chapter 3 introduces a rhetorical typology of brand marks. We distinguish six possibilities for arranging verbal and visual elements to construct a mark. Chapter 4 establishes how type of brand mark varies systematically with product category, and explores the implications. Chapter 5 discusses the evolution of brand marks over time.

In Part III, we examine other major devices used for visual branding. Chapter 6 examines typeface, Chapter 7 discusses spokes-characters, Chapter 8 explores color, and Chapter 9 reviews pictorial style. These chapters emphasize history less, and rhetorical analysis more, in part because historical discussion of these elements is woven through earlier chapters. The Epilogue returns to the conceptual issues broached in this Introduction.

NOTE ON STYLE, TONE, AND APPROACH

The tone is more relaxed than a journal article. The tie is loosened, slacks replace the suit, the arm drapes over the chair and gestures. We try to avoid the hedged and bland. Our commentary is more critical than would be allowed in a peer-reviewed journal article. McQuarrie has retired from university teaching and Phillips holds an endowed chair. We feel free to be blunt.

In terms of reference style, there are endnotes and a References section. In text and in the notes, we use the author (year) style of citation. In text, we strive to cite only protagonists, people such as Marchand (1985) or Pollay (1985), whose work is foundational, and to whom we must refer more than once. When we want to direct the reader to the literature on the topic, or provide background, we pack multiple author (year) citations into an endnote, in an effort not to litter the text with these citations.[30] All the citations, whether in-text or in the notes, can be found in the References.

AUDIENCE

Although we dream of being read widely, by anyone interested in brands, advertising, or visual design, in our sober moments we target a more narrow audience: young scholars. The highest and best use of the book is to have it assigned as reading in a graduate seminar. That seminar will probably be offered in a school of business, but may be offered in a school of communication, a school of design, or even in a history department. A good seminar reading is provocative. It adopts one perspective, which clashes with other perspectives also assigned. The diverse portfolio of seminar readings sets up an illuminating discussion.

A seminar reading may be contrasted with a textbook intended for a survey course. Textbooks have to give equal weight to all currently accepted perspectives, and to provide magisterial coverage for everything collectively considered important. Textbooks are expected to be comprehensive, and to address a topic large enough to justify a 15-week course. Branding might meet that breadth standard; marketing, advertising, and consumer psychology surely do; but visual branding, not so much. A seminar reading is free to narrow its coverage, and be more idiosyncratic in its treatment of controversial questions. It will be combined with other readings, and its student readers will be advanced. A seminar reading can attack; it can drill deep deep down; it can take one approach and push it to the hilt, without looking over its shoulder at bystanders, clucking that the authors skimped on this and glossed over that. A seminar reading is liberating to write.

Our second audience is the practical men and women engaged in visual branding at their day jobs. We don't presume to give brand managers or art directors advice about how to brand;[31] this book is a work of scholarship. But we do think that experienced practitioners might benefit from understanding the history of how they earn their daily bread. And we believe a rhetorical analysis of the space of possibilities for visual branding may be fruitful, again in the hands of a veteran, who has a moment of leisure to reflect on what works and why. That practitioner is ill-served by current academic accounts, which remain in thrall to a defunct psychological apparatus.

Because the audience spans disciplines, and stretches outside academia, we have tried to unburden the main text of most references, attempted to avoid statistical esoterica in-text, and minimized jargon. Endnotes provide expansions where needed; our target audience of young scholars includes assistant professors, out to make their own mark in one of these topic areas, and we owe them the extra background and technical information that notes supply.

Last, we've provided a companion website at https://www.e-elgar.com/ visual-branding-companion-site. This site contains 20 additional repro- ductions of ads, with these figures marked in-text by a WA prefix. The site also contains a bonus chapter, useful to instructors and students, describ- ing possible research projects. The suggested projects give pointers for work designed to challenge or extend the findings we report.

PART I

Historical perspectives on brand advertising

1. Overview: visual branding in historical perspective

When did advertising begin? This question distracts rather than enlightens. The rhetorician doesn't care.[1]

A better question is: by what point had magazine advertising for national brands fully emerged in the United States?[2] As rhetoricians, we are not interested in the dawn or even the sunrise, but the entire day, beginning in the morning, the earliest hour which enjoys the full light of day. For brand advertising, complete with visual branding, that point lies somewhere around the turn of the twentieth century. The sky was beginning to redden in the 1870s: Ivory Soap and other pioneer brands had been introduced, the American continent was being knit together into a national market, and printing technology and media custom were beginning to facilitate illustrations in advertising.[3] Sunrise, to continue the metaphor, can be securely dated to 1892–93. This period marked the launch of the low-priced, mass-circulation magazine whose revenue depended more on advertising dollars than subscription payments.[4] This is also the period when the better magazines began to refuse patent medicine ads; in other words, the point where ads could not all be dismissed as bunkum. By 1905, brands and trademarks had received major new legal protections.[5] The sun had moved completely above the horizon.

By the early years of the twentieth century, color printing in mass reproduction had been feasible for some years, although it was still uncommon in print advertisements. Mass circulation magazines like the *Ladies Home Journal* (*LHJ*) had flourished for over a decade, pulling in more than 1 million subscribers. Nationally distributed brands had proliferated since their advent after the Civil War. By 1900 the American economy, after devastating slumps that began in the early 1870s and continued through the middle 1890s, was booming again. The large corporation, promoting its brand to a national audience of millions, was in place.[6]

A remark sometimes attributed to Albert Einstein asserts that "everything should be made as simple as possible, but not simpler." Advertising from around the turn of the twentieth century is early enough to anchor a history of visual branding in advertising, and we need nothing earlier to establish trends. Hence, this will be history over 12 decades, from about 1893 to 2015. For brevity, we will call it a century.

HISTORICAL COMPARISONS

Although magazine advertising was fully formed by the early twentieth century, along with the mass-marketing of national brands, other innovations were yet to come. Many products, heavily advertised in later decades, had not as yet become mass-marketed goods: the automobile, for instance, is nearly absent from magazine ads in the early 1900s, but common in 1920s ads. Conversely, some product categories which were heavily advertised in the early years of the 1900s – corsets, for instance – are no longer mass-market goods.

From the standpoint of identifying change in rhetorical practices, if we were to compare a 2015 ad for cell phones, with a 1905 ad for corsets, we would have two variables in one equation. We could not solve for rhetorical practices that were specific to 1905, separate from practices that were specific to advertising corsets during the Edwardian era of dress and fashion. Historical differences would be confounded with product category differences. To keep the focus on how visual branding changed over the century, it helps if we constrain the set of products. Fortunately, many categories were heavily advertised throughout the period. These include: (1) packaged foods; (2) personal care products, from soap to toothpaste; (3) household cleaning products (for example, scouring powder); and (4) home furnishings and improvements, such as flooring, furniture, cabinetry, paint, and appliances.

We could obtain an even tighter comparison if we constrained brand as well as product. Many of the most famous brands, treated by historians as central players in the development of consumer culture, were already flourishing by early in the twentieth century: Campbell's, Heinz, Ivory, Jello. When we place a Campbell's soup ad from 1905 beside another from 2015, we hold both product category and brand constant. By imposing such constraints, differences over time in rhetorical practice more clearly emerge. Unfortunately, the turnover in brands across a period this lengthy made it impossible for us to fully observe this second guideline.[7]

Constraining brand, where possible, yields a second benefit. Do you remember Huyler's or Lowney's chocolates? Probably not; but at the beginning of the period, these vied with Hershey's as leading brands of chocolate. Ultimately these other brands disappeared or were reduced to minor status, and did not continue as leaders. Did bad advertising wreck the Huyler brand franchise? There is no way to tell. But if good advertising contributes to successful branding – an uncontroversial proposition – then the incidence of bad advertising, in the population of failed brands, must be higher than in the population of brands that have enjoyed long-term success. Hence, were we to compare a 1900 Huyler's chocolate ad to a 2015 Hershey's ad, we would risk comparing ignorant or mistaken rhetorical practice to effective and sound practice, and lose sight of the comparison on which we seek to focus, which is early versus later practice.

Rhetoricians haven't time to catalogue or collect. Rhetoricians are not antiquarians. Rhetoricians care only about what works. Plato condemned us for it. As a rule, we will try to avoid reproducing old ads for vanished product categories or for brands that have disappeared or dwindled into insignificance. We did look at these ads, and when we categorize the ads from a period, our global assessments will include them. But for the examples we reproduce, we strive to set a higher bar. On the other hand, it will not do to altogether exclude new brands in new product categories. These may introduce new rhetorical possibilities. We reiterate the fundamental assumption of classical rhetoric: in any rhetorical situation, the number of gambits – potentially successful moves in the game – is finite and even small. But new products may introduce a new persuasive situation, with newly possible gambits. We may skimp on vanished products and brands, but we cannot dismiss new products and new brands, if we are to grasp the full panoply of rhetorical practices in visual branding, and their trajectory over time.

PREREQUISITES FOR BRAND ADVERTISING

There is another reason to start a rhetorical history of brand advertising in the 1890s. Prior to the 1880s, the professions of copywriter and art director did not exist. There was plenty of print advertising before that point, but it was not produced by specialists. Numerous ad agencies predate 1890, but they primarily sold space in publications, placing material created by the advertiser.[8] The owners of firms, or one of their clerks, constructed those print ads. Copy was minimal, and visual elements were selected rather than constructed: type foundries offered an abundance of display typefaces and simple graphics.[9] If the business owner had some flair, as did Harley Procter of Procter & Gamble ("99 44/100% pure," "It floats"), ad copy might be creative, and stylistically astute; else, it tended toward boilerplate puffery, stiff announcements, or the shouts of the barker, with graphic support limited to canned elements.[10]

It was after 1890 that more and more of the ads appearing in the new magazines began to be written by specialists.[11] Art directors, who constructed the visual appearance of the ad, came later.[12] Before 1900, many ads changed no more frequently than packaging changes today. The same graphics and selling copy would be run again and again, for years. Only as the century turns do we see more and more ad campaigns take the form of ever-changing executions: newly written copy supported by newly constructed illustrations, ads made from scratch. Only from this point do we see professionals take charge of ad design. Professional rhetoricians begin to make a living from advertising.

Before 1898, new products had been introduced at a quickening pace for several decades. These new products always had names, and like Ivory or Quaker Oats, some of these names survived and thrived as brands. But it was only with the introduction of Nabisco crackers in that year that a business owner, head of the new cracker combine, tapped an ad agency and its staff of specialists to design a new name for a product that had already been manufactured and mass-distributed for years. Uneeda Biscuit may have been the first new brand to be launched, separate from the launch of the product it named.[13]

Last, why put so much weight on magazine advertising, when the topic is the broader one of visual branding in advertising? Here it helps to introduce a distinction with another form of advertising, one familiar to marketing scholars, but one that may pass over the heads of historians not trained in the business disciplines. Most advertising prior to the advent of advertising-supported magazines was direct response advertising: its purpose was to get the consumer to reach for her purse and buy, right now, as in direct mail advertising today. It is no accident that John Powers, widely recognized to be the first professional copywriter, came into his own while working for a department store, writing ads to be read in a daily newspaper, aimed at consumers about to go shopping.

Early magazine advertising, through the first years of the twentieth century, was sometimes designed as direct response advertising; but from the beginning, and increasingly, it advertised the brand, not the sale. Magazine ads, above all, built the brand in the eyes of those who might buy, not immediately but in the near future; and also those who had bought and sought reassurance; and even those who might, some years later, consider buying. Brand advertising builds brands; other forms of marketing sell the product thus branded.[14] Advertising, and brands, and magazines all predate the 1890s; nonetheless, the 1890s provide a defensible point of beginning for a sample designed to capture trends in visual branding over the long term, down to the present day.

CAPSULE SUMMARY: A CENTURY OF BRANDING IN PRINT

Before pursuing detailed comparisons using example ads, here is a broad brush picture of developments over time. In this account we periodically jump ahead 25 to 30 years (see Box 1.1 for details of the sampling strategy).

BOX 1.1 A PUNCTUATED INTERVAL SAMPLING STRATEGY

We stress again the importance, for historical studies of visual branding, of holding in the hand the physical magazine. True, in an age of digital archiving, it is increasingly possible to find old magazines digitized on the Internet; and the new archiving has largely avoided the foibles of past archivists, at whom Rowsome (1959, p. 1) railed: "[shame on] the nameless past librarians who in years gone by instructed the bindery to cut off and discard advertising sections before binding magazine volumes."

What you can't descry from an internet scan of an old ad is the exact caliber of the printing process, nor even the size of the original ad: about 6.5 inches by 9.5 inches for a *Munsey's, McClure's* or *Cosmopolitan*, but over 11 inches by 16 inches for a *Ladies Home Journal* or a *Saturday Evening Post*; a page almost three times as large. Few subsequent authors have been as scrupulous as Presbrey (1929), who noted the degree of photo enlargement or reduction for most of his reproductions. As a consequence, the modern reader may see what looks like a half-page ad reproduced in a book or digital archive, and not realize that the original was as small as a classified newspaper ad; or you may see a large and highly detailed ad and not be told that this ad appeared on the back cover, and was the only full-page ad in the entire magazine.

However, the imperative for obtaining physical copies, combined with their absence from many modern libraries, creates a dilemma: although it is easy to find old magazines for sale by searching the web, once you go back a century these may cost as much as $50 per issue. The initial impetus for our punctuated sample was this prohibitive cost. Rather than the rigorously specified date sampling of a Pollay (1985), we decided it would be acceptable to buy a 1907 issue, and assign it to the "around 1900" sample, because that issue had a nick on the cover and was available for half the price of any issue from the year 1900.

What makes this haphazard selection viable are the gaps in time we imposed: jumping ahead to buy a copy from 1921, and again to get a copy from 1954, using the same cost-minimization rule. Each loosely bounded in time sample serves as an instrument for clarifying what's different about the preceding and following sample. The length of the gap – two or three decades – improves the resolution. When we juxtapose two ads produced decades apart, the differences leap out. And with five punctuated samples, we had four opportunities to make that juxtaposition; which in turn made sustained trends easy to spot.

You don't have to obtain physical copies of old magazines to pore over examples of old ads. Most of the histories we consulted reproduce ads in copious quantities. But in addition to not capturing size information, reproduced ads tend not to be time-locked. Rather, the typical volume takes a thematic approach: here a chapter on breakfast food ads that might span one 20-year stretch, there a chapter on early automobile ads that might span a different 30-year stretch. It's impossible to extract trend lines from that hodgepodge. Another problem with collections: compilers are naturally drawn to the vivid, artistic, and prominent. Why reproduce that little black-and-white woodcut, from an ad one column wide, and all in agate type, when you can reproduce that lavishly engraved ad with color touches, that occupies the entire back cover, and gives just as much of a period feel? Problem: 117 of the 220 ads in that issue of 1898 may have been just like that unimpressive little woodcut; another 100 were a little bigger and nicer, but not by much; and the back cover ad was the only full-page, fully engraved, partially colored ad in the entire issue. You can't do history if someone else has filtered your sample of ads according to criteria unknown.

Last, there is a subtle problem with drawing continuous samples of ads in volume. Marchand (1985) looked at 180,000 ads; probably every ad in the magazines he sampled. Accordingly, he could only look across 15 years or so, making it impossible for him to see which changes of that era were sustained. Likewise, when an author samples from every decade, a story of fad and fashion, or cyclic change, becomes probable; and the fewer the number of decades sampled, the less likely that trends will emerge. It was easier, for us, to see how ads from the 1950s differed from 1980s ads, because 30 years is a long time in advertising. If we had had to tell a story about 1950s ads versus 1960s ads versus 1970s ads, we don't know that such clear patterns would have emerged. And it was also easier for us to pinpoint what changed from 1950 to 1980 because we could compare ads from both periods to those from later, in the 2000s, and earlier, from the 1920s.

Changes in branding practice are gradual. Sampling time periods separated by 25–30 years helps to make changes visible. From the standpoint of the individual human beings who laid out these ads, by means of these intervals we skip ahead about one generation each time. Although hidden from us (unlike the authors of books, the creators of ads do not sign their work) in each period we are discussing a new population of creators, new persons inhabiting a new generation raised under new circumstances, but confronting the same challenge: how to brand.

At the beginning of the twentieth century, many magazine ads were indistinguishable from newspaper ads: printed in black and white, rather than color; consisting mostly of text, including price; and occupying a column, rather than the whole page. Color was not absent, but rare: only the ads on the inside and back of the cover pages, which were printed on a thicker, glossier paper stock, may have been color; and this opportunity was not purchased every issue. Full-page ads, while also not absent, were similarly the exception: excluding the covers, there may only be 3–4 full-page ads in an 84-page issue of *LHJ*, but more than 100 column-length or fractional-column ads (December 1907). In our September 9, 1905 copy of the *Saturday Evening Post* (*SEP*), there is only one full-page ad, on the back cover; and it is the only ad with color.

The proportion of editorial material to advertising was still high around 1900. The short stories and self-help articles in *LHJ* filled a very large page – 11 inches by 16 inches – with what today would be called fine print: 9-, 8-or even 6-point typeface. To the modern eye, each issue of *LHJ* is stuffed with a textbook's worth of words, crowded with print. We see few visual elements anywhere, and these are rudimentary and small.

In the 1920s, everything exploded. Full-page ads in color became common rather than rare, distributed throughout the magazine rather than limited to the covers. The count of pages grew. A mid-decade issue of *LHJ* may have 200 or more pages in total, with dozens of full-page ads in color scattered throughout. The range of products advertised broadened: automobile ads proliferated, along with household appliances. The balance of pictures and words changed, both in the editorial matter and in the advertisements. To the modern eye, an *LHJ* from the 1920s remains print-heavy and wordy, especially in the advertisements; but visual elements, which had occupied 10 percent or even less of a typical page 20 years earlier, may now make up 20 percent, 50 percent or even more of some ads. White space appears in ads; layouts may (sometimes) be less crowded.

A typical 1920s ad will still appear old and dated to the contemporary viewer, primarily because the visual elements are mostly painted and drawn. Color photography for mass reproduction was not yet technically or economically feasible. Black and white photographs do appear in some ads, but illustrations, color or no, dominate.

Skipping ahead to the 1950s, the preceding depression and war years saw many changes in printing technology and its economics. Like the 1920s, the 1950s were an exuberant period of affluence, in which both consumer spending power, and the supply of things on which to spend, greatly expanded. As in the 1920s, magazines became thick again, and thick with ads. An *LHJ* issue may be 100–200 pages; a *Better Homes and Gardens* (*BHG*), or *Good Housekeeping* (*GH*), may contain 200 or even 300 pages, many devoted to advertising.

Color photographs begin to replace illustrations in the 1950s. Illustrations continued to be common; color photography would not dominate until later. Black and white ads also remained common. New in the 1950s was the frequent use of color text: headlines ceased to be black print only. Early in the decade, advertisers threw all kinds of color onto the page: the headline was put in red, a subhead in green, a diagram in blue. To the modern eye, the use of color appears noisy and undisciplined.

The indiscipline extended to layout in the narrow sense. Advertisers routinely had a full page with which to work, even two pages, and they threw in everything but the kitchen sink. These continued to be large pages by current standards; no longer 11 by 16 inches, but still 10 by 13 inches or so, rather than the 8 by 10 size that had dominated since the 1980s. A 1950s ad might include a close-up color photo, of the sort that would dominate later ads, but here that photo may be but one among half a dozen components. It may be accompanied by a diagram of how the product works, another picture with callouts of key features, another picture of the product in use, a package shot, or any number of things. There would still be hundreds of words of copy, a dozen subheads in three contrasting colors, and more. Layout tended toward the busy and cluttered.

A new element coalesced by the 1950s: the brand block. A brand block is a region of the ad page, typically at the bottom, reserved for brand identification. The brand block contains visual elements that appear across ads, as opposed to the remainder of the execution, which varies with each ad. Over time, the brand block grew more and more organized, and would become the primary means by which the advertiser self-identifies, declaring this ad message to be from this brand, this source, this entity whom you already know, and about whom you know a good bit from past encounters.

Earlier, in the 1920s, brand promotion had been more hit or miss. The brand name might or might not be rendered in a distinctive typeface. Even then, another iteration of the name, or maybe only that of the corporate owner, might be reproduced nearby in an ordinary or regular typeface, with a mailing address. As the brand block coalesced in the 1950s, advertisers exerted more control over how and where the brand was represented on the page. Logos – distinctive graphic elements that accompany or adorn the brand name – were also more likely to appear. However, by later standards, there was still not a lot of consistency in the presentation of the brand.

Moving forward, ads from the 1980s are of special note: during this decade any scholar older than 50 is likely to have acquired their tacit understanding of how an ad is supposed to look.[15] These 1980s ads would have dominated their consciousness when, as a student, an interest in pursuing advertising scholarship first took root. We mention this anchoring in the 1980s because of the danger that a psychologist – or any non-historically inclined person – will hypostatize the visual presentation of brands in advertising typical of the 1980s. The familiar gets misinterpreted as fundamental; temporary and era-specific features are treated as underlying structures that endure. We hope to break this pernicious habit. Ads from the 1980s are visually distinct from those that came before and after; the branding practices seen in the 1980s are not universal templates, but historically situated conjunctures.

If you put ads from the 1950s side by side with ads from the 1980s, you might conclude that advertisers had cleaned up their act. No longer do we see everything but the kitchen sink. In the prototypical 1980s ad, the visual portion of the ad has cohered into a single, large color photograph that may occupy half the page or more. We do mean occupy: the photo now fills the entire width of its part of the page. Below (and/or above) the picture is a text block or two. The headline, in large type, occupies a band above or below the picture; the body copy occupies another band, either directly beneath the headline, or with the picture sandwiched between. At the bottom, or in the bottom right corner, is a separate brand block containing the name in a large and characteristic typeface, the logo (if the brand has one, which many now do), and maybe a tagline, present across ad executions and sustained for some time. In many ads from the early 1980s, ad layouts are this schematic. Ads contain a small number of discrete elements – picture, headline, text, brand – each filling a separate region, often a horizontal band that extends across the page.

The 1980s are also the era of the bold-faced, large font headline; or better, the double-bolded extra-large mega-type headline, with letter strokes thick as a pinky finger. There's nothing artsy about the typeface in these headlines, and advertisers don't bother to color or embroider the typeface of the headline. The prototypical headline uses a plain san-serif typeface, prints as pitch black, and shouts as loud as silent print can. With the clutter of the 1950s cleared away, and with MBAs trained in management science now acquiring decision-making roles, in the 1980s advertisers honed in on the specific tasks the print ad layout was to accomplish. Catch the eye with a big color picture. Shout the claim in the headline. Identify the brand.

The characteristic 1980s layout has been naturalized in subsequent psychological treatments. But there is nothing natural or permanent about it. You have to put ads from the 2000s side by side with ads from the 1980s to break the spell. The 1980s layout, consisting of separate blocks of picture, text, and brand, was a temporary set of conventions. Not natural. Not permanent.

What happened to the 1980s layout? Photoshop happened. Computer graphics capability exploded in the later 1980s and early 1990s. The ability to create visual effects on a printed surface expanded far beyond what a photographer could accomplish in the darkroom by skillful airbrushing or superimposition. Also, the ability to design distinctive typefaces cheaply and quickly, and to lay them out easily, and to print them for no extra cost, expanded apace.

Two other technological developments were influential. If you can, get hold of a women's magazine from the early 1980s – neither black and white reproductions nor microfilm will do, it has to be the physical magazine – and find a cosmetics ad with a large color photo of a model (the norm in ads for cosmetics, then, now, and for some time before). Look closely at the skin, and at the flesh tone. It's not right. It doesn't look real to the contemporary eye. The 1980s ad attempts a photorealistic style that falls short of that goal. Next, repeat the exercise with a cosmetics ad published after 2005. The flesh tone will be beautifully rendered. The ad photo could be a clear glass window onto a real model: a girl born with an outstanding complexion, further groomed by the expert application of cosmetics, and improved further by judicious Photoshop treatment, but a real-looking girl nonetheless.[16]

This exercise suggests that knowledge of the chemistry of inks and paper coatings, and the technology of image transfer, measurably improved over the intervening decades. There may also have been changes in the technology of camera lens manufacture or studio lighting. The techno-logical details need not detain the rhetorician, but we must reiterate that the means of production, when it comes to printing images, continued to evolve following the 1980s. It may still be evolving today. The rhetorician wants to ask: what might be the effects of surpassing that threshold, that point where photorealism achieves its apotheosis? What might advertisers choose to do with pictures, once these can be made to look really, really, real?

The second technological development was the diffusion of the internet among ordinary consumers, beginning about the mid-1990s, along with the diffusion of screens: electronic surfaces for viewing images. By the mid-2000s, consumers were acclimated to high-resolution LCD screens, displaying full-color images pulled from the vast repository of the web. At about the same time, high-definition television took off, further increasing consumers' exposure to high-quality, photo-realistic images, but also to fictive, fantastic images, whether produced from hand-drawn animations, or as computer-generated visual effects. If we could count exposures per day to vivid high-resolution color imagery, among ordinary consumers, from 1950 to 2015, the curve would be exponential in some periods; and if we looked at the cost to deliver a color image to a mass audience, weighted by its photo-realism, we would see an exponential fall-off in that cost.

By the 2000s, the day-to-day existence of American consumers had become perfused by images. Under this deluge, printed magazine ads changed their layout exactly as you might expect. Pictures increasingly crowded out words. Pictures took over the entire ad. Words that remained were inscribed on the picture, rather than occupying a separate block beside or below the picture. Headlines stopped shouting; these reduced in size, often ceased to be bold black, and now graced the picture: they became captions rather than shout-outs.

The content of the pictures changed as well. Excepting cosmetic ads, which continue, as before, to feature photorealistic close-ups of face, hair, or lips, pictures are more likely to be visual effects, forged in software, rather than photos captured by a camera. Fictive and fantastic imagery has grown more common. Rhetorical devices of all kinds migrate to the picture: metaphor, personification, puns, hyperbole. In a word, images replace photographs in ads.

One final development, sociocultural rather than technological, helps to explain contemporary branding practice in print. From the 1950s, consumers' daily exposure to ads grew and grew and grew, waning a bit during recessions, but always rebounding. That may be why the bold screaming headlines seen in 1980s ads gradually disappeared. Thirty years ago, shouting in print might have served a branding purpose, have worked, been effective. But by the 2000s, consumers had become ever better at tuning out unwanted ad messages, especially the comparatively pallid messages of which print is capable (compare television, or web animations). A print ad that stooped to shouting was that much more easily spotted and screened out. Alluring pictures, beautiful and strange, now had better odds of stopping the consumer. Seduction, not command, became the preferred approach.

Now skip ahead to the 2030s. We can't, of course, at least not in this edition; the future hasn't happened yet. The point of this tease: it is unlikely that print advertising has ceased to evolve, has somehow reached a final state in which currently visible rhetorical strategies become fixed, to endure until advertisers cease to print on paper. On the contrary, we expect change to continue. Technological change has not ceased. The first generation of graphic designers to train on and use Photoshop throughout their careers is beginning to pass the mantle to a new generation. This next generation of advertising creatives, now moving into the mainstream of their careers and rising up the ranks, is the first to have grown up from birth inundated with web imagery; but they did not encounter the iPhone, and the explosion of mobile imagery, until late in their teens. The generation that grew up glued to a smartphone screen isn't in college yet, much less employed. Change will continue.

In the next chapter we introduce and discuss examples from each of the five eras briefly canvassed above. In capturing visual branding practice, words take us only so far.

2. An illustrated history of visual branding in magazine advertising

Before looking at magazine ads after 1895, it helps to see an example of what might be called pre-magazine advertising: print ads that preceded magazine ads. Print advertising is much older than magazine advertising; Dr. Samuel Johnson famously announced in 1759 that advertising skill had come "so near to perfection that it is not easy to propose any improvement."[1] Figures 2.1 and 2.2 show ads from 100 years after Dr. Johnson wrote, and several decades before the beginning of our period. These appeared in Henry V. Poor's first directory of railroads, published before the Civil War. Annual publication of this directory resumed after the war and continued through the 1920s. Railroads, as the first national enterprises, stimulated some of the earliest national advertising. These two ads help to reveal typical practices before magazine advertising came into its own.

The ad for the firm of A. Bridges in Figure 2.1 is text only. Counting italics, boldface, and changes in size, the ad mixes more than a dozen typefaces. The vocabulary is technical and descriptive. The ad presents itself as a display sign or announcement. The ad for New York Rail Road Chair Works uses similar technical language and the same profusion of typefaces, but these are confined to half the ad; the remainder is taken up by pictures of iron parts and a fully kitted-out locomotive. The pictures are black engravings presented full face, and about as photorealistic as a drawing can be. The rhetorical style is announcement. Look: here are the parts we have available for sale.

Poor's directories continued to carry ads up until the beginning of our period, and beyond, although their count, after waxing in the 1870s, began to wane after 1890. These later Poor's ads change little from the examples in Figures 2.1 and 2.2, with one exception: we see the first appearance of body copy (Figure 2.3). Although not the norm, an occasional ad will now include a block of prose intended as salesmanship in print: claims and arguments for the product, rather than announcements of availability and source. Two other, slighter changes are visible: in some ads from the 1880s and beyond, the picture, whether of locomotive or factory, grows larger, and even dominates a few ads; and the bewildering mash of typefaces seen in Figure 2.1 becomes less common.

Figure 2.2   Another early print ad

Figure 2.1   A print ad from before the explosion of consumer magazines

Figure 2.3   A somewhat later print ad containing body copy

With these baseline examples of print advertising in hand, the distinctive-
ness of early magazine advertising can emerge. In the sections that follow,
the discussion is built around specific examples, offered as representative
of their era.

1900s

Figures 2.4 and 2.5 show ads for Ivory Soap from the mid-1890s. Each
occupied a quarter page. These are primarily text ads, although the *Ladies
Home Journal* (*LHJ*) example contains a fair number of decorative elements, and a sketch of the soap bar. They are nonetheless distinctive,
relative to the Poor's directory ads, in three ways. First is the prominence
of the brand name, in what may be a custom or hand-drawn typeface,
printed much larger than anything in the early Poor's ads. Second is the
use of white space to make the already prominent name more so. Third is

IVORY SOAP

IVORY

"IT FLOATS"

FOR THE BATH.

THE PROCTER & GAMBLE CO., CIN'TI.

Figure 2.5   Another early magazine ad for Ivory Soap

IVORY SOAP

99⁴⁴⁄₁₀₀ PURE

When you pack for the sea shore or the mountains, fill a tray of your trunk with Ivory Soap and require your laundress to use it. Light summer garments should be washed only with pure white soap.

T⁻ᴇ PROCTER & GAMBLE CO., CIN'TI.

Figure 2.4   An early magazine ad for Ivory Soap

When the children's best clothes come from the wash with the colors faded and streaked, and with worn spots showing in places where there should be no wear, then you may know that your laundress is using something besides Ivory Soap.

You can save trouble and expense by furnishing her with Ivory Soap, and insisting that she use it and nothing else. The price of one ruined garment will buy Ivory Soap sufficient for months.

A WORD OF WARNING.—There are many white soaps, each represented to be "just as good as the 'Ivory';" they ARE NOT, but like all counterfeits, lack the peculiar and remarkable qualities of the genuine. Ask for "Ivory" Soap and insist upon getting it.

Copyright, 1898, by The Procter & Gamble Co., Cincinnati

Figure 2.6   Early Ivory Soap ad where the illustration is central

the inclusion of a sales point, in the form of a brief and distinctive claim meant to be repeated over and over: the already famous phrases, still recognizable today, stating "it floats," and "99 44/100 Pure."

Next, consider another Ivory ad from four years later (Figure 2.6). If anything, the changes across these four years dwarf those that separate the earlier Ivory ads from the Poor's ads from decades before. The prominent brand name has disappeared, as have the brief claims. An attractive illustration, possibly a touched-up photo half-tone, or alternatively a pen and ink drawing requiring some artistic skill, occupies more than half the ad (although this remains a quarter-page ad on the inside of the front cover, as had been true and would remain true of Ivory ads for several years to come). Most importantly, this is not a picture of the product or of wash day, but a lifestyle picture, of an outing at the shore with the children, a narrative picture that allows a story to be woven if the viewer chooses. Beneath the picture are several paragraphs of hard-sell, performance-based claims. There is no brand block; the brand name is buried in the body copy.

The first pair of Ivory ads could have appeared in a newspaper or other print outlet; but the later ad shows the distinctive qualities of the emerging magazine ad format, as it coalesced at the beginning of the twentieth century: large picture + discursive selling copy, in what will later be called the picture window layout.[2] The Ivory picture is much more advanced than many that we will see from this era; others will be as large, but much more mundane, and less pleasing to the eye. But all these magazine ad pictures are a long way from the still-life product shots, or static portraits of the founder, that had dominated earlier ad pictures – when a picture was included at all.

Figure 2.7 shows an ad for Andrews Heating Co.[3] It has moved a little distance away from the Poor's directory ads, but not by much. Less advanced than the Ivory soap ad of 1898, it is also more representative of the ads one might see by flipping through the back half of a magazine of this era. The first change is the lengthy copy: about 1000 words, most of it set in exceedingly small type. The Poor's ads had mostly remained announcements, but this ad is a sustained attempt at salesmanship in print. There is also a more sophisticated use of large type. Rather than using variations in type to shout in different registers all down the page, at the top of the Andrews heating ad the first bit of large type acts as a true headline. It gives a summary claim, intended to convey the sales message even if the consumer reads nothing else. Other instances of larger, bolder type act as subheads to organize the copy and provide support for the headline. There are five illustrations spaced through the ad, and these also show an advance over the Poor's ads, going beyond depictions of the part to put the product in context: you can find Andrews products heating fine homes like this one, and spreading through neighborhoods like this one. Nonetheless, the visual branding, such as it is, remains rudimentary. Words do the heavy lifting, along with facts: price and availability.

Figure 2.8 shows an ad for the National Cloak & Suit Company. The name is presented in ordinary type: there is no brand mark or trademark to be seen. Rather than a brand block at the bottom of the ad, there is an address block: the firm hopes the consumer will write back. Like the Andrews heater ad, this ad is heavy with words and prices, especially in comparison to any contemporary fashion clothing ad. But this clothing ad advances in one respect: it leads with a picture, and the illustration of the

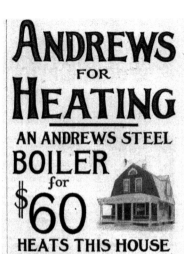

Note: The original ad is in a single column but has been split into two columns for the purposes of publication in this book.

Figure 2.7   A print-heavy magazine ad from the early 1900s

ice is unusually prompt, as we make your Suit, Skirt or Rain-Coat to order in ten days from receipt of your letter.

You get a perfect fit, and at the same time your garments have absolute distinction and individuality. You shop at home, save money, are dressed in the latest New York style and get absolute satisfaction, or your money back.

Winter Suits

MADE TO ORDER $6 to $25

Catalogue and Samples Will Be Sent You Free by Return Mail

Our Catalogue illustrates and describes the following garments, which we make to order:

Visiting Dresses	$6.00 to $20.00
Tailor-made Suits	7.50 to 25.00
Separate Skirts	3.50 to 15.00
Rain-Coats	8.75 to 18.00

OUR GUARANTEE:

If anything we send you is not entirely satisfactory, send back the goods at once, at our expense, and we will promptly refund your money. You take absolutely no risk.

Our Ready-Made Departments show the latest and best in each line at astonishingly low prices. Here are goods that you need right now. You could not shop elsewhere and duplicate our prices.

Our Catalogue illustrates and describes the following goods, which are ready-made:

Ladies' and Misses' Cloaks	$5.45 to $34.75
Children's Cloaks	4.75 to 9.95
Children's Dresses	1.98 to 5.48
Ladies' Shirt-Waists	.98 to 6.98
Fur Neck-Pieces and Muffs	2.25 to 13.50
Sweaters	.85 to 3.48
Underwear	.24 to 2.48
Corsets	1.00 to 3.00
Kimonos	.45 to 2.15
Handkerchiefs	.05 to .25

We prepay postage or express charges on anything you order from us to any part of the United States; this means a big saving to you.

Write to-day for our new Winter Style Book, sent free to any part of the United States, and if you desire Samples of Materials for a Suit, Skirt or Rain-Coat, be sure to mention the colors you prefer.

National Cloak & Suit Co.

221 West 24th St., New York City

Largest Ladies' Outfitting Establishment in the World

Mail Orders Only.   *No Agents or Branches.*

Style, Economy and Quick Service

The highest-priced New York tailor cannot give you better or more up-to-date styles than those shown in our Catalogue. A glance through it proves this. As for cost, comparison is convincing. No other house can approach our prices. Our serv-

Note: The original ad is in a single column but has been split into two columns for the purposes of publication in this book.

Figure 2.8   An ad from the 1900s where the illustration is key

two models occupies the entire top of the ad. We do not have a small illustration subordinate to the text, as in the Andrews ad, but a central, leading component. This layout strategy – big picture to start, with supporting text below – will have a bright future in magazine advertising. Although branding remains vestigial, this missive from National Cloak & Suit is markedly more visual than the Andrews ad, and on a par with the 1898 Ivory ad.

Figure 2.9   A cereal ad from the 1900s where illustration and text are balanced

The next two ads go further down the visual route seen in the Ivory ad. Both are for packaged food – breakfast cereals – leaders then, as now, in brand advertising. In Figure 2.9, Shredded Whole Wheat shouts its name in large type at the center. To the left is a lifestyle drawing that might be captioned "Studious maiden, contemplating the end of summer vacation." What has "Back to School" to do with breakfast cereal? The copy draws the connection: good food à well-functioning brain. The Shredded Wheat ad is an early instance of a rhetorical strategy that will later come to be labelled "sold like soap." A mundane product, based on no unique intellectual property and requiring no inimitable resource to manufacture – soap, cereal – is made the means to the end of a much loftier goal: here, success in school, and life. The picture, and its enjoyable character, underwrites the strategy. Without it, the argument would not be read through, and if skimmed, might be rejected as tendentious. Rhetorically speaking, the picture of the maiden provides the sugar coating; the visual element helps the copy medicine go down, per Mary Poppins.

The Grape Nuts ad in Figure 2.10, from five years later, uses the identical

Note: The original ad is in a single column but has been split into two columns for the purposes of publication in this book.

Figure 2.10   Another cereal ad from the early 1900s

visual strategy, although here we see a cheerful young boy playing outside, as preferred by middle-class mothers, a century ago as now. Without the sugar coating of the picture, calculated to make a mother smile, the argument would be a stretch, falling into what psychologists call the latitude of rejection. With the delicious picture, the maternal instincts are easily ensnared by the copy appeals.

The two ads share another feature, one which betrays their comparative antiquity and lack of modernity: there is no brand block, no separate region dedicated to presenting the brand identity in a prominent and favorable way. There is no brand mark of any kind, not even the fancy font that is otherwise common in this era. The brand name is large, but rendered in the same typeface as the rest of the ad; we have name as headline rather than as sponsor self-promotion.

Two Nabisco ads capture some of the evolution in visual branding already under way during the early 1900s. In Figure 2.11, there is no visual element other than a decorative frame; no picture. Such decoratively framed ads are common in this era. However, the brand name is rendered in a distinctive typeface, one that recalls stencil-cut dough. In Figure 2.12, an innovation is visible: branding via the package shot. The package is what the consumer must spot and recognize within the store.[4] Among packaged goods, depicting the package to present the name will gradually become the norm over the next century. In much later ads, plain font renderings of the brand name will disappear. The brand will be represented solely by its package and the distinctively printed name as presented there. Interestingly, in this earlier era the package may be more graphically intense than the ad as a whole. Only later will ad layouts catch up to packaging design in visual sophistication.

The Campbell's soup ad in Figure 2.13 shows an intriguing mix of older and more modern features. We have the lifestyle illustration at top: ladies at the dinner table, maid bowing forward to present. The name is set in a script typeface occupying a block in the center. The package – the can – provides further brand identification. On the other hand, the full corporate name still appears as an identifier in plain type. And color is not yet common enough, or cheap enough, for Campbell's to pay for a full-color rendition of its distinctive package. The character at the bottom is another modern touch, one of a stable of "Campbell's kids" who appeared across ads, serving collectively as spokes-characters.

Other examples of more advanced visual branding also crop up in this early period. Consider the ad for hosiery in Figure 2.14. It provides an early example of a trope that continues to be used today: the before and after illustration, showing problem and solution. First the older, haggard homemaker, with furniture from an earlier era, emotionally spent from

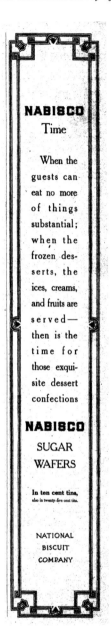

Figure 2.11   Nabisco ad from the early 1900s showing border

Figure 2.12   An early Nabisco ad featuring the package

*Figure 2.13   Campbell's soup ad
               from the early 1900s*

*Figure 2.14   Early 1900s ad with
               before and after
               photos*

Figure 2.15   Jello ad from early 1900s with busy, cluttered layout

darning; below, the younger, happier homemaker, living amid more modern décor, her problems solved by the hero product. From early on, these before-and-after ads tend to use photos, to draw on the still-believed expectation that "the camera doesn't lie." To make this ad look thoroughly modern, you would need only to make the photos larger; capitalize on a better lens and improved printing technology to make these sharp and clear and in color; juxtapose the photos side by side; cut the word count by 80 percent; switch to a modern product such as cosmetics; integrate the trademark with the name; *et voila*, you have an ad that would not excite comment in a 2015 issue of *Good Housekeeping*. The rhetorical strategy would remain identical.

Other layouts are less advanced. Consider the Jello ad in Figure 2.15. It is cluttered, and anticipates the even greater clutter that will be seen in the 1920s and 1950s, which only later gets winnowed down. It has a decorative frame, and a little lifestyle picture: a girl with a bow who visually anchors its claim: "Delicate. Delightful. Dainty."[5] There is a package shot and an illustration of the product in use, of a kind that later, once color photography had been perfected and become cheap, will dominate count-less food ads. The brand name is repeated three times in three different typefaces. The ad gives price information and offers a recipe booklet as a premium. In short, the Jello ad attempts almost everything.

The overall impression, after looking at hundreds of ads from this epoch: visually, with a few notable exceptions, advertisers didn't quite know what they were doing. Metaphorically, it's like watching a toddler of about one year old, who has recently learned to walk. The child can walk; he can even walk fast. But he also tumbles a lot, and seems as often to be falling forward as moving under his own power. It's an unsteady gait.

As a case in point, consider the ad for Pillsbury flour in Figure WA.1,[6] a rare early example of a full-page ad, doubly rare for containing photos, which have been colorized. Take a good, long look. We found it . . . disturbing.

The baby appears to have been photographed separately and pasted in; his head is as large as Mom's, and his wrist to elbow length about the same. The table is too high; the actress cannot have a knee to ankle length that long. Her posture is unnatural. These failures of realism, this igno-rance of staging, make it easy to see that spoon as an ornamental silver dagger. The painful grimace invites us to see her teeth filed to a point. The fingers clutching the baby's arm become dark claws. The steam from the cup resolves into Devil horns, and we see not mother and child at the breakfast table, but a baby about to be sacrificed. The advertiser does not yet know how to guide and channel visual inferences; these spin out of control.

In this era movies were still new; feature films scarcely existed. The Kodak camera was but a few years old. No one had much experience pho-tographing actors caught in the act of living and doing, models enacting a scene designed to promote desired inferences. Producer ignorance was matched by consumer ignorance: consumers hadn't yet seen many staged pictures, narrative stills, slice-of-life photos. Visual vocabularies were nascent; the consumer gaze had not yet been trained. Pillsbury knew what it wanted to show: a lifestyle photo; feeding depicted as love embodied; mother nourishing, warm, and protective; baby cooing with delight; buy this cereal because you love your baby. But the pasted-up photo gives, instead, a forced, unnatural, even horrific impression.

In a few years, much greater visual mastery would be evident. It was not that advertisers didn't know how to create a lifestyle image, a visual depic-tion which consumers would reliably interpret as desired, as in the 1898 Ivory ad; but as yet, advertisers only knew how to accomplish this with illustrations, by means of hand-drawn art and the control it gave. Even Kodak, in this early era, chose to use an illustration to convey successfully

Figure 2.16   Kodak ad from early 1900s relying on illustration rather than photo

the mother-and-baby ambience that Pillsbury failed to achieve photo-graphically (Figure 2.16).[7]

1920s

All histories of advertising agree that the 1920s were halcyon days. Magazine advertising burgeoned. By late in the decade, magazines of the modern type were fully established, with the count of ad pages on a par with the count of editorial pages. Also modern: more than half of all the pictorial and visual arrangements in the magazine appear in the ads rather than the editorial. Ads provide most of the visual treats. In the 1920s there were now many more national brands, not a few of which have maintained their leadership positions down to the present day. New product categories appeared, with new brands to be advertised to the consumer. World War I had left Europe prostrate; and as would happen again after World War II, the United States enjoyed a flush of post-war affluence after 1921. These were boom years.

However, from a visual standpoint one big technological development had yet to occur. Color abounds in ads from the 1920s, but these are color illustrations; color photography still lies in the future. Interestingly, although the technology was now decades old, even black and white photography remained uncommon in ads from this era. The visual element in advertising mostly consists of hand drawn illustrations, many colored, others not.

The eschewal of photography may be partly technological. The black and white photos that do appear in 1920s magazines, whether in editorial or advertising, do not look good to our eyes. Their grainy, pointillistic character could come from low resolution in the printing technology used to produce the magazine, or limits in the photographic process (see Box 2.1). The blurry quality, and the excessively flat depth of field, could reflect limits of the lens, or the shutter speed, or the film; or even lack of skill with lighting. Whatever the cause, the poor aesthetics of printed black and white photos go far to explain why many advertisers in the 1920s stuck with hand-drawn illustrations.

A second limitation emerged: although color became common, the use of color remained tentative and restricted. We sense that graphic designers were still exploring the territory of color, while remaining anchored in a black and white world. For instance, there are many richly colored illustrations, but the color stops there; all text, even the brand name, remains in black. Here and there, the brand block, including the name, will be printed in color; or at least, the package will be. Headlines set in colored type are not common, especially early in the decade. A color background also remains uncommon. And bleed pages, where the color extends all the way to the edge of the page, do not yet exist.

Figure WA.2 for Congoleum rugs shows a representative instance of an ad built around a large color illustration placed at the top of the page. This picture window layout will dominate by the 1980s, by which time a color photo will have replaced the illustration. Here in the 1920s, to control consumers' visual inferences, and shape them in the desired direction, the advertiser must use an illustration. The artist knows how to convey a bucolic suburban scene, with its handsome, successful husband, served by demure and contented wife.[8] The artist can convey the spaciousness of this kitchen, and show the product in use. The copy blocks are still large, but are moving

BOX 2.1   PRINTING TECHNOLOGY AND THE CONSTRUCTION OF ADVERTISEMENTS

It was apparent from our first perusal of old magazine ads that a technological gulf – maybe more than one – separated the infrastructure available for printing magazines in the 1890s from that underlying today's magazines. Identifying and grasping the extent of this technological gap was one of the first pay-offs from purchasing and examining physical copies of old magazines.

Many technologies have shown dramatic change since the fifteenth century, and not a few have changed dramatically since 1900. At a superficial level, any educated person knows that there was a digital printing revolution in the 1980s; and many people will be vaguely aware that the printing machines in use even by 1900 differed fundamentally from the sort of machine introduced by Gutenberg. Terms such as letterpress, lithography, and offset are not particularly obscure, even though most non-specialists would have difficulty if backed against the wall and challenged to explain exactly how each of these technologies worked.

Nonetheless, we found it challenging to pin down exactly: (1) what changed in printing technology during the nineteenth century, and also in the twentieth century prior to the digital revolution; (2) just when these technological changes occurred; and (3) how the technologies available in each era constrained or opened up rhetorical possibilities for advertisers.

Terms such as tymphan, frisket, make ready, rotary press, mangle, stereotype, electrotype, half-tone, intaglio, rotogravure, phototypesetting, linotype, CMYK, Pantone, and offset lithography had to be mastered. We're not ashamed to disclose that we found videos on YouTube helpful for grasping details of how machines worked.

The gist of the story: prior to 1890 or so, it was difficult to flexibly combine pictures and text in mass print production. By contrast, borders and decorative elements were easy. These were available from type foundries along with the lead type in which the words were set. Likewise, if the picture existed in the catalogue of a type foundry – a generic dog or sheaf of wheat, say – it could be purchased and locked into the case with type, making it easy to include. If an unvarying picture was to be used over and over again across ads, such as a portrait of the founder, one could pay the time and cost to have an engraving or woodcut made, which likewise could be locked onto a plate beside lead type, and then printed with ease on a letterpress machine.

What advertisers could not easily do was to create new pictures ad by ad; or snap a photo and have it print with clarity; or design custom typefaces; or integrate wording with pictures, as opposed to presenting pictures and words in separate blocks. As printing technology shifted from presses to offset, and as type, the same as pictures, came to exist primarily as photographic imagery rather than as pieces of lead; and as the cost curves for mass reproduction of photos, color, and everything else plunged; then and only then did the visual branding we see today become technologically and economically feasible.

The colorful ad you see in a 2015 magazine was not possible in 1890 because it required the accumulation of a stream of innovations in at least the following technologies: (1) camera lenses, shutter mechanics, lighting lamps, and the chemistry of photographic emulsions; (2) the chemistry of ink and of color separation and capture; (3) the manufacture of paper with the desired strength, absorbency, and smoothness of surface; (4) phototypesetting in place of lead type casting; (5) the mechanical devices by which the letter press, passed down little changed from Gutenberg, was replaced first by a cylinder press, then a rotary press, and then by rotogravure and offset lithography; (6) the development of half-tone screens and other devices for converting continuous photographic tone to discrete dots which could be printed. All of these developments had proceeded a good distance over the century prior to 1980. All continued to develop further, supplemented by: (7) developments in the new digital technologies of Photoshop and prepress design (a term that has replaced layout, now that no one pastes things up on boards anymore).

Practicing rhetoricians do not really need to study technology; they work with whatever communication techniques are available. Historians of rhetoric are not so fortunate; they need to understand how technology determined the means of persuasion that were available at any one point. And it is the student of visual rhetoric who feels this need most keenly.*

Note: * The following specialized references may be skimmed in order to get a sense of the depth and range of technologies that go into printing, and the enormous amount of innovation from 1800 to 2015. For printing presses, see Moran (1973); for historical perspectives on photography, see Newhall (1982), Sobieszek (1988), and Szarkowski (1989); for typesetting equipment, see Huss (1973); for rotogravure, see Cartwright and Mackay (1956); and for detailed case-by-case analyses of how an image would print differently under different printing technologies, see Jussim (1974)

toward subservience to the illustration. Conversely, this magazine ad has not decided whether it wants to be a catalogue page instead; it also presents color samples with ordering information. Unusually, the ad features an emblematic logo, the gold seal; also unusually, the brand name is printed in color, and occupies its own space at the lower right corner, anticipating the brand block that will later become routine. Unfortunately, there is no color consistency between the name in the logo and that in the brand block; the desirability of having the brand own a color has not yet taken hold.

Figure WA.3, for Colgate toothpaste, uses a similar layout that also leads with a color illustration. Those elements that are similar, across the Colgate and Congoleum ads, neatly capture a central tendency in 1920s ad layout: lead with a big color illustration; follow with a large text block; include only a small headline; and supply the rudiments of a separate brand block. Here there is even a tagline in the brand block: "cleans teeth the right way," a modern touch not yet common in the 1920s. Colgate, a packaged good, anticipates more recent practice by building the brand block around its package. The package design itself has ceased to be merely ornamental, and now contains, and brings into the ad, a selling message: "comes out a ribbon / lays flat on the brush." Also anticipating later layout designs, the package appears at the dynamic center of the illustration, the target of the girl's pointing finger, and again, stacked on the counter. Brand, brand, brand: advertisers are learning what to emphasize in an ad. But the Colgate and Congoleum ads also exhibit the clutter commonly seen in ads of this era, with multiple pictures and multiple text blocks. It will be a few decades before this clutter is pruned away.

Although black and white photography had been capable of mass reproduction for some decades, we found it to be comparatively rare in 1920s magazine advertisements.[9] The Libby's ad in Figure 2.17 conveys the

Figure 2.17   Libby's ad from the 1920s with unsuccessful photos

shortcomings: the photos are small, blurry, and do not have much depth of field. Nothing happens in these photos, and you can't see much. Even in the original 11 x 16 inch print size, the food plates aren't much more than stippled patterns of blacks and whites. Magazine photographic printing was not yet capable of photorealism, especially in the depiction of food.

Even in the case of machines, which lend themselves to visual reproduction via the camera, itself a machine, the black and white photos of the era are not successful. Consider the vacuum cleaner ad in Figure 2.18. The photo contains no visual drama, and can't even be said to reproduce the details of the machine. It just sits there. As yet, nobody knew how to

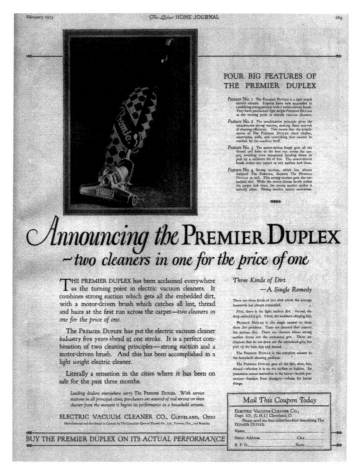

*Figure 2.18   Vacuum cleaner ad from the 1920s with uninspired
            photography*

photograph a thing, a machine, to make it appealing; there was no histori-cal tradition on which to draw.

The techniques for painting a beautiful still life, for presenting luscious fruit, were centuries old by this point; but the packaged food advertiser faces a different challenge. He has to show a delicious-appearing meal, prepared with a packaged ingredient which is subordinate to other com-ponents. Whole fruit is easy to paint in an appetizing way; this skill had been mastered by the Renaissance. But making a meal on a plate look deli-cious is a far different challenge, one that was beyond the ability of graphic designers of this era. Unintentionally hilarious examples abound.

Consider the Quaker ad for macaroni in Figure 2.19. It appears that

Figure 2.19   Quaker ad from the 1920s unsuccessful in depicting food

the designer started with a photograph of two packages, one spilling out product, and two plates with two meals built around the product. Taking the lower plate first, the sauce here looks more like primeval black ooze than something edible. The vegetable on the right appears radioactive, while the unrecognizable accompaniment above cues ancient jokes about cafeteria food. In the upper plate, the noodles must have appeared too blurred and indistinct; in an attempt to bring them out, stark white spaces in the shape of noodles have been punched out, not to good effect. The hope must have been that after a cursory glance to identify the product, the reader would dwell on the text instead.

The problem of how to portray a meal to make it look delicious was not a problem limited to photographers. Black and white illustrators weren't always successful either. Consider the ad for Crisco in Figure 2.20. Does this cherry pie make your stomach grumble with hunger? Or does that piece of pie, shoved at you, suggest worms, eyeballs, and dripping tar, more than sweet luscious fruit? The 1920s may have been boom times for most advertisers, but food advertisers of the era had to limp ahead, lacking the unmatched photorealism of color photography, and still awaiting improved camera set-ups and higher-resolution printing. The photographs of the era cannot and do not do much for the brand.

Black and white illustrations were common across categories in the 1920s, and could be successful when not attempting to make meals look appetizing. Figure 2.21, for Beech-Nut, shows what could be accomplished through the illustrator's art. The image of this boy will be interpreted as desired by most viewers. He's a healthy, happy boy child to warm a mother's heart. The advertiser was savvy enough to show a stack of bread, which could be drawn successfully, rather than attempt to show peanut butter spread over bread, as would become the norm once photorealistic color photography became possible. The ad is unusual for its time in having a brand block consisting of the package alone, and also for the brevity of its copy. Few ads in the 1920s made do with but 60 words of copy.

Much more typical is the ad for Mum deodorant in Figure 2.22, with its large black and white illustration, in place of the photo that would appear in any personal care ad by the 1980s, and its more than 500 words of copy. Also typical of the 1920s: the lack of any special type or graphic treatment of the Mum's brand name. Instead, the advertiser repeats the text of that name in the body copy, over and over, rather than enhancing it visually, or making it large and prominent, or giving it a block of space to own.

Although still uncommon, the 1920s do see some attempts to brand with color. These ads do not necessarily use a color illustration, but instead supply large swatches of color, with the choice of color keyed to the brand, and becoming owned by the brand, as part of its trade dress. For instance,

Figure 2.20 Crisco ad from the 1920s also unsuccessful in depicting food

Campbell's soup begins to reproduce its distinctive red and white can, its packaging, in color, as in Figure WA.4. Below the color illustration – a safe still-life arrangement of whole vegetables – and the can and the text, there is a brand block in Campbell's distinctive shade of red, with the tagline: "Look for the red and white label." The bowl of soup is less successful, but not as unappetizing as the other failed attempts discussed earlier. As late as 1921, this same brand block had appeared in black and white, although still featuring the then incongruous commandment to look for a red and white can.

Fels-Naptha presents a large close-up of its unwrapped soap bar next

*Figure 2.21   Beech-Nut ad from the 1920s showing successful black and
               white illustration*

to its package (Figure WA.5). The distinctive gold color of the soap, and
the blue green of its packaging, are reproduced and echoed in the two
borders added to frame the product shot. The ad foreshadows a staple of
later packaged goods advertising layouts: nothing but brand and text, with
the package and contents providing all the visual portion of the ad, which
nonetheless succeeds in conveying elements of the brand's trade dress.

On the other hand, in the 1920s we still find major consumer brands
advertising in black and white, in less than a full page, with no visual
adornment at all, as in the Heinz ad in Figure 2.23. But this is not the
norm; at least a black and white illustration is expected, as in the ad for
Scot toilet tissue in Figure 2.24, where the illustrator, in choosing an Art
Deco style, with modern (for the 1920s) hair style to match, visually suggests to whom the brand is positioned, and how the brand wishes to be
perceived by this target.[10]

To sum up: visual branding was nascent in the 1920s. Some tools, such
as blocks of color, had become available, and here and there, individual

Figure 2.22   Word-heavy Mum deodorant ad from the 1920s

advertisers, or maybe only art directors at select agencies, had begun to explore their use. Other visual tools, commonplace today, were as yet unavailable. The 1920s were still the age of copy. Most advertisers appeared to believe that hundreds of words were required to advertise the brand, and that these lengthy missives would be read by enough consumers to be

Figure 2.23 Heinz ad from the 1920s without color

Figure 2.24 ScotTissue ad from the 1920s showing potential of hand-drawn imagery

worth the space. Consumers were approached as readers, not viewers, and as highly involved, not indifferent. Advertisers did not try to seduce with pictures; they believed consumers could still be commanded with words. Visual branding had not got far.

1950s

The 1950s emerge from our examination as a transitional era. We see survivals of earlier styles side by side with the tentative appearance of new visual styles that will later become dominant. In the early 1950s, a single issue of *LHJ* may contain ads featuring: (1) a black and white illustration accompanied by copious text; (2) a color illustration with rather less text; (3) a now successful black and white photo – or three or four – supported by multiple chunks of body copy; and (4) a large color photo, alone or accompanied by additional photos, and supported by varying amounts of text. The first two are holdovers from the 1920s, while the last two, especially the latter, will become dominant by the 1980s. Here in the 1950s, a single ad layout may mix two or even three of these visual styles.

In another transitional marker, full page ads dominate the front half of the magazine, becoming even more common than in the 1920s, but fractional page ads continue to dominate the second half of the magazine. By the 1980s, fractional page ads will dwindle further, finally becoming uncommon in mass circulation magazines, except for a chunk appearing in the last few pages along with true classified ads, to use the terminology of newspapers.

The 1950s are transitional in other ways. Word count has measurably decreased, as Pollay (1985) found, but is still higher than today. Physical page size has shrunk a little, but remains much larger than the contemporary 8 by 10 inch norm, except in the case of *Good Housekeeping*, which has shrunk to near modern size. Printing resolution had improved relative to the 1920s, but will improve further; and paper stock does not yet have the true glossy surface that will emerge later. Camera and lighting technology have notably improved, as will become apparent in the photographic examples, but these also will continue to advance.

We begin the examples with a throwback or holdover. Figure 2.25, for a now-vanished clothing company, features a hand-drawn black and white illustration supported by lengthy copy. The copy has no subheads or other visual punctuation, and the brand sponsor is identified in plain type at the bottom of the ad. Even the trademarks are placed separately from the sponsor, as was the case in the 1920s. Figure 2.26, for Baldwin pianos, shows a second ad that could have appeared in the 1920s or before.

Figure 2.26 Baldwin Piano ad from the 1950s also using older styles

Figure 2.25 Clothing ad from the 1950s retaining older styles

The black and white hand-drawn illustrations are traditional in style, as is their lazy-S layout. The product name is called out in a title block, but the Baldwin brand is not visually enhanced or typographically set out.

A magazine reader in the 1950s would encounter many black and white ads, but not all would be as traditional or old-fashioned as these first two. Consider the ad for Chix diapers from Johnson and Johnson in Figure 2.27. The illustration style and the single-column width hark back decades; but the absence of body copy and the reliance on a short large-type headline are forward-looking, as is the organization of a brand block around the package. The ad for Nescafé coffee in Figure 2.28 departs from the 1920s to an even greater extent, despite its use of a hand-drawn illustration. There is, first, the disembodied head shot, a staple of this era. Second, the ad is busy: curved headline, package on the diagonal, coffee drops exploding upwards, copy framed in a sunburst, and multiple dispersed text blocks. Such noisy layouts are characteristic of the 1950s. A third point of departure from the 1920s is the large type headline stating a claim, in conjunction with a comparatively small amount of body copy.

More typical of the 1950s, and a good index of how far visual branding had got, or not, is the black and white illustrated Clorox ad in Figure 2.29. It is very busy, consistent with its era, but also organized, with four numbered blocks, using a style rarely seen in the 1920s. Every inch is put to work: there are six illustrations, including the animated package, and messages are highlighted in four separate blocks, such as the easel near the bottom. On the other hand, as we saw in the Jello ad from the 1920s, the brand name appears in three separate typefaces. The diamond background for the name on the package, which will evolve into the current Clorox brand mark, is not picked up in the ad, and there is not a separate brand block. Most of the creative energy behind this ad went into the copy, and then the arrangement of the copy on the page, with only a little going into the visuals.

In the early 1950s some brands give up on color, and revert to black and white. Compare the Fels-Naptha ad in Figure 2.30 to the earlier one in Figure WA.5. The Fels-Naptha brand has given up on, or its brand manager no longer wishes to pay for, the attempt to own the colors gold and teal. We likewise saw examples where Colgate gave up on red in favor of black and white ads, and Palmolive soap gave up on its green and gold representation. Color has not yet won the day in branding circles.

The 1950s saw the dawn of research into the effect of mechanical factors on advertising response. For a few decades, academics and consultants busied themselves attempting to measure the effects of color versus black and white, of larger versus smaller ad sizes, of using an illustration versus a photograph, and so forth.[11] These studies were possible and pertinent

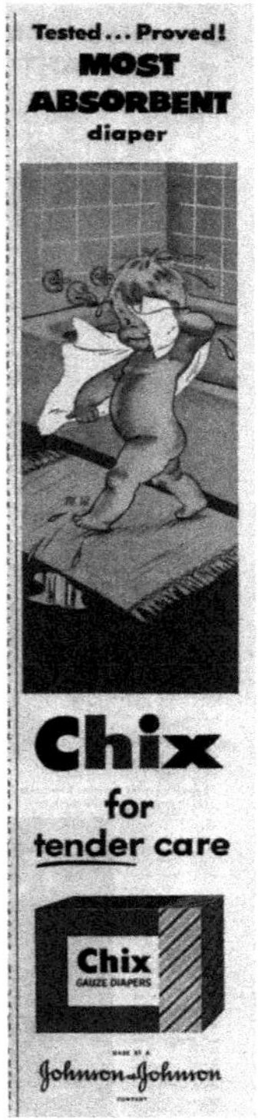

Figure 2.28   Nescafé ad from the 1950s using a busy style and newer elements

Figure 2.27   Chix diaper ad from the 1950s using a more contemporary style

Figure 2.29   Clorox ad showing characteristic 1950s styles

because all these formats were used in the 1950s, and for several decades after. Magazines also charged different rates for different formats, lending traction to cost–benefit analyses. However, by some point in the 1990s, full-page, full-color photographs had become so dominant a print ad format that these mechanical studies gradually had to be abandoned for lack of relevance. But back in the 1950s, it is easy to imagine a hard-bitten Fels-Naptha executive demanding to know why he had to pay for color if a cheaper black and white ad could get the name out there as well, and his minions responding meekly, "Yessir." There were not yet branding consultants who stood ready to preach the virtues of owning a color. Black and

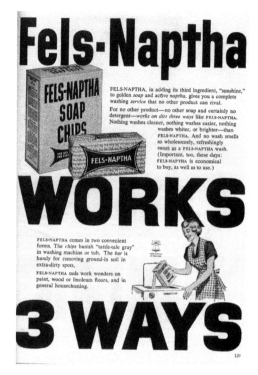

Figure 2.30   Fels-Naptha ad from the 1950s eschewing the use of color

white was the cheaper option, and that appears to have carried the day for some brand sponsors.

Not so much throwbacks, but certainly transitional, are ads from this era that feature black and white photographs. Camera technology had advanced enough by the 1950s for some of these photographs to succeed, during an era when color photography, while technically and economically feasible, was still not the norm. Figure 2.31, for Lux soap, provides an illustrative example. The use of celebrity endorsers for women's soap and cosmetic products dates back to the 1920s.[12] But here the large photograph beautifully and convincingly renders both Ann Sheridan's attractive visage and her personal force. By this point, most of the audience for this ad had been watching movies all their lives. Relative to the 1920s consumer, the viewer of this ad had seen thousands of black and white photographic close-ups on movie screens much larger than this page. The viewer was accustomed to the idea that a photograph is a window onto reality: that Ms. Sheridan looks exactly that way, and exactly that beautiful. The

Figure 2.31   Lux ad from the 1950s showing skillful use of photography

remaining limits on photographic and printing technology are put to good effect, to indicate a smooth and completely unblemished complexion. All that keeps this ad from being a perfectly modern skin cleanser ad, other than the use of black and white photography in place of color, is the amount of remaining body copy – about 100 words – and the use of multiple small pictures. For an audience not yet used to color imagery, the black and white photography in this ad probably succeeded in conveying a photorealistic effect.

The photographs are equally successful in the Campana ad in Figure 2.32. Printing technology now allows subtle enough half-tones to

Figure 2.32   Cosmetics ad from the 1950s with successful photos

suggest beautifully smooth complexions. However, the Campana ad is more true to its era, and less of an anticipation of the future, than the Lux ad: it contains about 500 words of body copy, and the pictures play only a supporting role.

Even manufacturers of mundane appliances had learned to shoot black and white photographs that flattered the product. Compare the General Electric (GE) ad for a clothes iron in Figure 2.33 to either the vacuum cleaner ad or the Libby's ad from the 1920s (Figures 2.17 and 2.18). This clothes iron gleams, and the product itself has benefited from the application of industrial design: it's a nice looking machine. The seven small inset photos do reflect the busyness of 1950s ad layout, but are high enough in resolution to succeed in conveying details of product usage and the benefits of specific design features. There is a brand block, which contains a tagline; conversely, in a bit of a throwback, the trademark GE circle is shown twice, as part of the name and separate from it. Other retrograde elements include a stated price and the less than full-page size.

Not every use of black and white photography was as successful. The ad for Drene shampoo in Figure 2.34 is modern in the use of a large photo dominating the page, combined with an inset brand block, and also modern in the minimal body copy. But the photo doesn't work. The woman's head is twisted off her torso, *Exorcist* movie style. Her complexion is muddy. It takes a while to read the scene: what is intended to be seen as hair glistening in starlight, amid a delicate spray of blossoms, comes across as black and white blobs and blurs. This shampoo advertiser's rhetorical strategy is clear, and appropriate for a branding effort in this product category: to show a dreamy scene of subtly shiny hair, romantic as starlight. But the available means of photographic reproduction were not up to the task.

The Johnson Wax ad in Figure 2.35 provides another instructive instance of failure. The goal is to show how a wood floor in a tasteful living room will gleam, if only the sponsor's product were to be purchased. But the depth of field afforded by the lens and lighting set-up is not up to the task. One sees a muddy image of a fireplace, blobs to the right suggesting a plant, and to the left, other blobs on the coffee table. The photograph fails its goal, which was to show a beautifully and tastefully decorated home of class and distinction, achieved by means of the product hero. It is too small and blurry. The advertiser falls back on a hand-drawn illustration for supplement. The displayed package is an afterthought, not a real image but a simplified sketch; another branding opportunity foregone.

In contrast to these atavisms and aborted moves forward, the prototypical ad from the early 1950s is a large and extremely cluttered layout that makes the head swim: a cornucopia of shouts, whistles, lures, and hustles. The Duz detergent ad in Figure WA.6 is representative. Headlines may

Figure 2.33   General Electric small appliance ad from the 1950s

Figure 2.34 Shampoo ad from the 1950s with unsuccessful photography

be in black, red, and blue, and underlined in black, red, and blue brush stroke. There are two color illustrations, two testimonials, three sub-headed blocks of copy, and over half a dozen separate benefits claimed. This kitchen-sink strategy does not stem from the ignorance or incompetence of a minor brand. An ad for Tide (p. 38 of the same issue, not reproduced) has two large and one small illustration, a color background for the headline that is not a color owned by the brand, other headlines in other colors, a banner background, a song, and four or five different claimed benefits.

This busyness applies across product categories. The Dole ad in Figure WA.7 uses a large color photograph overflowing with different items. The display is the negative apotheosis of Checkhov's famous dictum:[13] why the salt and pepper shakers, in that style, and why that many pieces of silverware, in that style? Not content with the photograph, a color sketch of a

*Figure 2.35   Johnson Wax ad from the 1950s with unsuccessful
            photography*

celebrity is added at the top, and not one but seven different Dole packages
are piled up.

In the examples thus far, we have seen only a few examples of color
photos. These are not uncommon here in the 1950s, a decade or two after
the mass reproduction of color photography became feasible, but still
account for a minority of all images, relative to black and white photos,
black and white illustrations, and color illustrations, such as those seen in
the Duz ad. Some of the color photos that appear in the 1950s do succeed.
Figure WA.8, an ad for a Max Factor cosmetic, shows off to good effect
the lovely complexion of the model, in not one but two color photos. Even

Figure 2.36   Ivory soap ad from the 1950s showcasing color photography

more modern is the successful posing, as she believably nuzzles the man in the large shot, and believably applies the makeup in the small shot. The viewer of these ads again had decades of experience viewing similar scenes in movies. The ad producer knew how to set up the shot, and the ad consumer knew how to view it. Visual literacy was much advanced.

The ad for Ivory soap in Figure 2.36 is similarly successful. The viewer will respond, reflexively: yes that is a darling little angel! Beautiful! The entire page is pleasing to the eye, with its enormous main image, the promise of the smaller supporting image (Mom can look as good if she uses Ivory too), the large swaths of color, and the plentiful use of white space. The brand color of blue is subtly emphasized throughout, down to the blue eyes of the little angel girl, picking up on the package color. This ad is among the most visually accomplished of any we have reproduced thus far. In 50 years, advertisers have come a long way from the horrific, unnatural poses and representations seen in the Pillsbury ad from 1907 in Figure WA.1.

In ads that must show a beautiful complexion, the limited development of color photography and printing as of the 1950s is more a feature than a bug: low resolution and soft focus make it easy to believe that the complexion shown is real, rather than extensively touched up. But even outside of cosmetic, soap, and skin care ads, we see increasing evidence of mastery of the art of communicating visually through color photography. The ad for Armstrong flooring in Figure WA.9 successfully shows a stylish living room (if you like pink), with windows admitting a generous amount of soft light. The room appears spacious and well lit; compare the Johnson wax ad (Figure 2.35), or the Congoleum ad from the 1920s section (Figure WA.2). Other modern touches include the separate brand block, and brand name adorned with letter art (see Chapter 3). The layout is characteristic of what will come later, with the photo occupying the top three-fourths of the ad, and bled to edge of the page; 30 years later, in the 1980s, all that will change is a further reduction in the body copy. Six decades ago, Armstrong was able to produce a primarily visual ad which gently promotes the brand by displaying an attractive lifestyle.

Alas, progress in bending color photography to advertising purpose remained fitful in this era. For every successful Armstrong ad, you can find others less so. The enormous two-page ad for Rinso detergent in Figure WA.10 is garish; that lipstick is more often seen on clowns. The sharp corners of the package cut into the cheeks of the models, and the boxes are out of scale with their faces and hanging unsupported, as these two women appear to grin stiffly at something over the reader's shoulder. It is as retrograde and unsuccessful as the Armstrong ad is polished and sure.[14]

Many food ads remain mired in a hell of low-resolution printing, poor lens quality, inept lighting, and ignorance of staging. Consider the Campbell's soup ad in Figure WA.11. It intends to show delicious chicken cooked in "heavenly gravy." But the image is as easily read as dead birds trapped in a mudslide; it's not easy, with the technology of the day, to make a cream sauce look good on the page. It comes across as goo.

Although many food ads fall short, others are more successful. Again, to avert the suspicion that we have picked out and picked on an unfortunate few designs sourced from minor no-talent agencies, we present a pair of ads for the same major brand, one successful in its use of color reproduction, the other less so. The Jello ad in Figure WA.12 convincingly portrays a rich mellow gold filling (butterscotch mocha, we might say today), a yummy chocolate filling, a believable pour of sugar, and a golden pie crust. Like the Armstrong ad, it uses a modern layout, with bleed color photo filling the top three-fourths of the ad, a minimum of body copy, and a separate brand block based on the package. Much less successful is the Jello ad in Figure WA.13. The lime mold glistens appropriately, provided the reader is not distracted by the white dots stenciled on top. But the mess in the center is both unrecognizable and unappetizing (we defy the reader to identify the filling without reading the copy). Yucch.

In short, despite the occasional successes seen in the use of color photography, we still see leading advertisers opting for the safer choice of color illustration. The portrait of the girl that dominates the Breck shampoo ad in Figure 2.37 may evoke the same admiration and pleasure as the photo of that Ivory baby girl, but here the visual pleasure rests on the illustrator's art. Likewise Pepsi-Cola, when it wanted to portray a fashionable woman, reverted to illustration rather than attempting color photography (not reproduced; see the same issue of *LHJ*, p. 176).

Finally, it is still rare to see a brand attempt to own a color. The Ivory ad gives a taste of what is to come; the Prell shampoo ad in Figure 2.38 goes further: green product, green packaging, key selling claim in green brush stroke text, green eyes on the model. Prell. You'll recognize it in the store. You'll know it in the shower.

1980s

The 1980s represent the triumph of color photography. Illustrations, especially black and white illustrations, nearly disappear from magazines such as *Good Housekeeping*. The use of color illustrations is sparing, relying as much on a contrast effect, within a sea of color photos, as any belief in the inherent selling efficacy of the artist's touch. Black and white photos also begin to disappear. A negative trend is visible even within the decade, as black and white ads go from a minority at the outset, to a rarity later.

Color photos both take over in population terms, becoming the norm, but also begin to take over each ad page where they appear. As the 1980s proceed, bleed pages become common: the photo, and color, go all the way to the edge of the page. Increasingly, we see a color background that covers the page, and/or a photo that takes up the entire page. This trend proceeds as the decade advances. In the early years, the photo may bleed to the edge, but it only covers the top half or top third of the ad; the remainder of the ad, with its block of body text, remains black printed on white, the same as

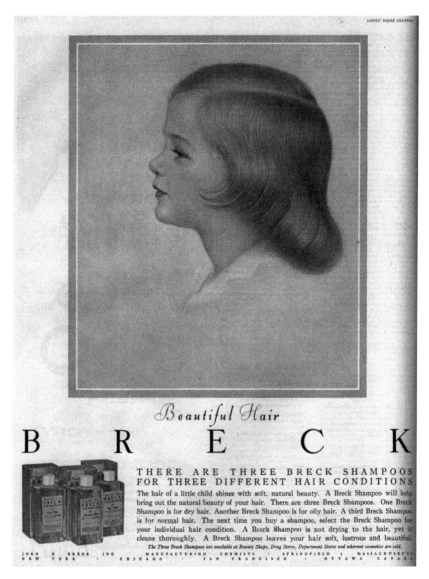

Figure 2.37   Breck shampoo ad from the 1950s

the rest of the magazine. By later in the decade, the color photo may take over the entire page, so that the small amount of text remaining is inscribed on the photo, and no longer a separate block printed on the white page. In other cases, that portion of the ad which does not contain an image will

Figure 2.38   Prell 1950s ad showing branding by color

nonetheless have a textured color background, so that there is no white area to be seen anywhere on the physical page.

The ad in Figure 2.39, for Volvo, is transitional.[15] The color photo occupies only half the page, and does not bleed to the edge. The quality of the printed photo is not great, but is adequate to capture the intended scene: a large family home somewhere in the Northeast, with differences in design

Figure 2.39   Volvo ad from the 1980s showing picture window layout

of the older cars made visible enough to support the headline. That head-line is typical of the 1980s in its size, its boldface, and its unadorned font. The body copy is set in two partial column blocks, and consists of more than 100 words.

Soon the consumer of the 1980s will encounter more visually dynamic and less text-intense layouts. Consider the ad for Revlon in Figure WA.14. The hair, complexion, eye color, and lipstick shade of each model are beautifully captured. The headline is in colored text within a contrasting color block. The brand in its package dominates the lower portion of the ad; the body copy has been reduced to less than 50 words, now presented in a fairly large typeface, and in reverse type on a colored background.

But the Revlon ad is still traditional in its organization into blocks. The 1980s consumer will begin to encounter more and more ads that are not organized as blocks. The ad for Emeraude fragrance in Figure 2.40 presents a single image that takes over the entire page. The skin tones of the model emerge beautifully. Skillful lighting produces a rich play of shadows which, aided by advances in lens, film, and printing technology, are successfully made present on the page. Not counting brand name and tagline, the text portion consists of only six words, inscribed on the picture rather than set separately in a block. The photography portrays a posture of passion: the model's hand covers her breast, her lips are parted, face lifted up: she's excited, passionate, and feels intensely. The technology of photographic reproduction has sufficiently advanced to allow the viewer to experience her image in this way. And in experiencing this image of passion, the consumer moves a long way from the screaming kids, the piles of laundry, the messy floor, and the perennial challenge of what to serve for dinner, which occupy so much of the rest of *Good Housekeeping* magazine, both editorial and advertising.

Most of the layouts from the early and mid-1980s based on color photography can be placed between the Volvo ad at one extreme, and the Emeraude ad at the other. The Volvo layout, a relatively pure case of the picture window format, was already becoming dated at the beginning of the decade; the Emeraude ad, almost totally pictorial, harks to the future. In between, we see ads like the Sara Lee ad in Figure 2.41. This ad uses a modified picture window format. The photo occupies only the top three-fifths of the ad, but bleeds to the edge of the page, and has an irregular bottom border. There is no block of body copy, only a long headline. And the brand block consists of packages lined up across the bottom. Finally, there is no longer a white background, but below the image, a shade of gray that ever so slightly darkens from left to right, and also toward the top of the image, where it becomes pitch black. That subtle darkening of the gray below, coupled with the intense black above (or visually, behind) makes the photograph successful: for what makes these snacks look so scrumptious, so real, is the studio lighting, which brings out the gold of the muffins, makes the chocolate and the coffee look darkly delicious, and gives the napkin folds their soft richness. With this ad, color photography in the food space reaches its acme. You can look at this image a long time, and only grow hungrier; it has no flaw to disrupt contemplation of how good these snacks might taste.

Food advertisers were not always this successful, especially earlier in the decade. The ad for Shake 'n Bake, in Figure WA.15, does not succeed.

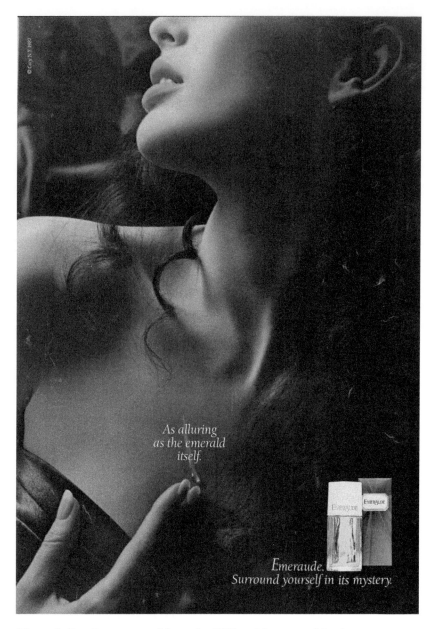

Figure 2.40   Fragrance ad from the 1980s with successful color photography

Figure 2.41   Sara Lee ad from the 1980s successfully depicting food

Where the Sara Lee ad is close to the Emeraude pole, the Shake 'n Bake
ad is closer to the Volvo pole. True, it has a large picture bled to the page
edge and not confined to a block; but it also has a separate text block and
the large type headline characteristic of the early 1980s and before. The
picture is a long way from the clutter of the 1950s; but alas, what is meant
to be seen as melted cheese could as easily be scum, and what is supposed
to be a mouth-watering tomato sauce coating looks more like red paint.
Photographic and printing technologies have not yet jelled.[16]

The same technological shortfalls undercut some personal care ads from
the early 1980s. In Figure WA.16, a famous actress is shown in extreme
close-up. We are meant to see her as a beautiful face, made that way by use
of the Raintree moisturizer product. But she could as easily be a manikin
or figure in a wax museum; the skin tones, as lighted in the studio and
printed with the technology of the day, don't quite cut it. She's uncomfort-
ably close to us, and does not look real. Overall, the ad hews to a straightforward picture window layout, again closer to the Volvo anchor, despite
the colored background and diagonal picture border. The advertiser still
feels a need for 50 words of copy set in two blocks.

Still other uses of color photography from the 1980s occur within even
more primitive layouts, while being not very successful as images. The ad
for Colgate in Figure 2.42 uses a cluttered layout more commonly seen in
the 1950s or even 1920s. There are four separate blocks of text, in small,
smaller, tiny, and tinier fonts, with a long headline in large boldface broken
into two by the picture. Everything is placed on a white background.
Although realistic, the photo of the young African-American boy is
problematic: why so sad? That is the face of a boy unjustly sent to deten-
tion instead of lunch. What's this got to do with toothpaste? And the small
photos of painted chalksticks offer support for the copy claims that, to be
generous, is a stretch too far. Colgate still hasn't figured out what to do
with the no longer new technology of color photographic reproduction. A
yawning gap separates Colgate from Emeraude.

Because 1980s ads mix more and less successful uses of photography,
this too may be considered a transitional decade. There are still ads using
black and white photographs in rigid picture window layouts, like the
Maytag ad in Figure 2.43, which has more than 100 words of copy set in
blocks, and a blurry supporting picture showing appliances. The people in
the main photo in the Maytag ad stand there trying to look like just folks.
To the jaundiced contemporary eye, it could be a still from a *Saturday
Night Live* skit. The most modern thing about the ad is the centered brand
block with large name and emblematic logo, albeit in black. Else, it's a
throwback.

A novel use of color photography, seen in the 1980s and down to the

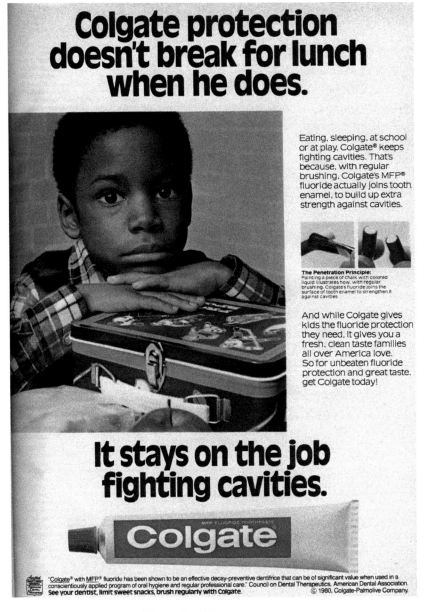

Figure 2.42   Colgate ad from the 1980s

George, Jr., Mrs. Lang, Maryelizabeth, Mr. Lang.

"A working mother's best friend is her Maytag," writes Mrs. Lang.

Between her family and her job, who has the time to wait around for repairmen?

"Thank you for making a washer a working housewife and mother can count on," writes Mrs. Nancy Lang, Hampton Bays, New York.

"11 years ago, I purchased a Maytag. It wasn't till just this past spring that it needed its first repair."

Mrs. Lang knows from experience that Maytag Washers are built to last longer and save you money with fewer repairs. She also knows that they can save you the hassle of waiting around for repairmen.

Mrs. Lang adds that she is also delighted with her Maytag Dryer. "As for my Maytag Dishwasher, I would be lost without it," she concludes.

Of course, we don't say all Maytags will equal that record. But long life with few repairs is what we try to build into every Maytag product.

See our washers, dryers, dishwashers and disposers.

MAYTAG
THE DEPENDABILITY PEOPLE

The Maytag Company, Newton, Iowa 50208.

Figure 2.43   Maytag ad from the 1980s with unsuccessful staging

present day, represents a variation on the product-as-hero theme. In these layouts, the package is photographed as large as life and as realistically as the technology will allow. The package may be the only visual element, as in the Pepto-Bismol ad in Figure 2.44, where the remainder of the ad, excepting a thumbnail diagram, consists of text, including the mega-type sans serif black headline so characteristic of the 1980s. The Pepto-Bismol ad may reflect the spread of management science. This ad has been

Figure 2.44   Pepto-Bismol ad from the 1980s

stripped to its selling essentials: state the claim in a headline so large they can't miss it; reiterate the claim in a few lines of copy; show the package so they can find it on the shelf; let the package name the brand. No need for anything else.

In other instances, the package will be photographed about as large, and made as central, but will be accompanied by other photographic imagery, which may be artful. Consider the Sanka ad in Figure WA.17. The package is as large as in the Pepto-Bismol ad, and even more photorealistic, consistent with the technological advances in reproduction during the intervening six years. But here, rather than a mega-type headline, the package brand is supported by a beautiful image: a splash. Blue water under a blue sky, pure as can be, rendered in a crystalline explosion. The result is pleasing to the eye, and as difficult to produce photographically as to make a meal on a plate appear delicious. The Sanka ad sells visually: a water process was used to perform the decaffeination, still a novel product feature at this time. And water, pure water, is what the large picture connotes, no less than the Emeraude picture connotes passion.

As the 1980s proceeded, advertisers were increasingly able to achieve the holy grail of persuasive photography: realism – indubitable, compelling realism. And because most of what is to be realistically portrayed consists of the pleasing and the sensual and the gratifying, advertisers also achieve, in the 1980s, the ability to give visual pleasure to the viewer by means of the photograph alone. Consider the Hunt's ad in Figure WA.18, or the Tree Top apple juice ad in Figure WA.19. That's one beautiful tomato; that's one crisp, ripe apple. These two ads are modern in their reliance on a dominant visual in the form of an impressively realistic color photograph; but these two ads are dated insofar as they still contain copious text in a separate block. As time proceeds, the image will stay, and the text will reduce further, and migrate from its separate block to an inscription on the picture. More and more, ads will present themselves as pretty pictures, vivid and alive, and not as a stale sales pitch, canned and frozen speech.

Finally, even as photorealism fulfills its promise, there are glimmerings of the next turn, to a post-Photoshop world, where images will harness color reproduction technology for fiction and fantasy. In Figure WA.20, Crest constructs an image of a bathroom wall broken through by a running boy. This image could not work without the realism provided by contemporary color reproduction technology; but here it is a fiction that has been made real. A child cannot run through a wall, and if he did, he would not leave that neat outline. But color photography makes us see that implausible event as something that really happened. As with all fiction, this fantasy image more vividly conveys the desired copy point, of how eager children will be to brush their teeth with this brand. Indeed, how could one successfully convey eagerness to brush, without use of fiction? A photo of children running to the bathroom would only indicate "running children" – or perhaps, children with the runs. Eager children at the bathroom sink would be one more portrayal of happy smiling faces in a magazine full of these. Only by drawing on a visual cliché diffused in comic books and cartoons – the run-through wall, the hole made in the shape of a running figure – in conjunction with the realism of color photography, can the desired copy point be visually conveyed. The image works because of technology, but also because of the vastly increased visual literacy of the 1980s consumer, the consumer who has watched color television for decades, who has watched movies all their life, and who, above all, has spent decades thumbing through 300-page magazines stuffed with imagery put to work, images designed to convey messages, eloquent images.

2005–15

Because contemporary examples appear elsewhere in the book, such as the Tide ad in Figure 0.1, we do not offer a set of examples here. Historical analysis is, in any case, difficult to do with materials that are still being produced, where we can claim no historical perspective, no future vantage point. Instead, here is a sketch of prominent tendencies in recent magazine advertising:

1. Visual elements dominate the page. If these do not compose a picture or image, there will at least be a colored background, maybe textured. Rarely do we see distinct visual and verbal elements separately grouped on a white page, as in the Volvo ad. Most often, the entire page is filled by a picture or a set of images and colors, as in the Emeraude ad. The ad is marked as a page apart from the magazine, because elsewhere editorial matter continues to take the form of (mostly) black text in blocks on a white page, supported or illustrated by pictures.
    a. The pictures are as likely to be fictive, or to contain fantastic elements, or to be confabulations, as to present realistic color photographs of people, scenes, and objects. Images are as likely to be constructed in computer graphics software as captured with a camera in a studio, as in the Crest ad.
    b. There remains some advantage to counter-programming; to being marked out as different from the common run of ads. Hence, ads with white space – allowing the white paper beneath to remain uncovered – do not disappear; rather, when present, white space takes up a large proportion of the ad.[17] A sea of white paper hosts a few small visual and verbal elements, and thereby, picks them out, gesticulates at them, yells for attention. What we seldom see any more is a white border confining the picture, and a text block on a white band across the page, as in the Volvo ad.
2. Text may be *de minimus*, presented as a caption, headline, or brief anchoring explanation, and not as a block of copy. For the product categories on which we focus, you are more likely to see an ad with fewer than 25 words than one with more than 100 words. For headlines, you are more likely to see a small-type caption than the

mega-type black headlines common in the 1980s. Special typefaces for headlines, in color and not overly large, are now more common than mega-type black text in a plain sans serif font.

3. Brands loom large, depicted by their packages if a packaged good, or by a color graphic design of their brand mark if not a packaged good. But the incessant repetition of the brand name in the text, as seen in the 1920s Mum ad, becomes rare. Brands are more present visually than verbally.

4. Text-heavy ads, black and white photography, and also black and white illustrations mostly disappear; but color illustrations, especially of spokes-characters, or in cartoon form, retain a role.

    a. By 2015 we begin to see faux roughness: the careful mimicry, by computer graphics software, of hand-lettering, chalkboard lettering, or pencil sketches. It's as if the ad visuals seek to deny their computer origins by migrating away from the perfect and slick. Time will tell if this is naught but a fashion of the moment.

CONCLUSION: HOW VISUAL BRANDING IN ADVERTISING CHANGED

Throughout the book we assume a one-way historical development: that advertising became more visual, decade after decade, and that branding became ever more visually sophisticated, advancing generation after generation, without significant backsliding. Our model of a linear development can be contested; alternative patterns, not taking the form of a linear trend, are described in the Appendix to this chapter. Although we cannot know what will happen in the future, we have implicitly argued that the following trends will not reverse: (1) magazine ads will not revert from color to black and white; (2) words will not expand to take up more and more of the page while pictures shrink back to play a smaller role; (3) ads will not become less creative in their use of type; (4) pictures will not revert to straightforward photorealism; and more. In the strong form of our assertion, there may be pauses and equivocation along this route, but there will be no significant reversals that endure for a decade or more. The trend is set.[18]

Not all historians of advertising would be comfortable with this hypothesis of a long-term unbroken trend. Fox (1984) sees cycles, identifying an oscillation between the dominance of hard-sell copy in ads, versus that of soft-sell, picture-supported persuasion. Pollay (1985) notes a vacillation toward and away from what he scores as more versus less informative advertising. There is no necessary contradiction between our findings and those of Fox and Pollay. Their cycles revolve around copy, and what advertisers do or don't do with words in ads; whereas our investigation centers on the visual element, with words serving only as a foil. Pictorial persuasion is orthogonal to the categories of Fox and Pollay: a picture can sell hard or soft, be informative or emotional.

To conclude the chapter, we summarize the elements that distinguish our historical account from those of our predecessors. First, our sample is longer, with a later endpoint. Pollay's sample starts a decade after ours, and ends 40 years earlier. The Leiss et al. (2005) sample starts ten years after Pollay, and also concludes in the 1970s. Both sampled every decade. Neither Goodrum and Dalrymple (1990) nor Rowsome (1959) choose to tell a time-locked story; they group ads by theme more than date. Most ads reproduced in Marchand date to between 1919 and 1936. Presbrey starts centuries earlier but ends in the 1920s.

A second point of difference is our exclusive focus on visual elements. Most histories of advertising look at all elements, and give plentiful attention to the words, and through them to the appeals used, along with authors' speculations about the psychology behind these appeals. The pattern of change may be different for words. More boldly, between 1890 and 2015, there may have been no change at all in the words available for constructing a print advertisement, or in the available semantic content, the specific branding appeals advanced in words. Consider soap as an example. In the attempt to promote the brand, there are lots of different things that might be said about soap. Some words, like pure, may have enjoyed time-limited vogues; others, like gentle, may be perennial; but the set of words and the corresponding appeals relevant to soap are no different today than a century ago. By contrast, the visual resources available today are far different than what Ivory soap could muster in 1890.

A third point of difference is our restricted product focus, especially the restriction to branded convenience goods and household durables advertised in women's magazines. As marketing scholars, we have a healthy respect for how different product categories may require different advertising strategies. Absent a careful sampling strategy keyed to product categories, historians risk wandering in a daze. Haphazard selection from heterogeneous product categories produces conceptual mush. Whatever temporal developments may be present get lost.

A fourth and more subtle point of difference is our contention that brand advertisers got better at it with time; and that this improvement in capabilities continued for decades. The tendency in many histories is to treat brand advertising as like Athena, sprung forth fully formed, and in complete possession of all its faculties from the outset. To our knowledge, no previous account has highlighted the limitations of the graphic means available in the early decades, or the rudimentary design of brand marks, or the slow emergence of a brand block. Equally rare is the idea that advertising techniques and visual branding continued to evolve after the 1970s (although here, we enjoy the unfair advantage of writing decades after most of our predecessors).

We give unceasing change and ongoing development a central role in the story of brand advertising. And it is the focus on visual branding, rather than advertising in general, which drives our conclusions down this different path.

APPENDIX: ALTERNATIVE PATTERNS OF HISTORICAL CHANGE

In this chapter we have discussed two patterns commonly asserted in historical work: that advertising shows a cycling back and forth, as in an oscillation between poles; or that it shows a one-way trend, stated in terms of an increase or decrease in some factor. But these two patterns are not the only lenses applied by historians to social and cultural phenomena.

A rather different pattern posits an inflection point. In this account some activity, which has continued for a while, suddenly changes direction. The activity, which may have had one nature for decades, over a short interval acquires a different nature; which it sustains thereafter. We've identified such an inflection point for American magazines, arguing that in the early 1890s these publications changed from being small journals directed at an elite audience, and priced to match, to mass circulation publications, now aimed at the ordinary person, and priced low enough to reach a mass audience, because financially supported by advertising revenue. Consistent with the idea of an inflection point, a century later there continue to be mass circulation American magazines, supported primarily by advertising. There was no cycling back.

Marchand (1985) hypothesizes an inflection point. He argues that magazine advertising assumed its modern form in the 1920s and 1930s, and implicitly, that advertising has continued ever since along the tracks then laid down. The problem: Marchand doesn't collect, exhibit, or analyze ads that appeared either earlier than, or much later, than his chosen period. Although he makes much of the turn to modern art in the latter 1920s, we don't see it in ads from the 1950s. From a long-term perspective, it appears to have been only a temporary phase.

Samples concentrated in time are convenient to the historian; a short span makes it possible to examine intensively a broad range of social phenomena. Unfortunately, point samples can't rule out either a cycle or a trend line as an alternative explanation for what is observed to occur in the focal decade. Every advertising textbook mentions the "Creative Revolution" of the 1960s; but few bother to put samples of ads from two decades earlier, and two decades later, side by side with ads from the 1960s. This neglect renders dubious the idea of a revolution, which is only a dramatic label for an inflection point. Without sampling ads from a lengthy period, and holding other factors constant, transient fluctuations may be misread as enduring inflection points.

Another pattern of historical change is the fashion pattern. Here we see ongoing variation which does not correspond to either a cycle or a line. Because the variation continues, there is also no inflection point. To be clear: hemlines may rise and fall, but that's a cycle, not a fashion pattern. Fashion is manifest as powdered wigs for men at one point, full beards at another, clean-shaven and short hair at a third point, and shaved heads and beards at still another; or corsets for women at one point, brassieres at another, arms bared or arms covered, hair curled or straight, put up or let fall. Fashion means fluctuation without direction.

One advantage of a periodic sampling strategy: continuous sampling tends to foreground changes in fashion, changes that wash out in a periodic sample when the intervening periods are long. In our opinion, print advertising is prone to fashion and to vogues for one appeal or another. There has been a lot of fluctuation year by year and decade by decade. There was at least a "Creative" fashion in advertising in the 1960s, even if not a revolution. Only by stepping back to a 30-year interval do trend lines readily emerge. The modern art that cropped up repeatedly in ads from around 1929, which was central to Marchand's (1985) account, had disappeared by the 1950s. But the increased reliance on photography, which Marchand also noted in passing, both endured and continued to wax. Only long-term samples, periodic or otherwise, can winnow fluctuations in fashion from enduring trends.

The final historical pattern of note combines elements of the inflection point, cycle, and trend line patterns. It may be labelled the life cycle pattern. The conceit: the phenomenon has a beginning point, styled as a birth; goes through a period of development, which is indistinguishable from a rising trend line; tops out; and ultimately declines and disappears, with the beginning of the decline indistinguishable from a cycle turning point.

The life cycle pattern is a bit too metaphorical for our taste. We don't find it useful to analogize historical phenomena to living things.[19] But the metaphor is popular in marketing thought (for example, product life cycle), and worth a mention in this catalogue of patterns of historical change.

A more viable version might be labelled the finite pattern. Magazines, and brands, are launched – they do have a beginning; these may grow strongly in circulation or sales for a time; and then in many cases these fizzle out, or just stop. There doesn't have to be a distinct decline; the magazine or brand stops growing, or stops growing rapidly enough to remain a viable business enterprise in the eyes of its owner (who may not be perfectly rational in making the decision to terminate). The finite pattern involves less heroic assumptions than the life cycle pattern, and shows more direction than the fashion pattern. It is a distinctively capitalist form of historical being: entities launch, thrive for a period, and then meet their demise. This demise is probabilistic rather than inevitable. *Harper's Magazine* is still going strong after almost two centuries, and Ivory soap is coming up on 150 years. Hundreds of other magazines, and thousands of other brands, disappeared during those intervals.

The finite pattern is the least intellectually appealing. Trend lines make for nice graphs, cycles are fascinating, inflection points are heroic, and fashion is weird and wonderful. Large heaps of finite durations of varying length, fitting no other pattern, are dull. That humdrum quality counts in favor of the realism of this last hypothesized pattern of historical change.

PART II

Brand marks

3. A typology of brand marks

In much of this book we refer to brand logos. Logo reflects familiar, conventional usage, but is impermissibly vague for our purposes. Here in Part II we use the more general term: the brand's mark, its licensed trademark. The United States Patent and Trademark Office offers this definition: "A trademark is a word, phrase, symbol or design, or a combination of words, phrases, symbols or designs, that identifies and distinguishes the source of the goods of one party from those of others."

The term logo is problematic because it suggests a symbol or design – a visual element – even as many brands do not include any symbol or design as part of their trademark. Here is a familiar example:

There is no symbol or design in the Kellogg's mark. If you object that its distinctive typeface constitutes a graphic design, or point to its vibrant color, then here is a second example:

Morgan Stanley

The brand mark of Morgan Stanley contains no symbol or design, and although it must appear in some typeface, the sans serif font used is not obviously marked or special. To call it a logo risks confusion; it is best termed a brand mark.

DIFFERENTIATING BRAND MARKS

A rhetorical analysis of brand marks seeks to identify the available means of persuasion: the short list of options for designing a brand mark. The first option is whether to include anything other than the name in the brand mark. Many brands choose to include a symbol or design in their marks, some visual element other than typeface; but many others do not.

This distinction has not always been observed in marketing scholarship, nor handled properly when noted. Henderson and Cote (1998), in a treatment that has been foundational for recent thinking, ignore the name-only category of mark.[1] By contrast, Park et al. (2013) build their discussion around the idea that there are two kinds of mark, and only two: name-only, and name + symbol.[2] However, Park et al. make this comparison invidious: they assert that name-only marks represent a failure to seize the opportunities that could have been gained by including a separate visual element. A name-only mark, in their view, is a defective attempt at persuasion, one that a skilled rhetor would know to avoid. As an aside, a rhetorician will seldom be enthused about yes–no distinctions, or other binary cuts, as in the Park et al. work. Yes, the rhetor seeks a short list of persuasive devices, but not that short.

Our goal in this chapter, and in all the typologies advanced in the book, is a scheme more like the periodic table of elements in chemistry.[3] An unordered list will not be proof against Samuel Butler's famous jibe: "For all a rhetorician's rules / Teach nothing but to name his tools." Although we write in the tradition of classical rhetoric, we write following the scientific revolution, and regard that revolution, and its intellectual accomplishments, with respect. An ordered set of conceptually distinguished devices will offer more insight than a polyglot list or catalogue.

The organization of the periodic table provides an exemplar for a conceptually ordered finite set of persuasive devices. There are not infinitely many physical elements; fewer than 100 occur naturally. These elements are also not a haphazard agglomeration of dozens of diverse atomic arrangements. All the chemical elements can be arranged into about half a dozen rows and somewhat more than a dozen columns, each calling out a key property; within these rows and columns there are also distinct blocks. If you know the row, column, and block position of an element, you can predict what other elements it can combine with, whether it will be a liquid, solid, or gas at standard temperature and pressure, act as a metal, and much more. The periodic table is not a catalogue or list. Position in the table stems in part from the number of electron shells in the atom of that element, and the number of empty positions on the outermost shell, and these physical facts determine how each element behaves.

The periodic table gives a discrete count of the fundamental elements of material stuff, and arranges these elements into a pattern that gives insight into the capabilities of each. Elements are distinguished on multiple dimensions, not least the linear axis of atomic weight. A classical rhetoric, redesigned for the modern era, aims to do the same for the stuff of persuasion.

Imagine a scientifically trained chemist who sniffed about iron's lack of luster as compared to gold, or who disparaged carbon as a promiscuous element, too prone to combine with others. That would be silly. It likewise makes no sense to treat the abundant use of name-only marks as some dereliction of marketing management or a failure of branding. Name-only marks exist, and have endured, for a reason. Too bad if students in a class-room, using seven-point rating scales, rate these name-only marks lower than visually enhanced marks. True, a name-only mark represents a deci-sion not to push visual branding to the hilt, within that piece of the firm's marketing effort; but there will be other opportunities to visually brand elsewhere in the promotions mix.

To illuminate why there must be more than two categories of brand marks, we next present a range of cases (Table 3.1).[4] Examining first the

Table 3.1   Difficulties with the dichotomous classification of brand marks

Brand mark	Park et al. (2013) categorization	
	Name-only	Name + symbol
ESTĒE LAUDER	√	
Honeywell	√	
COSTCO WHOLESALE	√	
LEXMARK	√	
Colgate	√	
MATTEL		√
JOHN DEERE		√

Notes: See text for discussion. Name and symbol classifications were graciously provided to the authors by C.W. Park and Andreas B. Eisingerich. Caveat: marks shown may not be the same as the designs rated some years ago by Park et al. (2013).

marks at the top and bottom of the table, and applying the Park et al. classification, Estée Lauder is easy to classify as a name-only mark, while John Deere clearly uses a name + symbol mark. But with these extremes set aside, classification grows more difficult. Consider Costco: do the three horizontal lines constitute a graphic design, or should this be deemed a name-only mark? Next consider Lexmark. Does a red diamond completing a capital A constitute a separate graphic design, as defined by Henderson and Cote in their treatment of logos? Neither Costco nor Lexmark contain only text, but likewise, neither approaches in complexity the emblem of a deer about to leap. Next consider Colgate and Mattel. In both cases, the graphic portion is larger and more prominent than for Costco or Lexmark; but does the red trapezoidal background of the Colgate mark rise to the level of a separate graphic design? Conversely, if the presence of color is determinative, is Colgate, where the color appears as a field, any different than Honeywell, where the letters provide the color? Turning to Mattel, its mark displays more design than the red trapezoid of Colgate; but does the tooth-edged gear of Mattel constitute a symbol to the same degree as the deer of Deere?

Examples of such difficult-to-classify marks are legion, once a scholar goes to the trouble of searching out and examining hundreds of real brand marks. A good typology of marks must have at least three categories, and maybe more, if it is to handle cases such as Costco, Lexmark, Colgate, and Mattel. In Table 3.1, only John Deere can be classified, without qualm, as a name + symbol mark, and depending on the position taken concerning color, only Estée Lauder fits the bill for a name-only mark. All the other marks in Table 3.1 have to be differentiated by introducing additional terms.

To develop the typology described next, we compiled a sample of marks from 217 leading brands, as described in Box 3.1. We aimed for a grounded approach: a typology that would emerge from a zero-based examination of a large sample of contemporary brands, rather than being imposed from without as an a priori conceptual scheme. Separately and together, we sorted and resorted the 217 marks, until a stable pattern emerged upon which we could agree.[5]

THE TYPOLOGY

We propose a six-category typology of brand marks, organized by an underlying gradient that parallels the role played by atomic weight in the periodic table of elements (Table 3.2). If it weren't such an ugly neologism, we might label this gradient as "visualness;" but that is too bare and clumsy

---

BOX 3.1   SAMPLING BRAND MARKS

We sought a sizable collection of marks of leading brands. An internet search revealed half a dozen compilations that purported to contain the top 100 or top 50 brands (the effort by Interbrand, updated annually, is among the best known). After eliminating duplications across compilations, we had 217 marks in the sample. For subsequent samples (see boxes in Chapter 4), we added category-based compilations (for example, top financial services brands, top retailer brands, and so on).

Most of these compilations use a secret sauce to determine ranking, but virtually all used a financial criterion to determine which brands made the initial cut, that is, which brands were "top," "large," or "leading," and thus eligible for ranking. This selection criterion introduces biases, as discussed in Chapter 4.

All samples were collected in 2014, and the marks contained were current as of the end of 2013 or thereabouts. If you are reading this book years hence, many of these marks will have been updated or changed in the interval; and the longer the interval, the greater the turnover.

Table 3.2   A typology of brand marks arrayed along an eidos *gradient*

Zone	Type	Definition	Position on *eidos* gradient
C: Logos proper	Emblem	A stand-alone graphic design accompanies the name	More visually stimulating
	Emblazoned	The name is placed on a graphically rich background	
B: Graphicized logotypes	Letter art	One or more letters in the name is graphically elaborated	
	Lined, bordered or fielded	The name is accompanied by or placed on a simple graphic element: a line, border, or field	
A. Logotypes	Colored text	Text of the brand name only, but in color	
	Black and white text	Text of the brand name in black and white	Less

Note: See text for expanded definitions, and Tables 3.3 through 3.7 for examples of each type.

a term. Reverting to Greek, we call it the *eidos* gradient. Brand marks vary as to how visually stimulating and rich an experience each makes available to the consumer. Put mechanically, marks vary in the amount of non-textual material included, which is to say, marks vary as to how many and how complex are the visual elements that accompany the text of the name. Each mark can be placed higher or lower on this *eidos* gradient, and this placement contributes to consumer response to the brand. The higher the placement, the greater the amount of visual branding work the mark can accomplish for the brand.

Text-only, black and white brand marks are plentiful; Estée Lauder is not an outlier or oddity. This type of mark anchors the bottom of the *eidos* gradient. Every other mark in Table 3.1 adds visual elements not present in the Estée Lauder mark. We argue that these additional visual elements – the red color of Honeywell, the red shape behind Colgate, the red letter replacement in Lexmark, the red gear surrounding Mattel, the deer emblem accompanying John Deere – can be placed in ascending order on the *eidos* gradient. The deer emblem potentially offers the most visual stimulation: it is more visually interesting than a generic background shape, such as a trapezoid. Likewise, embossing the Mattel name on a toy gear offers more visual stimulation than embossing the Colgate name on a generic trapezoid. Moving further down the gradient, adding color makes the Honeywell mark more visually interesting than the Estée Lauder mark.

To assert an *eidos* gradient is to rule out a three-category scheme as sufficient for organizing brand marks. Absent that gradient, the marks in Table 3.1 could readily be placed in three groups: name-only, name + visual element(s), and name + symbol. Absent an underlying gradient, there would be no grounds for distinguishing the impact on consumers of bare visual elements (a red trapezoid shape) versus true graphic designs (a red toy gear). In turn, the middle category would become a catch-all, a coding convenience conceptually equivalent to "other."

A rhetorician is offended by polyglot, heterogeneous catch-all categories that call out for further differentiation. Anyone with an orderly mind should be put off by an "other" category that is as numerous, in the field, as the supposedly root categories, conceptually defined, of name-only and name + symbol.

Conversely, if it were not for the idea of discrete types of marks, the *eidos* gradient would be indistinguishable from the dimensions that comprise the Henderson and Cote (1998) conceptual scheme, which typifies psychological accounts of visual stimuli (see also the discussion of Henderson et al. 2004 in Chapter 6). Hence, taken alone, the *eidos* gradient would provide a psychological rather than a rhetorical account of brand marks. To combine the *eidos* gradient with the assertion that there are discrete types of marks – that Colgate represents one type and Mattel another – brings together classical rhetoric and scientific thinking about causation. Only such a combination can produce a conceptual framework that bears comparison with the periodic table of elements. Consumers will respond differently to brand marks located high and low on the *eidos* gradient, and consumers will respond to the discrete locations on that gradient identified through rhetorical analysis of the space of possibilities for brand mark design.

Finally, the six discrete locations on the gradient are organized into three zones, defined again by whether only text is present, or something more. We identify two different ways to visually enhance the name of the brand: either stand-alone visual elements may be added, or graphic designs introduced. We label these zones along the *eidos* axis as follows: (1) logotypes, where only text is present; (2) graphicized logotypes, where graphic elements are present and supplement the name; and (3) logos proper, in which there is a graphical design in addition to the alphanumeric text of the name.

Whether it is meaningful to speak of zones stands or falls on whether graphic designs can be distinguished from mere visual elements. We encourage readers to look at the many examples of each type of mark, reproduced later in this chapter and grouped into zones, and then decide whether the zones provide a workable and useful overlay on the base distinction between six types. There are limits to the linguistic description of visual phenomena. We must show as well as tell.

Within the zones, each subtype represents a distinct avenue along which black and white alphanumeric text may be graphically enhanced, beginning with the addition of color, and extending to stand-alone graphic designs. Each of the six subtypes identifies one of the available means for constructing a persuasive brand mark. Two of these available means are not particularly visual. We believe it useful to discover that not all brands use their marks to visually brand. Later we will show that the decision to eschew visually branding through the mark is defensible. The value and limits of visual branding emerge more clearly by noting cases where it is minimal or absent.

Every claim asserted by the typology is subject to *ceteris paribus* conditions: the *eidos* gradient indicates only the potential for visual stimulation. How much visual enhancement actually occurs will vary in accordance with brand, consumer, and situational factors. Each type has a central tendency with respect to the *eidos* gradient, allowing us to rank the types; but visually speaking, any one instance of a type may be relatively rich or impoverished. It is easy to imagine overlap between the types, in which an impoverished mark from a higher type provides less visual interest, to some consumers who encounter it in the marketplace, than would a rich instance of a lower type. Finally, there must be a large number of additional factors, unrelated to the typology, that also shape the intensity of visual experience. One example: the sheer size of the graphic portion of the mark. Some logos are tiny emblems, while some graphicized logotypes contain large swatches of color. Size variation can blur the effects specific to each type (see Box 3.2).

BOX 3.2   TEST OF SUBTYPE PLACEMENT ALONG THE *EIDOS* GRADIENT

We had 20 undergraduate student judges rate the marks from the main sample described in Box 3.1. Each judge received printed cards with half the sample of marks. The judges sorted the marks into six bins according to how "visually rewarding and stimulating" each mark was, beginning with the two extremes, and then iteratively sorting out marks remaining in the middle on two additional passes. Each mark received a score based on its position in the sort for a given judge, and an average score was computed across the ten judges who saw it. These scores were in turn averaged for every member of each of the subtypes of marks. Table 3.8 gives means and descriptive data for the three zones and the six sub-types.* The zones and the subtypes showed the expected linear effect.

We also found a disproportionate negative effect associated with subtype #1, black and white text-only logos. The difference in visual stimulation for that type of mark versus the next one up (colored text) is so great that it slightly exceeds the difference between subtype #2 and the most visually stimulating subtype in the set (Table 3.8). This again raises the question of why any brand would content itself with a black and white text-only mark, a question which will become more pointed when the cross-category comparisons are examined in Chapter 4. In sum, black and white marks, to which the Henderson and Cote (1998) study was confined, were judged as significantly less stimulating and rewarding, and black and white text marks even more so.

Second, note the inversion of the expected ordering of means of the embla-zoned versus emblematic subtypes (Table 3.8). We take this to be a salutary reminder of the importance of the *ceteris paribus* clause in predicting the visual reward and stimulation to be expected from any given type of brand mark. Compare below the emblazoned Sprite mark to the marks of Ernst & Young and ConocoPhillips, which are members of the emblematic set, a subtype which we have located above emblazonment on the *eidos* axis:

The Sprite mark, although placed in the lower subtype, is much more colorful and the graphic portion is much larger (as will generally be true for a background). The Ernst & Young mark is black and white and sparse, while the graphic portion of the ConocoPhillips ad is miniscule. Anticipating this issue, we had the research assistants rate each mark according to the relative size of the graphic portion. If only colored marks where the graphic portion accounts for half or more of the mark are included, the expected ordering of emblematic marks over emblazoned marks is restored (Table 3.8).

Note: * Given our disparaging remarks about student raters elsewhere, we'll spare the reader the MANOVA *F* tests, which we did perform and which supported the stated conclusions. The point of this box is to illustrate the importance of *ceteris paribus* conditions in placing any individual brand mark on the *eidos* gradient.

A final complication: color. Any type of brand mark can be represented in black and white or in color. We stipulate that the colored version is more visually stimulating than the black and white version. Likewise, the central tendency, across the population of all colored marks, falls higher on the *eidos* gradient than the central tendency for black and white marks. Color adds visual interest. Always.

THE SIX TYPES OF BRAND MARK

Zone A: Logotypes

Subtype #1: Black text-only

Morgan Stanley's brand mark provides one example of this subtype, but was far from the only such instance among leading brands; other examples include Duracell and Gucci (Table 3.3). A total of 15, or about 7 percent of the sample of marks of leading brands, fell into this category.

The brand marks in this category use a range of fonts: sans serif or serif, script, bold or italic, and so on. We acknowledge that typeface may contribute to brand meaning, per Henderson et al. (2004), and as established by prior research (see Chapter 6 on typefaces). Our contention: all purely

Table 3.3   Examples of brand marks categorized as Zone A, logotypes

Black and white text-only	Colored text-only
SONY.	**PHILIPS**
Cartier	jetBlue
G U C C I	**Panasonic**
Z A R A	ORACLE˙
DURACELL˙	*Walgreens*
PRADA	*H&M*

Note: In these tables, we try to select exemplary instances, rather than attempting to capture the range of variation within each type. See Table 4.4 in Chapter 4 for more examples of Zone A logotypes.

black, alphanumeric-only brand marks have the same *de minimus* capacity
to provide a visually rewarding and stimulating experience, separate from
the reading of text. The typology focuses on visual experience beyond
textual processing of the brand name and its associations. In our view,
typeface plays no role in this visual experience, even as it may well play a
role in the semantic inferences drawn about brands from their marks.

We will address in detail the contribution of typeface to visual branding in Chapter 6. Here, we dismiss the claim that selection of a serif, bold,
italic, or script face can move a logotype up or down the *eidos* gradient.
In brand marks, text is text, and text does not provide a visual experience.
Text is read.

Subtype #2: Colored text-only

The typology distinguishes, and places higher on the *eidos* axis, brand
marks printed in a color other than black, such as Kellogg's, or Philips
(Table 3.3). In this we follow a burgeoning literature on the effects of color
on psychological functioning (see Chapter 8). About 11 percent of the
main sample fell into this category. Interestingly, all of the mono-colored
marks in this subtype were either blue or red (Labrecque and Milne 2012).
Other disproportions in the color choices made by brands are discussed in
Chapter 8.

Altogether, about 18 percent of the marks of leading brands were categorized as name-only, with no graphic elements other than color, and
thus impossible to locate within the dimensional space of Henderson and
Cote (1998). These are the marks disparaged in Park et al. (2013). This
finding that almost one in five marks of leading brands contained no visual
element other than color argues that this was a strategic choice, and not
a missed bet. The next chapter will show that logotypes are much more
common in some product categories. We'll build on that disproportion
to explain why name-only logotypes, lying low on the *eidos* gradient, may
nonetheless represent a smart strategic choice for a brand.

Zone B: Graphicized Logotypes

Subtype #3: Bordered, lined, or fielded

We locate this branch at the base of Zone B, because fields, borders,
and lining represent the simplest and most basic graphic supplements to
alphanumeric text beyond coloring. Metlife and Nintendo are examples
of bordered marks, and Tesco and Olay are examples of lining (Table 3.4).
Strictly speaking, a field is a more complex graphic element than a border
or line: fields have both color and shape. There may also be position: Gap
is centered, but Goldman Sachs is on top. With shape, there may also be

Table 3.4 Examples of brand marks categorized as Zone B, graphicized logotypes

Bordered, lined, or fielded	Letter art
MetLife	*SUBWAY*
(Nintendo)	**W**estpac
TESCO	*Coca-Cola*
OLAY	(comcast.
GAP	(KIA)
Goldman Sachs	SAMSUNG
hp	**VISA**

Note: See note to Table 3.3.

sharp angles (Colgate) or soft curves (HP – Hewlett-Packard). Given line, shape, position, and angularity, the consumer can now do more than read the brand name or experience the brand as deep blue or a bold red; they can now experience a brand as square, sharp, or rounded, and as at the top or pressing forward. The potential for a visually stimulating experience of the brand is greater. About 11 percent of the sample fell into this category.

Subtype #4: Letter art
This subtype is located further up the *eidos* axis to reflect the complexity, and potential visual stimulation, that come from integrating graphic design elements into one or more alphabetical characters making up the name. A letter may be turned into a graphical element (Coca-Cola), a graphic element may be added to a letter (Comcast), or a stand-alone graphic

design may replace a letter (Westpac). All of these represent instances of artful deviation from expectation.[6] About 12 percent of the marks fell into this category (Table 3.4).

The category of letter art helps to explain why serif, bold, italic, and script typefaces fail to shift a brand mark up the *eidos* gradient. Letter art is a deviation; it marks the text, in the semiotic terminology of Mukarovsky. Boldface and italic logotypes aren't marked enough to shift position on the *eidos* axis.

Because letter art presents a design, rather than a simple visual element like color or shape, we place it at the top of Zone B, above other instances of graphicized logotypes. Ultimately, however, placement on the *eidos* axis is an empirical question. Future research might suggest a different position.

In total, 23 percent of the marks of leading brands were categorized as graphicized logotypes, relying on lines, shapes, and embellishments of letters to accompany the brand name. With reference to Table 3.1 and the prior literature on brand marks, most but not all of the marks in Zone B would be classified as name-only and lacking a separate graphic design, and would therefore be disparaged in the Park et al. (2013) account.

Zone C: Logos Proper

Subtype #5: Emblazoned

Zone C marks the point where the graphical elements come to be as prominent or more prominent than text. At the base of Zone C lie brand marks where the text of the name is displayed against an elaborate background or surrounded by ornamentation (Table 3.5). The test for placing a mark here rather than in the next-highest subtype is whether the graphic elements constitute a stand-alone design which could serve as a visual sign in the absence of the brand name. If the removal of the name leaves an image that would instead be read as an empty background awaiting text – as visually incomplete and unable to stand on its own without a name – the mark is placed here. In turn, subtype #5 is a more complex version of subtype #3, with emblazonment distinguished from fielding by the presence of multiple shapes and colors, complex shapes, rhythmic repetition of contours, and so forth. The additional visual complexity justifies a higher placement on the *eidos* axis for emblazoned versus fielded marks. About 14 percent of the sample fell into the emblazoned category.

Subtype #6: Stand-alone graphic designs

With this subtype, the graphical elements in the brand mark possess enough coherence and cohesion to stand alone as an emblem, image, or picture. As a design, rather than as mere background or ornament, the non-text

Table 3.5   *Examples of emblazoned brand marks in Zone C, logos proper*

Kroger	RITE AID
Ford	ups
Cadbury	UNION PACIFIC
GE	LOWE'S Let's Build Something Together
Sam's CLUB	BEST BUY

Note: See note to Table 3.3.

portion of the mark gains the capability to replace the text: it can act as a sign of the brand, in the semiotic sense (Mick 1986). Unsurprisingly, since this category reflects what most people have in mind when the term logo is used, it was by far the single most common type here in the main sample, with about 46 percent of the marks.

Consistent with the challenge we raised to open the chapter, the marks in Zone C comprised only about 60 percent of the sample; put another way, two-fifths of the sample cannot readily be analyzed along the dimensions of Henderson and Cote (1998), because those marks, in Zones A and B, contain no separable graphic design.

REFLECTIONS: STAND-ALONE GRAPHIC DESIGNS

The large number of marks placed in subtype #6, at the top of the *eidos* gradient, poses a challenge to rhetorical analysis. This type begs to be subdivided into smaller and more cohesive subsets. But the scientifically minded classical rhetorician must beware superficial differences. At the end of that path lies the catalogue, rather than the periodic table.

In the next few paragraphs, we lay out a few ways to subdivide further the emblematic type of brand mark. At present, we reject all of these

Table 3.6   Examples of emblematic brand marks from Zone C, logos proper

MERCK	BT	xerox	CenturyLink	Time Warner Cable	Standard Chartered
McLANE	AMD	pwc	ERNST & YOUNG Quality In Everything We Do	BLACK & DECKER	Commonwealth Bank
	Red Bull	CISCO	TRAVELERS	SOUTHWEST AIRLINES	Aflac
Chevron	BURBERRY	RBC		COACH	HERMÈS PARIS

Note: The top two rows show abstract emblems, curved or angular; the bottom two rows show more representational emblems, with the bottommost row showing more canned or generic representations. See Table 4.2 in Chapter 4 for another set of emblematic logos.

attempts as superficial variations. Our reasoning: we can't find an argument for placing any of these subdivisions higher or lower on the *eidos* gradient, and we cannot satisfy ourselves that any of these subdivisions rises to the level of a distinct gambit within the space of possible designs for brand marks. But these judgments are provisional. Down the road, better rhetoricians than we might espy a robust set of subcategories within the emblematic subtype. Or, subsequent empirical work might find a reliable difference in visual stimulation across one or more of the discarded subcategorization schemes discussed next. If this were a journal paper, the following material would be discussed under "Limitations and Future Research."

This first subset we rejected distinguishes brand marks where the stand-alone graphic design does, indeed, stand alone in the common everyday presentation of the brand. AT&T, Nike, and Starbucks provide illustrative examples (Table 3.7). For these brands, in 2015 a consumer is likely to see only the graphic design, with no alphanumeric text identifier. In the Park et al. (2013) scheme, these might be described as symbol-only brand marks. There were only a half dozen such instances in the sample.

Table 3.7   Examples of emblematic logos with no text component

Notes: These six appeared to be the only ones in the main sample, and none of the category samples in Chapter 4 unearthed any more. See the text for a discussion of why these text-free emblematic logos were not considered to be a separate subtype.

Table 3.8   Visual stimulation and reward provided by different subtypes of brand marks

	N	Mean	Minimum	Maximum
Zone A (logotypes)				
#1: Black and white text-only	15	−1.72	−2.00	−1.25
#2: Colored text-only	23	−0.50	−1.35	1.15
Zone B (graphicized logotypes)				
#3: Lined, bordered, or fielded	23	−0.23	−1.50	0.60
#4: Letter art	26	−0.05	−1.55	1.50
Zone C (logos)				
#5: Emblazoned (all)	30	0.62	.00	1.65
Subset: color + large	*20*	*0.52*	*.00*	*1.45*
#6: Emblem (all)	100	0.27	−1.65	1.80
Subset: color + large	*44*	*0.68*	*−1.00*	*1.80*
Total sample	217	0.01	−2.00	1.80

Note: Judges sorted out marks located high and low on the *eidos* gradient on three passes, with the first two passes allowing for an "in the middle" judgment, with those middling marks rated on the next pass. Extremes on the first pass were coded +/− 2, on the second pass +/− 1, and on the third pass, the remaining marks were coded + / − 0.5. The score for each individual mark represents the average rating given by the ten judges who saw it; minimum (maximum) refers to the ten-judge average for individual marks in the subtype. See Box 3.2 for more information; the rationale for subsetting emblazoned and emblematic brands is also given there.

We set this subcategorization aside for two reasons. First, it is not stable or absolute. Much of the time, the consumer encounters the Starbucks mermaid emblem alone; but on plenty of other occasions – most store-fronts, for instance – the consumer will encounter symbol with name. Likewise, most official presentations of the Mercedes-Benz mark include the name; but we have seen a 100 foot pillar, standing beside a freeway, that showed only the trine circle. Second, the ability of the graphic design to stand alone defines the type: any brand whose mark falls here could go the Starbucks or Nike route, should it wish to do so. Whether a consumer will encounter the design without text appears to depend on the situation, and on whether enough money has been spent promoting the mark to allow the graphic design portion to be recognized without accompanying text, as in the case of the Nike swoosh.

Next, we dismissed a subcategorization based on the shape of the stand-alone design. A close look at Table 3.6 will show that many marks of this type take a roughly circular shape. We could therefore mark out a medallion subtype within the emblematic type. Unfortunately, we do not see how circles can provide either more visual stimulation, or unusual visual interest, relative to rectangles, triangles, diamonds, stars, or shields – which account for most of the nameable shapes that were not circles. Definitional difficulties also loom. Consider CenturyLink, where the design consists of 12 inwardly pointing triangles arranged in a circle. Where would that design be placed? Would it be classified under circles or triangles? And what about designs that contain an arc, but not a complete circle? And at what degree of bending do we speak of an arc rather than a gently curved line?

Alternatively, instead of distinguishing shapes, we could draw on one of the dimensions identified by Henderson and Cote, who distinguish whether a design is more curved or angular. Unfortunately, few marks categorized as stand-alone graphic designs contain no curve of any kind. That empirical disproportion is interesting. Perhaps there is something about curved shapes that conduces to visual branding; we leave this hypothesis to future research.

But here too there are definitional problems. Another look at Table 3.6 shows that while designs with no curve at all are rare, designs with no angles, corners, or tapering points are also rare. Most designs contain both soft curves and sharp angles. Consider again the CenturyLink mark: 36 small sharp angles and one big round shape are present. So how would that design be scored?: (1) give it a middling score on a curved versus angular polarity; (2) score it as neither curved nor angular ("other"); or (3) score it as moderately high on both curved and angular metrics, treated now as two oblique dimensions? Until such questions are resolved, no empirical study can be conducted of the impact, on the consumer, of designing a brand mark to contain curves versus angles.[7]

A third subcategorization that we dismissed would distinguish representational designs from those that do not depict any person, animal, object, or scene (this corresponds in part to Henderson and Cote's abstraction dimension). Here, coding difficulties do not appear insurmountable, although there will be some difficult cases (for example, does the Cisco mark show the Golden Gate bridge, a sine wave on an oscilloscope, or is it only a pleasing pattern of vertical line segments?). Most of the marks can be readily categorized as representational or not. CenturyLink's mark is not representational, while KFC and Burberry surely are.

We debated, in the case of this subcategory, whether our one-dimensional scheme, postulating only an *eidos* gradient, should be supplemented with a second dimension which, to stick with Greek, might be labelled a *semiosis* gradient. Representational marks have more sign value. As well as providing pleasure from design, they act as meaningful signs even as they point to the brand. When John Deere shows a deer leaping, a wide range of connotations are made available to the consumer. Deer are fast, agile, graceful; deer are avidly hunted but hard to bag; might the machines that John Deere manufactures be the same? Bulls are strong, powerful, indomitable; people stay out of their way; perhaps the Red Bull beverage will give me the same potency.

In short, a representational design of a brand mark enables the graphic design to act like a name, to secure specific meanings over and beyond vaguer connotations such as curvaceous or sharp, bold or pastel, daring or tame, traditional or modern. Representational marks can assume some of the functions of text. KFC has its Southern gentleman Colonel; Ferrari has its rearing stallion; Target has its bullseye. Hence, of all the subcategorizations we have tentatively dismissed, the idea that marks might be arrayed on two dimensions rather than one, on *semiosis* as well as *eidos*, seems most promising.

Some nagging problems remain, however, when it comes to the representational category. While many representational designs are unique – no other leading brand besides KFC contains the image of a culturally locatable visage, like Colonel Sanders – many others contain more generic representations. Heineken has a red star, and Macy's has a red star; but is either one intended to culturally implicate the Soviet Union or its Red Army? That seems unlikely. But how do we know that KFC *does* mean to invoke a courtly Southern hospitality, while Heineken does *not* mean to invoke the Bolshevik takeover of Russia, or the tanks that entered Berlin in 1945? These are semiotic questions.

Corona has its crown, and Moet & Chandon has its rather different crown. Burberry, Ferrari, and Porsche have a horse; Hermes and Coach have a horse and carriage. ING has a lion, but so does RBC. In all these examples the representational design is generic: crown, horse, lion. But brands are about differentiation. These crowns, horses, and lions are all visually distinct; but in terms of the object represented, they are not. Representational marks may not make up a unitary category. Therefore, we choose not to offer a two-dimensional typology of brand marks, pending a resolution of these conundrums.

4. How and why brand marks vary across product categories

In the previous chapter, we presented a typology of brand marks. We argued that all marks could be arrayed along an *eidos* gradient according to how much visual enhancement the mark conferred on its brand. We distinguished three broad zones along the *eidos* gradient: (1) logotypes that contain only text; (2) graphicized logotypes, where visual elements enhance the text, which remains primary; and (3) true logos, in which stand-alone graphic designs accompany, and may dominate or even replace, the text of the brand name. With further subdivision, we identified six distinct rhetorical options, two per zone, for constructing a brand mark. Finally, we argued that although discrete, these rhetorical options could nonetheless be ordered on a linear axis indexing the theoretical capacity to provide a rewarding and stimulating visual experience to consumers.

The typology is grounded on marks of leading brands. Each of these marks is the product of decades of design refinement and many millions of dollars of design expenditure by some of the global economy's largest and most successful firms. It seems unlikely that any of these brand marks is incompetently designed, or reflects a slapdash and hasty effort, or represents an arbitrary choice made on a whim.

Problem: one empirical piece of our work supports a contrary finding of Park et al. (2013). Our student judges consistently downrated text-only marks, especially black and white text-only marks (see Box 3.2 in Chapter 3). These marks didn't provide them much visual pleasure. Conceptual and empirical analyses combine to suggest that marks that fall low on the *eidos* gradient are less pleasing to consumers. So why do some of the world's leading brands, with a wealth of design talent at their beck and call, persist in using marks that are not visually enhanced?

There must be a good reason why many brands only minimally enhance their brand names with graphic elements, and why some brands do not graphically enhance their brand names at all, not even with color, in contradiction of the recommendations found in the literature.[1] We propose that category dynamics – the requirements for success that distinguish one product category from another – explain this contradiction. These dynamics may make successful text processing of the brand name more important than visual enhancement.

In this chapter we state and test propositions about product category differences in brand mark design. We believe brands may have good reason to locate their marks either low or high on the *eidos* axis, and even to select a subtype. Contrary to one conclusion of Park et al. (2013), we will argue that name-only marks are not less successful than graphically intense marks; but in keeping with other findings of Park et al. (2013), in some categories brands are well advised to craft what they called a name + symbol mark, and what we describe as an emblematic mark. Likewise, the benefits of color, and the fitness of a color for use in branding, are also category-dependent, as developed subsequently in Chapter 8.

Because of these category differences, which tie back to purchasing conditions and the nature of competition, black and white text marks have their place. It is not per se a mistake for a brand to stick with a black and white, text-only mark. Minimal graphic enhancement of the mark does not represent a management failure. The utility and necessity of visual enhancement depends on the category. Visual branding can be carried out elsewhere than in the mark.

Visual branding via design of the mark is an option, not a necessity. Sometimes, for some brands, visual branding is an imperative, and every opportunity to do it must be seized. At other times, and for other brands, visual branding is not as powerful and may not be necessary; other routes to marketing success are more important. Few books or papers written about visual branding take such a diffident attitude toward their subject. But as scholars, we have to call it as we see it.

PROPOSITIONS ABOUT PRODUCT CATEGORY DIFFERENCES

P1 (financial services): The greater the intangibility of the good, the more likely that the brand will select a mark of the emblematic type.

From the beginning of work on services marketing, theorists have argued that services face distinct challenges in branding and promotion. Services are intangible. You can't touch banking, and you can't depict insurance; only their appurtenances can be shown.[2] Therefore, brands in services categories are routinely advised to emphasize tangible cues in their persuasive communications. Prudential has its rock, and you are in good hands with Allstate. A standalone graphic design, offering a rich sensory experience, and built on appropriate and desirable imagery, provides such a tangible

---

BOX 4.1   SAMPLING OF MARKS WITHIN PRODUCT CATEGORIES

Using lists from the branding consultancies and web sources as before (see Box 3.1 in Chapter 3), in the financial services category we identified 50 leading banks, 40 leading insurance companies, and 10 large mutual fund families. Using the same sources, we identified 120 leading retailers, including 61 clothing retailers. These were compared to the main sample with services and retailers removed (any financial services or retailer brands that had been in the main sample were reassigned to the category samples). We use this same comparison strategy throughout this chapter: marks from the focal category are compared to the main sample, after removing marks from the focal category. Therefore, the count of marks remaining in the main sample changes with each comparison. See Boxes 4.2 and 4.3 for the procedures used to collect marks in the remaining categories.

As before, our undergraduate research assistants coded each mark for position in the typology and for color, with disagreements resolved by discussion (see note 5 in Chapter 3). The likelihood ratio chi-square was used to compare the distribution of marks across zones and subtypes between samples, and across color versus black and white, and also for particular colors. In this book, we do not state the chi-squares or the probability level; suffice to say, all comparisons reported were significant at $p < 0.05$. The reader who cares about this sort of thing can recapture these and other test statistics by analyzing the frequency counts in the tables.

---

cue. Hence, the distribution of marks in a sample of services brands should be shifted up the *eidos* gradient, making marks of the emblematic type more frequent. See Box 4.1 for a description of how we tested this proposition and the others that follow.

P2 (retailers): The less visually distinguishable the brand offerings in a category, the more necessary it will be to identify the brand through the alphanumeric text of the name.

The unanswered question remains: why would any brand forego the powerful positive impact of including a stand-alone graphic design in its mark? The second proposition provides a rationale for such decisions that does not treat these as instances of management failure or errors of execution. Consider the storefront of a clothing retailer in a shopping mall. Is it possible to identify such a retailer by name, by only examining the assortment of clothing displayed in the window, without reference to any signage? We argue, no. Similarly, although Lowes and Home Depot, CVS and Walgreen's, do not carry identical assortments, they carry large assortments not easily distinguishable at a glance. Many retailers face this dilemma. Large assortments of diverse goods must produce an impression of overall sameness, when housed in the same big box or displayed behind the same large plate glass windows. The rule: if consumers cannot distinguish between brands at a glance, then a prominent, legible rendition of the name is advisable. Hence, retailer brands should be distributed low on the *eidos* axis. The typical retailer brand will use a text-dominant brand mark located in subtype #4 (letter art) or below.

A subsidiary prediction: clothing and fashion retailers will be located even lower on the *eidos* axis. In addition to facing the assortment conundrum, these retailers face an additional challenge: their merchandise itself consists of stand-alone graphic designs (that is, clothing and accessories). Here, a graphically intensive, highly colorful brand mark risks stylistic conflict or rivalry with the merchandise. Hence, clothing retailers will migrate toward plain text renditions of the brand name, often in black and white.

To pace the chapter, and avoid monotony, we next present results for these first two propositions. After a brief discussion, additional propositions follow.

Findings for Financial Services and Retailer Marks

Services
The distribution across the typology, of marks of financial services firms, differed as predicted: 72 percent of financial services marks, as compared to 38 percent of the non-services marks in the main sample, fell into the emblematic subtype (Table 4.1). Text-only marks were also comparatively rare (10 percent versus 23 percent). This is consistent with the idea that brands of intangible services are more likely to resort to graphic enhancement of the brand mark in order to provide tangible cues with positive associations. Representative examples of emblematic financial services marks are in Table 4.2.

Retailers
As predicted, retailer marks tended to be located lower on the *eidos* axis, with 47.5 percent falling into the text-only Zone A, as compared to 15 percent of the main sample with retailers removed (Table 4.3). This shift mostly comes at the expense of Zone C, logos proper, which accounted for only 28 percent of retailer marks, versus 62 percent in the main sample. Notable is the relatively high proportion of black and white text-only retailer marks (26 percent versus 5 percent). The distinctive profile of retailer brand marks was accentuated in the case of clothing and fashion retailers: in this subset, almost 61 percent of marks were located in Zone A, with 41 percent consisting of black and white text-only marks lying at the bottom of the *eidos* gradient. See Table 4.4 for representative examples of text-only retailer marks.

Table 4.1   Comparative distribution of brand marks for financial services

	Financial services	Bar chart showing relative %	Main sample comparison set
Typology	Incidence (#)		Incidence (#)
Zone A (logotypes)			
#1: Black and white text-only	3		13
#2: Colored text-only	7		20
Zone B (graphicized logotypes)			
#3: Lined, bordered, or fielded	4		14
#4: Letter art	8		14
Zone C (logos)			
#5: Emblazoned	6		24
#6: Emblem	72		61

Note: See Box 4.1 for a description of the sampling and analysis strategies. To facilitate comparison, the embedded bar chart shows percentages.

Discussion: Marks in the Financial Services and Retailing Categories

We identified two broad categories, financial services and retailers, where a priori we could predict a distribution of brand marks that was higher (lower) on the *eidos* axis. Both predictions were confirmed, using two fresh samples of brand marks. The high incidence of text-only, black and white marks among clothing and fashion retailers casts doubt on the Park et al. (2013) claim that name-only brand marks are per se inferior from the standpoint of achieving a strong financial performance for the parent firm. The higher incidence of graphically enhanced marks among financial services firms likewise suggests that the utility of crafting a name + symbol brand mark may be a function of category. One size does not fit all. Within the space of brand mark designs, there may not be per se superior types. Mark design is driven by fit; visual enhancement is not an absolute or unalloyed good. Visually bare and scanty marks, relying on text only, may be the best choice for a brand.

Table 4.2   Characteristic examples of brand marks seen in financial services

Banks	Insurance
CHASE ⬡	🦅 Prudential
⟁ **PNC**	◗ UnitedHealth Group
CREDIT SUISSE	**ING** 🦁
WACHOVIA	(ⵡ) **Allstate.** You're in good hands.
Bank of America 〜	G—🖼 **Great-West** LIFE & ANNUITY INSURANCE COMPANY
ANZ 🦊	🦌 THE HARTFORD

Note: This table and also Tables 4.4, 4.6. and 4.8 are rhetorically structured: in each case we've selected the cleanest examples of the most frequent type of mark in each category. Where possible, we've also selected marks in the color that dominates the category (see Chapter 8). These tables thus contain exemplary rather than representative instances.

For both services and retailers, the category differences were hypothesized to flow from different consumer search and decision processes (that is, the intangibility of services, versus the text-reliant search by name for a retailer). Next we focus on a new metric: the motivation for purchase, as defined by Fennell (1978).[3] She argued that diverse purchasing motives could be grouped into two embracing categories: whether the motive was fundamentally positive, aimed at garnering more of some desirable element (for example, the sensory gratification provided by tasty food); or fundamentally negative, aimed at the getting rid of a problem (for example, cleaning products that remove dirt).

The larger point: it is not some intrinsic property of the product category that drives the design of brand mark. Choice of design option is driven by the consumer decision processes and competitor dynamics that

Table 4.3   Comparative distribution of brand marks for retailers

	Clothing and fashion retailers	Other retailers	Bar chart showing relative %	Main sample comparison set
Typology	Incidence (#)	Incidence (#)		Incidence (#)
Zone A (logotypes)				
#1: Black and white text-only	25	6		10
#2: Colored text-only	12	14		18
Zone B (graphicized logotypes)				
#3: Fielded	10	7		18
#4: Letter art	6	6		25
Zone C (logos)				
#5: Emblazoned	1	11		24
#6: Emblem	7	15		93

Note: See Box 4.1 for a description of the sampling and analysis strategies. To facilitate comparison, the embedded bar chart shows percentages. Black bars are clothing retailers, hatched bars are other retailers.

shape that category. It is slipshod to say that "banks prefer emblematic marks." The prevalence of emblems among bank marks stems from the intangibility of banking, a trait shared with other service categories. Intangibility drives the design of brand marks for banks. Any category where the good on offer is intangible will develop brand marks like those in banking. Likewise, black and white text-only marks are not unique to clothing retailers; rather, brands will gravitate toward this design option whenever legibility of the name is an overarching concern in the category where that brand competes.

Switching the focus to purchase motives, and setting aside intangibility and legibility concerns, reinforces the point. Brand mark design is never about the category. It rests on the consumer decision process, or the manner in which brands compete, which predominates in that category. Sampling on product category is only a convenience: banks are good places to observe the effects of intangibility, while retailers provided a convenient opportunity to study legibility.

Table 4.4   Characteristic examples of brand marks used by retailers

Clothing retailers	General retailers
DSW.	TIFFANY & CO.
Carson's	*Cartier*
ANN TAYLOR	**CVS**
FOREVER 21	**BARNES&NOBLE** BOOKSELLERS
MICHAEL KORS	**FredMeyer.** Save time, money & gas.
J.CREW	**Pier1 imports**

Note: See note to Table 4.2.

P3 (food versus irritating categories): Food products purchased from positive motives will be shifted up the eidos *axis, as compared to cleaning and hygiene products purchased from a negative motivation, which will be shifted down the* eidos *axis.*

The intuition behind this proposition rests on a point made by Park et al. (2013). They argued that the purpose of brand marks need not be brand identification, but could instead be value expression, that is, providing the brand with valuable associations. However, rather than framing these goals as alternatives that vie for primacy in mark design, we prefer to pair promotion with identification, as the twin goals of brand mark design and of visual branding. Marks may identify the brand, but can also promote it. One or the other goal may dominate in a category, but neither goal is primary in any absolute or overriding sense. Brands are opportunistic, and invest in identification or promotion, or both, as their situation requires.

Yes, you can promote a brand by linking it to consumers' desired self-expression by means of positive associations and shared values. But value expression is easier in some categories than others. Delicious snacks are easy; but scouring powder presents more of a challenge. The rule: products purchased out of a positive motivation are far more likely to serve

---

BOX 4.2   SAMPLING MARKS IN PACKAGED GOODS
          CATEGORIES

We obtained a list of the 20 top-selling packaged food categories from a
Supermarket News compilation, and identified three leading brands for each category, based on market share or other indices of prominence (for example,
IBISWorld), subject to the constraint of selecting only one brand per manufacturer
within a category. Several of the 60 brands identified were already present in the
main sample; we then added any other packaged food brands already in the main
sample, but not in the 20 top-selling categories, for a total of 71 food brands.

To find products purchased out of a negative, problem-removal motivation, we
identified irritating product categories using the list of Aaker and Bruzzone (1985).
We then added other cleaning and hygiene product categories, again based on best-
selling supermarket categories, to get an adequate sample size, sampling three
brands per category. This produced a sample of 54 marks, including four brands that
had been in the main sample. Combining the food and irritating product samples
yielded a total of 125 packaged goods brands. Marks for these brands were obtained
from the web, and the research assistants categorized and coded these marks and
their colors, resolving any disagreements by discussion (see Box 3.1 in Chapter 3).
As before, likelihood chi-square ratios provided a statistical test; in reporting the findings, we again dispense with the individual tests and significance levels.

---

consumers' self-expression needs. Products purchased out of a negative
motivation, where the brand promises to remove or prevent some bother-
some blemish, mess, odor, or other source of discomfort, do not present
the same opportunity for consumer self-expression. Absent a positive
purchase motivation, brands have less incentive to graphically enhance
their brand marks, and may focus instead on establishing brand identification. Accordingly, like retailers, but for a different reason, the marks of
negatively purchased brands should be shifted downward into the text-
dominant zones.

Both food and cleaning products fit within the super-category termed
packaged goods (Box 4.2), most of which are low-priced, frequently purchased, and carry little risk; unlike purchase of an insurance product or
an expensive dress. Such packaged goods brands have been scarce in the
samples analyzed thus far. This is not an accident: any sample of "top
brands" or "leading brands" will systematically exclude many packaged
goods brands, for reasons explained next.

Park et al. (2013) note that they had to exclude any brand that was
not co-extensive with its corporate parent. It appears that the branding
consultancies (for example, Interbrand) likewise use corporate financial metrics in selecting top brands. As a result, one of two theoretical
branding strategies has dominated samples of leading brands: only

firms using a family brand name strategy made the cut. General Electric appears, but not the Tide brand of Proctor & Gamble; Kellogg's was included, but not the Cheerios brand of General Mills. In the enormous global economy of 2015, even a billion-dollar, individually named brand like Tide can't make the top 100 cut; only corporations promoting a single brand can satisfy the financial metrics. This paradoxically leads to excluding firms normally celebrated in the marketing literature as leaders of modern branding (for example, P&G, General Mills). Tests of Proposition 3 correct this omission, by focusing specifically on consumer packaged goods brands.

The focus on packaged goods suggests an additional proposition. Just as the search process for retailers is distinctive, so also point-of-purchase activities for packaged goods are distinctive: here a consumer faces a crowded and visually noisy supermarket aisle, where brands shout for attention by means of their packaging. A typical package provides a large surface which may be covered by swaths of intense colors outlining bold shapes. Hence, relative to most other categories of goods, packaging makes available a large surface for graphic enhancement beyond the space that will be devoted to the brand mark.

Might the design of brand marks be sensitive to this context? For instance, a brand mark of the emblazoned type can merge seamlessly into a surrounding package design. This allows the entire package to be an extension of the background design on which the name is emblazoned, making the mark co-extensive with the package. By contrast, a small stand-alone emblem, however intricately designed, may get lost on a supermarket shelf crowded with bold shapes and large expanses of bright color.

P4 (packaged goods collectively): Emblazoned marks will be more common, and emblematic marks less common, in packaged goods categories.

Findings for Packaged Goods Categories

Negatively versus positively purchased products
As predicted, marks of irritating product categories were located lower on the *eidos* axis than food marks (Table 4.5). About 39 percent of the irritating marks were in the text-only zone, versus 7 percent of the food marks. Irritating marks were also more likely to be black and white (17 percent versus 4 percent).

Packaged goods collectively
The centrality of packaging in the supermarket does favor one subtype of marks: 38 percent of the packaged goods sample (food and irritating

Table 4.5   Comparative distribution of brand marks for positively and negatively purchased consumer packaged goods

	Food products	Irritating products	Bar chart showing relative %	Main sample comparison set
Typology	Incidence (#)	Incidence (#)		Incidence (#)
Zone A (logotypes)				
#1: Black and white text-only	1	7		8
#2: Colored text-only	3	14		20
Zone B (graphicized logotypes)				
#3: Lined, bordered or fielded	6	6		19
#4: Letter art	10	5		24
Zone C (logos)				
#5: Emblazoned	29	16		20
#6: Emblem	12	6		87

Note: See Box 4.2 for a description of the sampling and analysis strategies. To facilitate comparison, the embedded bar chart shows percentages. Black bars are food products and hatched bars are irritating products.

products together) were categorized as emblazoned, versus 19 percent emblematic; while in the main sample, with packaged goods brands removed, emblazoned marks accounted for 11 percent and emblematic marks accounted for 44 percent. This was the only notable point of difference in the distribution of subtypes for packaged goods (Table 4.5). See Table 4.6 for representative examples.

Discussion of Packaged Goods Findings

The findings for positively and negatively purchased packaged goods indicate that the design of brand marks may vary with the nature of the consumer's purchase motivation. Visual enhancement of the brand mark emerges as an optional strategy; one most appropriate to product

Table 4.6   Characteristic examples of packaged goods brand marks

Food categories	Irritating categories
Heinz	PREPARATION H®
Stouffer's	TUCKS®
Kraft	Gas-X
CHEEZ-IT — REAL CHEESE MATTERS™	TUMS
ARMOUR	Mucinex
Pure Wesson	Scope

Note: See note to Table 4.2.

categories where consumer value expression is likely. When the product is only a means to the end of avoiding or removing an unpleasant problem, brand marks are less likely to be graphically enhanced. Aggregating over purchase motivations, the results also show that the design of brand marks is sensitive to the nature of the purchase occasion; in this case, the role played by packaging in appealing to a consumer who faces the challenge of navigating a crowded supermarket aisle.

Emblazonment represents an innovation specific to our typology: an example of the neglected middle ground between the name-only and name + symbol poles that had dominated past academic discussions (Park et al. 2013). The relative scarcity of packaged goods in past academic and practitioner discussions of brand marks, due to the financial criterion used to select top brands, may explain why emblazonment has not heretofore been called out as a distinct type of brand mark. Failure to formulate the limits of the name + symbol type (termed emblematic marks in our typology) may likewise reflect a neglect of the diverse circumstances under which brand marks must fulfill their purpose. With different consumer decision processes foregrounded, it is easy to recognize that an intangible service may require a different brand mark than a packaged snack.

Next, we acknowledge a necessary limitation of using category-based samples to test theories of the constraints placed on brand marks: some other factor, distinctive to the product category, might instead be driving the results. In addition to instantiating a negative purchase motive, hemorrhoid remedies, gas relief, and so forth are categories with many other distinguishing features. Even the idea of a negative purchase motive is only one instance of a consumer decision in which value-expression is not likely to be important; and it is the relative importance of value expression that matters. To establish the robustness of predictions from the typology, we broaden the statement of Proposition 3, and test this statement on a product category that differs from those examined before.

P5 (business-to-business manufacturers): The less the importance of value expression in the category, the lower on the eidos *axis brand marks will be located.*

Papers that laud the power of visual branding make a tacit assumption: that out in the market there are customers who can be swayed by promotional differentiation, in this case by a visually attractive brand mark. The consumer is susceptible because the amount of money at risk is low and the desired product benefits may be largely subjective.

Business-to-business (B2B) categories are different (Box 4.3): here we find small concentrated markets, high financial risk, and a rationalized

---

BOX 4.3   SAMPLING MARKS OF BUSINESS-TO-BUSINESS MANUFACTURERS

To identify B2B manufacturers, we sampled from the lists of holdings in two sector-based Exchange Traded Funds (iShares Materials and iShares Industrials). This gave us a list of the largest such B2B firms in the Standard & Poor's 500 index by market capitalization. We pruned from this list any firm that we thought had a significant consumer presence (for example, removing General Electric, but retaining General Dynamics), and smaller firms (less than 1 percent of sector capitalization), leaving 53 firms. As before, the research assistants coded each logo for position in the typology and for color (see Box 3.1 in Chapter 3).

sales process based on spreadsheet analyses that lay bare the cost of ownership and performance relative to specification. On the face of it, having a colorful and cleverly designed brand mark ought not to be a material factor in B2B marketing success. Accordingly, we predict marks of B2B durables manufacturers will be distributed lower on the *eidos* axis, because clear communication of the identifying name will be the goal of the brand mark. Hence, there should be little impetus to invest in visual enhancement.

Findings for B2B Manufacturers

Marks of B2B manufacturers were shifted down the *eidos* axis relative to the main sample. Here the shift was evenly distributed, with a decrease in Zone C counts (only 36 percent of marks, versus 61 percent in the main sample) spread down to augment both Zone B and Zone A counts. These results are consistent with the idea that there is less to be gained by graphic enhancement of the mark in the B2B category.

Table 4.7   Comparative distribution of marks used by B2B manufacturers

	B2B	Bar chart showing relative %	Main sample comparison set
Typology	Incidence (#)		Incidence (#)
Zone A (logotypes)			
#1: Black and white text-only	1		15
#2: Colored text-only	14		19
Zone B (graphicized logotypes)			
#3: Fielded	8		23
#4: Letter art	11		24
Zone C (logos)			
#5: Emblazoned	2		30
#6: Emblem	17		97

Note: See Box 4.3 for a description of the sampling and analysis strategies. To facilitate comparison, the embedded bar chart shows percentages.

Table 4.8   Characteristic examples of B2B manufacturer brand marks

Note: See note to Table 4.2

DISCUSSION

We found substantial differences across product categories in the distribution of types of brand marks. These category differences tie back to characteristic differences in consumer decision processes and the nature of the purchase occasion. Rather than providing a universal benefit relevant to all brands, it now appears that graphic enhancement of the brand mark – that is, going beyond printing of the name in a characteristic typeface – is of benefit only when specific contingencies are met. We adopt the resource-advantage (R-A) theory of Hunt and Morgan (1995) to develop the circumstances under which graphic enhancement may be advantageous.

Under R-A theory, firms seek competitive advantage through accumulating resources that either lower firm costs or increase the value delivered to customers.

The application of R-A theory to brand marks is straightforward: brands will only seek visually enhanced marks under circumstances where graphic enhancement is advantageous. Particular types of graphic enhancement (for example, use of a stand-alone graphic design) will likewise be sought out when these provide an advantage, and will not otherwise occur. In short, brand marks will be graphically enhanced, and in specific ways, when the surplus of the advantages gained over the costs incurred for this gambit appears attractive, relative to other gambits, each of which represents a drawdown on the firm's limited investment capacity.

Application of R-A theory suggests two shortcomings in contemporary discussions of visual branding. Authors tend to forget that the brand is fundamental, while any representation of the brand is secondary. Any representation has the power to evoke the *brand*: the complex knot of associations that make up that brand's equity. Accordingly, no graphic enhancement of the brand mark is necessary to promote it. The name alone suffices to tap its equity.

Past research on visual branding can be criticized for lauding the value of the visual while denigrating the power of a name. This ignores the powerful role played by names in magic and other pre-scientific attempts to control the world.[4] A name is an extremely compact and potent means of making available a host of semantic meaning, and a plain text rendition of a name, especially one that is readily legible, is an efficient means of cueing those semantic associations. Universally, the name gives the brand to the consumer; the contingent issue is when it may be advantageous to enhance, or reinforce and emphasize, elements of the brand by means of graphic design.

A second shortcoming stems from what Hunt and Morgan (1995) decry as the bane of the neoclassical approach to competition, and what we deem to be the continued baleful impact of academic psychology on the discipline of marketing: the fiction of homogeneity. In the present context, homogeneity flags an all too common assumption: that there is one single consumer decision process, and one role only for brand marks. If assumed to be homogeneous, this process can be studied by having college students fill out scales in response to brand marks drawn haphazardly from a few categories, not made subject to purchase, and free of any history (that is, having zero brand equity). With homogeneity assumed, there is no need to model particulars, such as the effect of navigating a crowded supermarket shelf while a child tugs at one's leg, or the embarrassment of buying hemorrhoid relief in public, or any factor specific to a product category.

Psychological theory can be universal and non-contingent to the extent that consumer decision-making is homogeneous, with brand marks having one purpose and one route to effectiveness. But once particulars intervene, a contingent formulation is required. Theory must grow subtle. Nuances count.

We identified three contingencies that appeared to make graphic enhancement of the brand mark an advantageous resource. The first was intangibility, as in financial services. Here graphic enhancement of the brand mark may be advantageous because of the tangibility inherent in a visual representation. Conversely, because packaging design is available to packaged goods firms as an alternative resource for visual branding, the brand mark may not need to be graphically enhanced to the same degree. The emblematic type of mark, so helpful to intangible services, is unnecessary for packaged goods. Small, elaborate emblems would get lost in the bright colors and large designs of the packaging itself. At the same time, emblazoned designs lend themselves to placement on packaging and integration with that larger package design.

The second contingency rests on the relative difficulty of securing brand identification. If competitors are not visually differentiated by their storefronts or merchandising displays, then graphic enhancement of the brand mark will be minimal because legibility of the name comes first. Retailers typically fit this specification because of the homogenizing effect of large assortments, and hence had marks located lower on the *eidos* axis. Likewise, when products in a category themselves consist of visual designs, as in the case of retailers of clothing and fashion goods, then graphic enhancement of the brand mark may be disadvantageous insofar as it has the potential to clash with, or limit the range of expression in, the graphically designed merchandise itself. Here the advantage lies with black and white, text-only marks, insofar as the color black is as versatile as a "little black dress."

The third contingency identified was the nature of the purchase motivation, in Fennell's (1978) terms. When this motivation is positive, as with food products consumed for taste pleasure, then graphic enhancement may be advantageous. When motivation is negative, as in the case of remedies and cleaning products, or the rationally purchased problem solutions seen in B2B categories, then graphic enhancement is less likely, either because the visual attractiveness of the brand mark is not a material factor in purchases, or because it would not be advantageous to visually enhance or attempt to make comely the problem which the brand solves. Graphic enhancement may not help either brands of hemorrhoid relief or manufacturers of industrial solvents.

Application of R-A theory suggests one additional consideration or overriding contingency, which may be pertinent to understanding the observed distribution of types of brand marks. Park et al. (2013) highlighted the issue of the comparative importance, in the design of brand marks, of securing brand identification and differentiation versus linking the brand to goals valued by the consumer. Park et al. labeled these linkages as the value expressive function and Brakus et al. (2009) described them as the experiential function of brand marks. Brand marks can identify brands, but marks also can build brand equity by contributing and emphasizing desirable associations and promoting an overall positive experience of the brand. The net of our cross-category comparisons indicates that where brand identification is a pressing concern, design of the mark will abstain from graphic enhancement and prioritize a legible presentation of the text of the brand name. Conversely, in categories where graphic enhancement of the mark is observed, there, value-expression may be primary.

The upshot of our empirical findings: firms may have less discretion in the design of brand marks than conventionally assumed. The type of brand mark that can be advantageous to a firm is set in large part by category dynamics that are not within the control of managers. The details of designs and typefaces remain a matter of discretion, but the degree of graphic enhancement that will be advantageous is constrained by external contingencies. Text-only brand marks should not be dismissed as a lapse in judgment, but accepted as an appropriate response to contingencies that govern the category where the firm competes.

MANAGERIAL IMPLICATIONS

This chapter can act as a prophylactic for executives of retailers and B2B firms, and for any executive in a category where products are purchased from a negative motivation. It provides protection against pitches from branding consultants, who may call for a redesign that pumps up the graphic portion of the brand mark, citing past academic literature on the financial threat posed by name-only marks lacking an attractive graphic design (Henderson and Cote 1998; Park et al. 2013). It encourages marketing executives to stand their ground, based on their own judgment of how customers decide, and the role played by value expression in the purchase. A legible text-only presentation of a good brand name, possibly enhanced by a color popular in the local culture, may provide a more than adequate brand mark.

Conversely, an executive responsible for an intangible service, or a lifestyle product, or any good purchased out of a positive motivation, who inherited a drab brand mark, now has additional grounds to request funds for a rebranding. The rejoinder that "at least our plain and unadorned mark helps to set us apart from the fancy marks used by so many others" can be rebutted. The practical implication: if most other brands in the category have graphically enhanced marks, it behooves a firm to arm itself with the same. The laudatory treatment accorded to visual branding is apt; but only in some product categories.

5. Rhetorical evolution of brand marks

To recapitulate: a brand mark is the trademark that universally accompanies the brand. It appears in ads across all media, on the packaging and maybe the product itself, in corporate signage, and elsewhere. Today all brands have a mark.

RHETORICAL AND HISTORICAL CRITIQUE OF PSYCHOLOGICAL APPROACHES TO MARKS

Psychological theory, whether concerning brand marks or anything else, strives to be universal and context-free. On a naïve psychological view, all brands have elaborate, colorful marks; brands have always had these marks; and there have always been brands, for as long as human beings have participated in markets. Like any other natural phenomenon, brands and branding are assumed to conform to scientific laws, which are universal and timeless.

If we wrote that last paragraph well, by its end you were shaking your head. Universal laws of branding? Timeless brands lying outside of history? Balderdash! The besetting sin of psychology is to naturalize: to take human constructions out of history and treat them as timeless things that subsist unchanged. The urge to do psychological science, when applied to brand marks, hypostasizes these human, local, very recent design efforts. It leads to the careless assumption that brand marks have always looked like they do today, removing the need to go back and examine brand marks from decades ago.

The rhetorician knows better. We seek the available means of persuasion in any situation. The means available for branding in 2015 need not be the same as those available in 1900. And what becomes available by 2055 may be different yet. Where once there were a few dozen designers engaged in branding activity, by the 1920s there were hundreds, by the 1950s thousands, and today, tens of thousands of creative individuals employed to design marks and other branding devices. Each generation went to school on the efforts of its predecessors. Each generation slid down the cost curve of existing technologies, and enjoyed access to new technologies.

The conceptual issue here is the same as our critique, earlier in Part II, of the Henderson and Cote (1998) and Park et al. (2013) efforts to taxonomize brand marks. Henderson and Cote do not acknowledge the existence and prevalence of logotypes where graphic design is absent. Park et al. acknowledge but disparage such logotypes. Both author teams, consistent with the main thrust of modern psychology, have an ideal type in mind; the one true brand mark, the optimal mark, toward which all designers should strive: colorful, pleasing to the eye, cleverly designed, and rich in positive brand associations.

Historians, like post-Darwinian biologists, see a different picture. Before Darwin, species were thought to be permanent features of the world. Each had an ideal form, an essence which endured, and many earthly expressions, all of which were approximations to that essence. Returning to brand marks, historians, like modern evolutionary biologists, do not see one ideal form emerging as the dross is chipped away. Historians see initial groping efforts, temporary expedients that fall away, slow refinement followed by abandonment, wholesale replacement, and seesaw motion, as gambits for brand mark design appear and then wax and wane in popularity. Historians can acknowledge long-term trends in select aspects of brand mark design, the same as biologists can acknowledge the increased size and elaboration of the mammalian form, and the emergence of primates as a mammalian form with new capabilities. But in neither case is it correct to postulate a teleology. Direction, yes; destination, no.

EARLY HISTORY AND PREDECESSORS OF BRAND MARKS

Not all the components of visual branding share the same history or developed at the same pace. For instance, the history of emblems – stand-alone graphic designs incorporated into the brand mark – differs from that of color and type.

Heraldry shaped the early history of emblematic brand marks.[1] Coats of arms, borne by aristocrats and noble families, predate branding, and printing. A coat of arms is an emblem or graphic design that identifies a family or lineage without giving the text of their name. Such a coat is not a brand; the ontology is not the same. It would be a gross solecism to speak of branding the Tudors or Hapsburgs. Noble families did not brand themselves; that verb has no meaning in the historical context in which heraldry originated.

Nonetheless, because coats of arms preceded the development of corporate brands, heraldry provided accessible and compelling cultural resources. In heraldry, the founders of early brands had available a template for how a graphic design could both act as a name, and attest to the illustrious character of what was named. As the earliest brands were often the creation of entrepreneurs – and inasmuch as wealthy merchants had been entering the European aristocracy for centuries, purchasing coats of arms along the way – therefore it was almost inevitable that early brand marks, especially in Europe, would initially not be distinguishable in design from coats of arms. Here we have a captain of industry, joining the upper ranks of society; there is his creation, and his mark on it, to show who made it; how could this mark take any other form than the coats of arms historically associated with the elite?[2] And how could a brand, a new thing struggling for legitimacy, as corporate capitalism disrupted and remade society, not associate itself with all that is noble and good, and thus with aristocratic identifiers?

Returning to the facts, and a more sober appraisal: there needs to be an "if" placed in front of this claim. If a brand chose to supplement its name with graphic elements, then this supplement would likely take the form of an emblem, rather than one of the other ways to graphically supplement and visually enhance a name discussed in Chapter 3. And if the brand originated early on, during the nineteenth century, when branding was nascent, and if the brand was European, then brand marks are most likely to resemble coats of arms, by incorporating standalone graphic designs: emblems.

If instead the brand is American, and originated around 1900, and we are looking at early examples of its mark prior to about 1920, then it is likely that there will be no emblem, no stand-alone graphic design at all. At that early date, and that early state of technology, unadorned brand names, possibly but not necessarily set in an ornamental typeface, were common (see Figures 2.3 through 2.17 in Chapter 2, for example). Because it was America not Europe, heraldry did not represent the same cultural resource, and did not beckon so enticingly. Instead, brand marks drew on traditions of display type: the larger sizes used in newspaper headlines, and the fancy typefaces seen on signage.

The point: zones within the typology of brand marks were populated at different points in history. In America, Zone C marks were initially the exception, rather than the most common type as today. The design of brand marks shows a historical trend: over time, the distribution of marks shifted up the *eidos* gradient. Once this historical movement is grasped, there is no reason to believe it has reached some final state. It is an error to treat brand marks, these human creations in history, as natural phenomena subject to laws like those that govern matter in motion.

BRAND MARKS AROUND 1900

To identify the sponsor, many brands list the company name, in black, and in the same font as the rest of the ad, along with a mailing address. We see identification, but as yet no promotion. Advertisers appeared to imagine that consumers were reading the ad, even poring over it, and could be stimulated to write in response. It was the era of salesmanship in print; magazine ads were not yet the mass media vehicles they would later become, aimed at subtly shifting the mindset of millions, but instead were direct response sales messages, aimed at converting readers to action by shaping their deliberate scrutiny of what was said in the ad.

The haphazard element – or more kindly, the tentative and exploratory character of early branding – is visible in the profusion of typefaces applied to a single brand. Jello, in one ad, uses three different fonts to name itself (Figure 2.15). Examples of this haphazard style are legion, even in the next period of the 1920s. The branding potential of typeface had not yet been recognized. Brands do not strive to own a typeface through an insistent consistency, but try on typefaces like suits of clothes. True, as time goes on, the brand name becomes less likely to be presented in plain text; but the large or fancy fonts used for the name in a print ad come and go, and may not be repeated on the package, if shown. Distinct typefaces are not attached to the brand, and owned by it, but rather, are intended to highlight and call out the name, in the spirit of applying boldface or italic. The text of the brand name is treated as a headline, something to be foregrounded and made prominent. Typeface has not yet been mastered as a resource for visual branding. No matter how marked the headlined name, a plain text rendition of the name, in normal size font, may be affixed above the mailing address. Branding remains fitful, within each advertisement as well as over time.

Since any color remained rare, colored logotypes are also rare. Letter art, and some bordering or fielding, is as visually intense as brand marks get. There are scattered instances of coats of arms type emblems, especially if the package is reproduced in the ad (this has not yet become the norm). We sense that the people who designed the package, or other corporate signage, weren't the same as the people designing the ads. No one yet acted as a steward of the brand's trade dress; the concept itself did not appear to exist. Sometimes, the emblem is present, but not integrated with the name; it is treated as a stand alone trademark, and announced as such; but it may be inches away on the page, and not a part of the name.

1920s

Brand marks in the 1920s are harder to summarize. It is a transition period, where some marks look the same as those seen 20 years before, some marks begin to acquire at least color, and a few take on modern form. Overall, the population of marks in the 1920s seems closer in its central tendency to the marks seen during the 1900s, rather than to marks that appear in the 1980s and after.

In rough order of descending frequency, brand marks in the 1920s are either: (1) black text-only and plain; (2) decorated, prominent black text-only; (3) black text in the ad, but with a more elaborate brand mark appearing in a package shot, or somewhere outside the identification region; (4) a more modern mark, located higher up the *eidos* gradient – emblazoned or even emblematic; or (5) color text-only. Although color ads become common in the 1920s, the ownership of color for purposes of branding lags behind, as seen in the rarity of color text brand marks.

The brand is still represented primarily by its name; it belongs to the copywriter, not the graphic artist. The copywriter sprinkles the name throughout the text of the ad (see Figure 2.22), and strives to set the name in a large and distinctive typeface at least once. But that large and distinctive typeface does not belong to the brand. We see typesetting, rather than type ownership; the large fancy fonts that appear are drawn from a common set, and used promiscuously across brands. The text of the brand name continues to act as a headline, and not a signature. The name is raised to prominence through selection of type, but that typeface is not owned by the brand. Ads print the name rather than display the mark; the brand block may consist of no more than the name in plain small text placed above a mailing address.

We continue to see lack of control over the repertoire of branding devices. As in the 1900s, the brand name may appear in multiple typefaces within a single ad: one font for its headline function, a different font elsewhere in the text, and a third font on the package. The same indiscipline holds for color: the package may be shown in one color, even as the brand name appears beside it in another color.

On a more modern note, the package shot starts to come into its own in the 1920s. As in modern ads, the package shot may serve as the brand block, the primary means of identifying the sponsor of the ad (although we may still see a plain text address block, in contrast to modern ads, where this has fallen away). Interestingly, the graphic design of the package may be more forward-looking, in presenting the brand mark, than the ad as a whole. Packages more often display emblazoned, emblematic marks than the rest of the ad (see Figures 2.17 and 2.20). It appears the team that designs the ad has little contact with the team that designs the package; these two promotional efforts are not integrated. In terms of graphic design, packaging leads: here the brand's visual presentation is managed with a stronger hand.

We can draw on economic history to explain why the package began to serve as the brand block at about this point. The first self-service super-markets appeared after World War I.[3] Before then, the customer had to ask for a product by name; they might or might not be able to see it displayed on the wall behind the clerk. Once self-service shopping became the norm, it became imperative that the consumer recognized the package on the shelf; they did not have to recall the name any longer, but only recognize it as they wheeled by its shelf display.[4] Immediately, the package became a key part of brand advertising. The branding dictum was no longer "get the name out there and keep it on the tip of the customer's tongue," but became instead, "show them the package, over and over, until they can't miss it in the store."

A curious feature of ads from this era is the isolated display of a trade-mark outside of the brand block. By this juncture brand managers knew that they owned a trademark, knew that this mark was valuable, and knew that it had to be protected; so it got tossed into the ad somewhere. These trademarks may be emblematic in design, or at least emblazoned, typically medallion-like; but they do not accompany the brand name, and do not appear in the brand block. Trademarks sit off to the side, sometimes accompanied by the exhortation: "look for it," or "accept no other." These exhortations disappear after the 1920s.

Quite a few leading brands today have roots dating back to the 1920s or earlier. A final impression, visible only to the modern reader, is of the gap that separates the presentation, then, of these brands from their presenta-tion now. Typeface may differ, of course, since ownership of type came much later; but brand colors, and even marks, also differ. Colgate does not yet own its red. And it is not only absence then, versus presence now: elements disappear too. But there is also continuity: Coca-Cola's mark appears similar, then and now. Campbell's had a red and white can then, too.

Finally, it is melancholy to see brands, clearly vigorous and promi-nent here in the 1920s, which have since disappeared, to the point of no longer being familiar even to someone born in the 1950s. Might brands be mortal, with finite life spans?[5] Or are these now vanished brands the losers, the flawed and weak efforts left on the cutting room floor, tailings from the capitalist mine, with the survivors of that era now ensconced in a permanent sinecure? That's the bane and beauty of writing recent history: it isn't over yet.

1950s

The big change in the 1950s was the spread of color, as touched upon in Chapter 2. By the early 1950s, many ads in a *Ladies Home Journal* (*LHJ*) or *Good Housekeeping* (*GH*) magazine used color. However, black and white ads had not yet become rare.

The consequence, for brand marks: the frequency of names rendered in colored text begins to increase. Unfortunately, many advertisers appear to have paid only for two-color printing. As a result the color, typically red, stays exactly the same shade across multiple brands. Every brand uses the one color this magazine allows them to print, rather than a color specific to and owned by one brand. Although by the 1950s color had increasingly entered the branding repertoire, its use had not been mastered. Color, in the design of marks, remained like type in the 1920s: an available resource, one whose potential a few brands had begun to explore, but one which most brands continued to ignore or slight.

Overall the 1950s, to our eye, is as much a transition period as the 1920s, but one where the transition is farther along. As in the 1920s, the American economy was booming, and new consumer goods appeared and diffused. Magazines are stuffed with ads for a wide range of branded goods. But, like the 1920s, the products advertised are mostly tangible things, not intangible services. Unlike the 1920s, competition after World War II became more intense across a wide variety of categories – multiple brands, each with a heritage and some prominence, each holding on to equity precipitated from decades of promotion, all vie for the consumer's eye.

During the 1950s the full typology laid out in Chapter 3 begins to be populated. Emblematic and emblazoned marks grow more frequent, along with bordered and fielded text, and the occasional piece of letter art. The block giving the address in plain black and white text has mostly disappeared; advertisers no longer approach the reader of the magazine as someone who will write back. But plain black and white text marks are still present in minimally developed brand blocks. And where type is manipulated, much of the time it proceeds as in the 1920s: the text of the brand name is marked, made prominent, by a fancy font, or by enlargement, or by boldface or by italics, and even by a print in color. But these are headline typefaces, not the brand's own typeface.

The separate, structured brand block becomes more common in the 1950s, containing a designed mark, maybe a package shot, and even a tagline. But these are still not the mode. Likewise, a brand block that consists solely of a package shot, with the name of the brand appearing nowhere else in the ad except on the package, becomes a little more common. However, some of the package shots in these 1950s ads strike the modern eye as odd. They are so bare of ornament and design as to resemble a student project in an advertising course, where the assignment had been "mock up an ad for your fictitious brand," and a rush job on the imagery was done end-of-term. Alternatively, the package in the ad is not the real package in the store, or a photo of it, but only a rough sketch, a simulacrum which the advertiser judged to be adequate for a low resolution thumbnail of subsidiary importance within the economy of the overall ad page (see Figure 2.35). These 1950s packages in ads look nothing like the heavily designed and graphically intense packages that populate a supermarket shelf in 2015.

It appears that advertisers did not always take the package seriously as part of the overall visual branding effort; in fact, we doubt that "overall visual branding effort" as yet had any meaning or familiarity. The concept of visual branding still had not taken root. Brand is a meaningful concept by the 1950s;[6] but the overall visual branding effort, comprised of brand mark design, brand colors, packaging, ad imagery, and all other visual expressions, has not yet cohered into a single activity to be managed as a whole.

Where some packages in ads from the 1920s showed a more intense graphic design effort than the ad itself, here in the 1950s that impression is reversed. Perhaps in the 1920s, the package had been designed first, and was older, developed over the decades after 1880, when many branded packaged goods had begun to appear, but when advertising effort was still only fitful. By contrast, here in the 1950s, after a flurry of new product introductions, the corporate brand may now be decades older than the package design.

It is still possible to find a confusion of typefaces in a single ad, with the brand rendered one way when appearing in the headline, in a different typeface in the brand block, and a third typeface on the package. But these occur less commonly now, and we may see a modern level of discipline, with the name rendered in a unique, brand-owned typeface in the brand block, and an identical rendering nearby on the package.

1980s

By 1980 advertisers and designers had accumulated over 80 years of experience with branding. With respect to brand marks, we now have fourth-generation graphic designers. Graphic design had long since become a career path; schools of advertising and of design were well-established. Color had been a staple of advertising for decades. But the design textbooks of this era (Nelson 1981) still emphasize the physical activities of cutting and pasting, proceeding in the same way as decades earlier.[7] And Nelson's own book is printed in black and white.

Nonetheless, by the 1980s the transition to modern brand marks is far along. Colored text, unique to that brand, is commonly used in marks. The full range of types is present: emblematic, emblazoned, letter art, and color fielded marks can all be seen. The address block is gone, except in direct response ads. The brand block has been perfected: a dedicated area at the bottom or bottom right of the ad, containing a uniquely designed mark, and even a tagline. The use of a package as the brand block has also been perfected.

In our judgment, the distribution of marks was still shifted down the *eidos* axis relative to the present, with emblematic marks manifest but not the mode. However, a confound vitiates this comparison. Recall that we are chiefly examining women's magazines, and focusing on ads for packaged foods, soap, and personal care products, with some attention to consumer durables advertised to women, especially household furnishings. There were not many ads for services in the publications we viewed; few banks or insurance companies advertised in these women's magazines in that era. In short, product categories where emblematic marks are now favored, such as services, were not advertised there; and some of the products that were heavily advertised, such as cleaning products, even today favor marks lower on the *eidos* gradient, as explained in Chapter 4.

Two conclusions follow from this perusal of brand marks and blocks from the early 1980s: First, once technology and cost trends made it possible, many brands chose to move up the *eidos* gradient. It was not necessary to have Photoshop software; earlier design technologies sufficed to produce marks with a modern appearance. Second, brands in categories where value expression is unlikely to occur did not participate in this modernizing trend; but food brands, and other categories where positive motives predominate, did seize the new opportunities opened up. Category matters to the design of brand marks.

2000s

As in Chapter 2, it is not necessary to produce many examples of contemporary brand marks and brand blocks (see Chapters 3 and 4 for examples). A brief statement of major elements of contemporary usage will suffice.

First, every brand manager today is familiar with the concept of visual branding, and accepts the need to integrate all visual presentations of the brand and maintain consistency across executions and over time. An entire industry of branding consultants has grown up, and visual branding (and rebranding) is among the services provided to clients. At a guess, each year more than a dozen Fortune 500 firms will rebrand or update their brand.[8] In a late capitalist economy, profits fluctuate, and the fortunes of firms and brands gyrate up and down without cease. Hence, "we need to refresh the brand" becomes a ready response for any executive pressed to account for a shortfall. Branding consultants and chief marketing officers set up a mutually beneficial feedback loop. The decision to refresh the brand is easy because the resources to do it are widely and readily available, and the underlying belief, that the brand is the firm's most important asset, is held with conviction.

As academics, removed from the daily whirl, and serving under no profit imperative, we can opine that some of this rebranding looks more like flailing about, or the rearrangement of deck chairs on the *Titanic*, or newly appointed executives lifting their leg to mark territory. Nonetheless, brands are in flux, so that few brands remain unchanged over the decades, willynilly. We return to these issues of how much a brand can change visually, and what can change versus what must remain unchanged, in the Epilogue. Next, we summarize the contemporary scene with respect to brand marks, and then look for trends in the rebranding that now regularly occurs in response to economic vicissitudes.

First, black and white text-only marks are now a special case, concentrated in a few product categories, as noted in Chapter 4. Most brand marks will include some color.

Second, text-only marks, colored or not, are now a minority, especially in packaged goods categories. On the package, the brand's name is going to be placed on a graphically designed surface; in the supermarket, plain white packages containing only black text are seldom seen. Given the graphically designed package surface, and the brand name in relatively large text, framing inevitably occurs: there has to be a color shape of some kind on which the name is inscribed, because the entire package surface consists of colored shapes. Because the package is the primary visual presentation of a packaged good brand, managers will gravitate to lifting off the immediate color background made to surround the brand name on the package, and carrying that color backing over to any display of the brand name.[9] Likewise, to maintain consistency in visual branding, ads for packaged goods end up presenting the brand by means of its package; it would be silly to have one brand mark that appeared in ads, but not on the packaging, and another that appeared only on the package. In short: text-only brand marks disappear from entire categories, making them uncommon overall.

Third, the trend over time is for brand marks to move up the *eidos* axis. Again, it's not because more eidetic brand marks are inherently and universally superior, but because, for broad sets of product categories, the lower reaches of the *eidos* gradient are inferior with respect to the imperatives faced by these brands. But, in a nuance missing from earlier accounts, not every product category requires a mark at the top of the *eidos* gradient. Packaged goods brands do fine with fielded and emblazoned marks, which we place in the middle of the *eidos* gradient. It is service marks that benefit from designs at the top of the *eidos* gradient.

Fourth, rather than a uniform seepage up the *eidos* gradient at all points, the trend line, to invoke Weber, reflects an ongoing process of rationalization, which is likely to have a terminus. No brand in the early 1900s could easily place a colored emblematic mark in its magazine advertising. The necessary technologies either did not exist or were not cost-effective. In time, the technologies (and the needed talent) for designing and reproducing graphically intense brand marks became available. Brands, beginning in packaged goods categories, some of which had moved early to graphically rich package designs, also began to put the new technologies to work in the design of their marks, and to engage in broader efforts at visual branding (for example, developing spokes-characters, and taking ownership of color and type). The efforts of these pioneers contribute the first component to the trend toward climbing up the *eidos* gradient.

The second contribution comes from brands in service categories. This contribution was twofold. As noted in Chapter 4, intangible services, as they begin to market themselves, seek to present tangible cues of their excellence. The brand marks of firms in service categories benefit most from the emblematic designs found at the top of the *eidos* gradient. Undergoing rationalization, more and more brands in service categories acquire emblematic marks; at the population level, consisting of all brands of products and services, this is visible, net, as a shift up the *eidos* gradient.

But services also became a bigger and bigger part of the United States and world economy over the century under study. Likewise, major advertisers came to include more and more service brands. As rationalization drives these increasingly common service brands toward an emblematic mark, the perception gets reinforced that the population of all marks is shifting up the *eidos* gradient.[10]

In summary, in America many brands started with a black and white text mark located at the bottom of the *eidos* gradient, supplemented in a few cases by a black and white emblem, by letter art, by bordering and fielding, or by other accoutrements of visual branding, such as an elaborate package design, or a spokes-character. As technology made more elaborate brand marks possible and cost-effective, rationalization lifted brand marks up the *eidos* gradient until they found the optimum spot relative to the imperatives imposed by their category: higher for services, middling for packaged foods, and lowest for retailers, business-to-business (B2B) marketers, and irritating and annoying packaged items. The shift upwards is most dramatic in moderately recent service categories, such as the mutual fund industry, where brands were launched before rationalization had gotten very far, so that these brands simultaneously rode up the curve of advancing technology and, as services, rationalized their marks toward the upper end of the *eidos* gradient, giving the illusory appearance, at the population level, of a rapid shift upwards across many brands.

By contrast, brands in more recent service industries, whose advent postdates both technological change and widespread rationalization, were likely launched with brand marks located high up the *eidos* gradient. No internet services firm in Silicon Valley launches without a professionally designed brand mark. Logo designers are as much a part of the infrastructure of Silicon Valley as venture capitalists. These brands begin their existence high up the *eidos* gradient, near to their optimum location, a spot toward which older service brands only gradually moved, as rationalization proceeded.

Fifth, the prototypical brand mark in 2015 uses color; and probably presents its name either on a color field, often elaborate, or accompanied by an emblem of some type. The brand name will be presented in a custom typeface. That typeface may appear to be a rather ordinary face, like the Ariel or New Times Roman familiar to all users of Microsoft Word; but in most cases close examination, even by an amateur, will reveal that the typeface has been customized to some degree, if only by an extra-bolding of letter strokes, or a change to the serifs. To a professional eye, all brand marks will be obvious instances of custom-designed typefaces. Likewise, brands will not be printed in any hue a fifth-grader might deem "red," but will have a Pantone or other specification of the exact shade of red to be printed.[11]

Sixth, all packaged good brands will have packaging that shows as much attention to branding considerations and to graphic design as any print ad. Most of these brands will use a photorealistic presentation of the package as the brand block in their print ads, which may be the only iteration of the brand name on the page.

To sum up this evolution with a metaphor: if the consumer swims about in a sea of brands, then 100 years ago the ocean bottom was a drab affair, mostly silt and pebbles, corresponding to black and white text-only marks. Here and there was a colorful starfish, or a sea cucumber moving slowly; but the ocean floor was mostly bare. Today the swimmer snorkels through a vibrant coral reef thronged with colorful creatures. And tomorrow? Three-dimensional (3D) television is here, and virtual reality is on its way. Today's colorful, emblematic, but two-dimensional brand mark may one day appear as primitive as a trilobite.

LOOKING TOWARD THE FUTURE

Predictions are always hazardous; but predictions pose a useful test for anyone writing a history of an ongoing enterprise. If our historical investigation has produced knowledge, then we should be able to predict future developments, at least in broad outline. We hazard two guesses:

1. The population of brand marks in 2035, in terms of the frequency count of each level of the *eidos* gradient, will be more similar to marks circa 2010, than 2010 was to 1985. Change will slow; rationalization is already mostly complete.
2. The first prediction applies only to magazine brand advertisers; that is, brands that continue to advertise on a two-dimensional printed surface. However, the overall population of brand marks will begin to shift to a new paradigm: the animated brand mark, the mark that moves, has a voice and maybe even a face. The argument: just as brands exploited the new technology of color printing once it became available, so also will brands exploit the new design technologies made available by the web.

Today only movie studios, and some cinema and video brands, use animated marks. Consider the credits that appear at the beginning of any film. We use the MGM lion as our sole example, but there are dozens more like it. This lion moves; he roars as he snaps his head around. That motion and sound cannot be captured on a printed page. But in the world of the Web, and the smartphone, that movement and roar could be captured on any screen. As business models shift to the virtual – as Google and Facebook become the exemplars of profitable enterprise, replacing General Motors and Procter & Gamble – then we can expect to see brand marks and trademark law evolve accordingly. Increasingly, it will not be the static graphic representation that is protected, but the entire complex of image, sound, and movement. And brands that live primarily in the Cloud will increasingly mark themselves not only by an image, but by a moving image with sound. That technology-fueled evolution will produce a new situation with newly available means of persuasion, and require new rhetorical typologies.

PART III

Visual elements

6. Typeface in visual branding

Type represents a large class: all those non-linguistic elements that can carry semantic meaning. Type, which is the visual element in text, can strike consumers as forthright or demure, energetic or calm, edgy or smooth; and such personality qualities can be transferred to the brand by the regular and consistent use of one typeface versus another. Typeface is the visual equivalent of tone of voice and sound symbolism, which are other instances of non-linguistic elements that nonetheless can be made to convey meaning, and reliably so; at least, locally, within the culture of origin.[1] Whether type, or any non-linguistic element, can also carry cross-cultural or universal meanings is a fraught question.[2]

As with all visual elements, the meaning of typeface has to be inferred by the consumer, and this meaning cannot be controlled as tightly as when properly semantic elements, such as words, are deployed. Here as elsewhere, we call it an error to assert a language of type, a language of pictures, a language of color, a language of animation, yada yada. The quixotic quest to construct a visual linguistics sent many a structuralist semiotician astray in the late twentieth century.[3] This metaphorical usage is as sticky and confining as molasses, and about as clear. Avoid it. There is only one language, composed of words, and supplemented by many alternative carriers of semantic meaning. Each non-linguistic alternative has to be approached in its own terms. We have not got one ring to rule them all. The activity of inferring meaning, to which all humans are prone, is enormously subtle and flexible, and proceeds along culturally set pathways using whatever material is to hand.[4]

The rhetorical perspective, as compared to competing semiotic and aesthetic perspectives, is ruthlessly pragmatic: what can the brand manager do with type? There can be no printed text without type; the brand manager cannot skip this choice. There will be type.

PSYCHOLOGICAL VERSUS RHETORICAL PERSPECTIVES ON TYPE

Rhetoricians begin by assuming that a small number of discrete choices exist: here, a short list of options for using type to brand. By contrast, psychologists begin by assuming that an infinite number of gradations will distinguish the manifold type options available to brand managers. These gradations can be organized in terms of dimensions, of which there may be dozens, which in turn can be organized hierarchically into a handful of master dimensions. Next, regions in type space can be linked to consumer response: typefaces in this region will strike consumers as pleasing–calm, typefaces over here as active–hot, typefaces over there as strong–solid, and so forth. Viewed from this psychological stance the brand manager can dial up brand perceptions as needed, by selecting, or having designed, a typeface that is moderately, markedly, or extremely far out on one of these dimensions. Because the space is infinitely gradated, competitive differentiation can also be achieved. If the brand needs to be positioned as strong, but a competitor has already gotten hold of a strong–solid typeface, the psychologist advises the brand manager to select a typeface that scores high on strong but also scores well on a second dimension, that is, supple as well as strong.

Exemplar

We can make this contrast concrete by drawing on Henderson et al. (2004), who provide an exemplary psychological account of typeface, structured in terms of a dimensional space. To generate these dimensions they gathered a sample of 210 commercially available typefaces. These typefaces were selected using researcher judgment to capture the diversity evident across existing typefaces. In their studies typefaces were presented specimen style "on white paper in 16-point font size in full alphabetic (uppercase and lowercase) and numeric forms" (p. 62).

Henderson et al. draw on a combination of universal design characteristics and features specific to type-design to identify 24 dimensions along which a typeface can vary (ornate–plain, heavy–light, and so on). Factor analysis reduced these design dimensions to six (for example, how elaborate, how weighty).[5] A second factor analysis, based on consumer ratings, reduced potential consumer responses to four: perceptions that a typeface was pleasing, engaging, reassuring, or prominent.[6] Additional data collection produced a numerical score on each design factor and each response dimension for each of the 210 typefaces. A series of regression analyses then identified the design characteristics, and thus the kinds of typeface, that were most highly associated with each of the four broad consumer responses. Practical implications for the brand manager follow directly. To achieve more of this desired consumer response, choose a typeface that has more of these design characteristics, that is, is located farther out on this theoretical dimension; to get this other desired response, choose this other typeface.

A complication: design characteristics that drive up one response (for example, reassuring) may drive down another (for example, prominence). The high–high–high–high cell – typefaces which optimized all four consumer responses – was empty. Hence, the brand manager has first to choose what vector of consumer responses is desired for the brand. This four-place vector holds values of high, moderate, or low for each of the four consumer responses. The idea of a vector captures the trade-offs facing the brand manager: a typeface that is highly effective in stimulating one consumer response must be relatively ineffective in stimulating some other response. Managers have to decide whether a high–high–low–low response vector, or a low–average–average–high vector, or any other permutation, would best promote the brand's strategic objectives.

We reiterate that the Henderson et al. (2004) study is exemplary among psychological studies of typeface. Other researchers either use the same approach with fewer dimensions, or work within a dimensional template to pursue more specific questions.[7] Therefore, a critique of the Henderson et al. (2004) work can stand in for a critique of the overall psychological approach to type, providing a foil for highlighting the features that distinguish rhetorical from psychological approaches to branding with type. In addition, because it was published in a top marketing journal, we don't have to worry about methodological flaws: the Henderson et al. statistics survived a rigorous peer review. Problems, if any, will have to be found with the assumptions and the input to their statistical analysis.

Critique

The underlying problem that bedevils psychological approaches is their commitment to universality. By contrast, the rhetorician works for a client who operates in some one human domain among the many that exist. The rhetorician focuses on the means of persuasion available here. The only universalist assumptions made by the rhetorician are: (1) there exist multiple human domains, each with its own rhetoric, so that there must always be a rhetoric to be found; (2) only a short list of means will be available in each of the domains to which rhetoric pertains; and (3) these means will be specific to that domain. Branding, and marketing, and profit-seeking firms, belong to the domain of the capitalist economy. A rhetoric of the marketplace need not be the same as a rhetoric of politics, a rhetoric of prophecy, or a rhetoric of protest.

The first problem, then, with the Henderson research stems from their sampling strategy: they sought a comprehensive sample from among all extant typefaces. Their analysis is intended to apply across the universe of realized and potential typefaces used to print Western alphabets.

A rhetorician would proceed otherwise. The goal would be to sample only the typefaces used in branding, with a preference for those used by the most successful brands. The rationale: in a capitalist economy, the very best type designers, defined as those most capable of achieving the objectives set by owners of brands, will gravitate to where the financial rewards are greatest.[8] Large corporations spend millions on visual branding, including the design of type. Brands search for highly skilled designers, and will pay more for what their managers believe to be more promising and lucrative designs. In turn, brands are disciplined by the marketplace: lousy choices in visual branding, including a defective or insipid type design, make brand failure more likely. Good choices, in visual branding and in all aspects of the marketing effort, make success more likely, and more likely to be sustained.

It follows that leading brands, really successful brands, are likely to employ now, and to have employed in the past, the best designers of type. The typefaces used by the entire population of leading brands are likely to be among the most effective typefaces now deployed – for branding. This argument is only probabilistic, and applies best at the population level. Brands can succeed for many reasons, and can thrive and endure in spite of a poor choice of typeface. Errors are always possible, and if enough other branding decisions, apart from type choice, have been sound, typeface mistakes need not fatally impair the brand. Hence, there can be no guarantee that any one successful brand will make an excellent choice of typeface.

But all of these considerations drop away at the population level. If typeface can make a difference in branding – if there are better versus worse choices, for each brand, at any point – then the population of leading brands, especially those that have endured, will exhibit mostly successful choices of type. Moreover the proportion of good, smart type choices, in this population of leading brands, will itself be proportional to the strength of the typeface effect. If type makes little difference to branding success, then the population of leaders will show only a small tendency toward smarter type choices; but if type choice is crucial to branding success, then most of the typefaces found in a population of leading brands must represent effective choices.

You may recognize this as a Darwinian argument. A kind of natural selection – market selection – applies within an Adam Smith marketplace. If a capitalist economy does select for success – if success among brands is not haphazard or random – then thriving survivors will tend to consist of brands that developed more effective adaptations to their environment. Mistakes die out at a greater rate. The fittest are more likely to survive and reproduce; or in this domain, sustain a presence in the market. When we come on the scene a century later, we can expect to see effective typeface adaptations among thriving brands. The logic is as ironclad as Darwin's.[9]

The rhetorician has no intention of remaining blissfully ignorant of the full range of typefaces available; we welcome anything psychologists, economists, evolutionary biologists, and the rest can tell us; but we expect to find the typefaces used by leading brands to be concentrated in one region of that vast space of possibilities, and to gain insight by noting where, within the macro-space of all possible typefaces, thriving brands with a long pedigree have chosen to pitch their tent.

Suppose the typefaces used by successful brands were to cluster all in one region of multidimensional type space. Such a clustering would call into question the usefulness, for branding, of the overall dimensional scheme advanced by Henderson et al. The dimensional scheme could still be an accurate representation of the diverse typefaces that exist in the Western world; but it won't help brand managers in pursuing their narrow charge, which is to enhance the financial value of their brand property by drawing on the best typefaces, those few most suited to their aims.

Henderson et al. (2004) provide 46 example typefaces in their Table 1, corresponding to the 23 bipolar design dimensions that survived in their analyses.[10] We encourage you to look at their table, and then go back to the brand marks reproduced in our Chapter 3, beginning with the text-only logotypes, paying close attention now to the typefaces used.

When we look at the typefaces in our set of marks, and then look at the typeface examples presented by Henderson et al., the contrast is stark: in our brand mark sample, most of the universal design dimensions have a missing pole. Only one end is present; its extreme opposite is either rare or altogether absent. As a case in point, there are no leading brand marks that would score high on the "not readable" pole. Duh! Brand identification may not be the only goal in mark design, but must be a minimum or threshold goal. No successful brand is going to deliberately construct a logotype that is all but unreadable. Outside of the branding domain, however, such inscrutable typefaces may serve artistic purposes. The psychologist's commitment to universality entails costs: a universal scheme must include typefaces unlikely to appear in the branding domain.

By contrast, design characteristics in the Henderson et al. sample deemed specific to typefaces do have both poles present. For instance, logos in both serif and sans serif typefaces are plentiful. It is the universal design characteristics in Henderson et al., deemed applicable to all graphical designs, whether type or image, which account for most of the absent poles in our brand sample.

Unfortunately, as can be seen from examining the regression results in Henderson et al.'s Table 4, the universal design characteristics, and the factors built from these dimensions, account for most of the variance explained in consumer response. In terms of effect size (R^2), dimensions specific to typeface mostly fail to surmount Cohen and Cohen's (1983) suggested threshold of 2 percent (these were successful in 4 out of 12 Henderson regressions). By contrast, the universal design characteristics meet this standard for 9 out of 12 opportunities. Compounding the problem, most of the effect sizes shown for universal characteristics are an order of magnitude greater than those shown for typeface design characteristics.[11]

To sum this up in non-mathematical terms: most of the variation in consumer response to typefaces is explained by dimensions that are truncated among the marks of leading brands. More bluntly: the weird typefaces drive the Henderson et al. results, but brand managers avoid weird-looking typefaces.

The Henderson et al. study suffers from two additional shortcomings which are worth noting, insofar as they reflect general tendencies in psychological work, predilections that become problematic for a rhetorician committed to success in the domain of branding. First, in their tests Henderson et al. presented their typeface stimuli as specimens, and not as meaningful text. They followed standard practice in experimental psychology: remove extraneous elements. Simplify and abstract, to isolate the effect of typeface per se. An enormous methodological literature has grown up to defend this practice.[12] The first step in the argument for favoring abstracted experimental stimuli is purely logical, and impeccable: if you test A + B together, and get effect X, you cannot know whether A, B or their conjoint presence is the cause of X. You could disentangle the cause by separately testing, A, B and A + B. Unfortunately, if your interest lies with A (type properties, in this case) there are uncountable instances of properties B, C, D, and so on, and even more permutations of A, B, C, D, and so forth: A + C, A + D, A + B + C, A + B + C + D . . .

The fateful decision, made decades ago when psychologists first decided that they wanted to build a science akin to physics: isolate element A. Ignore B, C, D and all the other properties; in fact, remove them. To construct a good experiment, present typeface in isolation from semantically meaningful text – and everything else. There's too much risk of contamination from uncontrolled semantic inference on the part of experimental subjects. Show only type specimens, and make all specimens the same size.

The final step in defending the practice of abstraction and isolation again rests on impeccable logic. We can test the effect of A, isolated from B, and still infer the contribution of A to any effect of A + B, as long as A and B – typeface and semantic meaning – do not interact in shaping consumer response. Experimental isolation works when effects are additive.

The tendentious piece slips in right after this triumphant assertion of basic logic: that we have no reason to expect an interaction between typeface design and semantic meaning. In fact, we can reasonably assume that these two do not interact. After all, we have no evidence for their interaction.

Did you catch it? Did you spot the dodge, there at the end of the last paragraph? We have no evidence that typeface design and semantic meaning interact, because we never test for that interaction! Experimenters always assume additive effects. The circle is unbreakable: (1) there's no good laboratory evidence for contextual interactions; (2) therefore, we can assume an additive model; (3) which insures that there never will be any good evidence for an interaction between stimulus properties and the context in which these stimuli may be encountered in the world outside the laboratory.

A diehard laboratory experimenter confronted with the argument thus far may be nonplussed, but only for a moment, until a Popperian smile settles on his face: "Alright Mr. Fancy-pants-know-it-all. Tell me, which of the uncountable contextual factors should I begin to test? Where do I start, when I have no theory about any such context, given the absence of evidence for contextual effects?"[13]

Victorious, the psychological experimenter drives to the conclusion he needs: "By investigating typeface in isolation, free of any context, I gain results which can be generalized to all contexts. If my laboratory scrubs out brand, and art, and education, and every other context in which words are printed in type, then I can generalize to the brand domain, same as any other domain." The more context can be scrubbed out, the larger the number of contexts in which the laboratory results will hold true. Gravity works the same on Earth, the moon, and out among the stars; psychology must strive for no less universal results, if it would count itself among the sciences.

The rhetorician who has selected brand as his domain of practice will be quite bemused by this bravura display. Rousing himself, he makes this rejoinder: "There may be uncountably many contexts for you, the psychologist committed to universal laws; but I have a simpler task: to promote this brand. To do that, I have to name it, and position it as a soap [or cereal, or whatever] that satisfies the needs of a large enough segment of consumers. Therefore, when it comes to understanding the rhetorical possibilities of type, I can point to two contextual factors that loom above all the rest. I need to render a name in some typeface, a name which may carry additional semantic meaning (for example, Ivory); and I need that typeface to line up with the qualities desired from soap [or cereal or whatever category] – the qualities on which I've positioned my brand."

Pausing for thought, the rhetorician continues by adducing one more context, a third prime candidate for an interaction effect: "In my work, most of the time I am thrown, in Heidegger's sense. My assignment is to redesign the typeface for a brand that has a history. I don't get to create a brand de novo. That history has already shaped an identity, a personality for my brand client; and that identity is positional, deriving some of its meaning from the identity of the other brands against which my brand competes. Therefore, my interest lies with comparing alternative typeface treatments of Ivory soap, those two words, with all their heritage and semantic freight."

The Popperian assault rolls off the rhetorician's back because he is a practical fellow who only has to care about success in one single domain. So focused, he easily identifies a small number of contextual factors that might moderate the impact of typeface design, and that have to be addressed in laboratory work that aspires to be useful in this domain. He insists that the desired causal knowledge has to reflect these contingencies: What is the effect of [typeface design characteristic] when a name is printed, within some product category, and when these names have a history, and when these names also carry surplus semantic freight (that is, ivory, which is pure, rare, valuable). The rhetorician of type can insist on these contingencies because most branding tasks are performed within these confines. He doesn't much care how student subjects over at the university respond to type specimens stripped of context.

The other conceptual failing in the psychological paradigm applied by Henderson et al. (2004) is more subtle: the search for optima. It's a failing because if it were successful, then the recommendation would be that all brands whatsoever should use the same small set of typefaces, those revealed to have the optimal characteristics for achieving one of the four desired consumer responses. Intrinsic to this failing is the convergence on exactly four desired consumer responses, a set that, as acknowledged by Henderson et al., bears a close resemblance to the work of Osgood et al. (1964). Those authors showed that if you rated any object on a diverse set of descriptors, and if you applied factor analysis to those ratings, the same three factors would fall out. It's the sort of universal finding that psychologists love.

But branding requires something more specific than a favorable shift along one of the three fundamental factors along which stimuli can be arrayed. There are hundreds of leading brands, and thousands that have some economic importance. Within any category there may be five, ten or 20 brands contending for a viable and sustainable position. Accordingly, establishing difference will often be a goal in branding. Differentiation is the flip side of having a clear identity. It is no accident that Pepsi, which once used the same sort of flowing script typeface as Coca-Cola, ultimately shifted to a stripped-down, sans serif typeface. The plain and even sterile typeface used by Pepsi may not be suitable, universally, or optimal within the soft drink category, but may be advantageous for a newcomer brand that has to compete against Coca-Cola, the original category leader (see Epilogue).

The rhetorician doubts there is any such thing as an optimal typeface design; he intuits that considerations of fit may be primary.[14] He further allows that when branding with typeface, the goal may not be to boost some broad consumer response like pleasure – to optimize – but rather, to push brand perceptions in a specific direction, here to make the brand appear tender, there to make it edgy; or alternatively, to push the brand away from a position already locked down by a competitor, get it out of that shadow.

In conclusion, we want to emphasize that we did not and do not intend to criticize the scholarly achievements of Pamela Henderson, Joan Giese, or Joseph Cote. Their paper represents the best psychological scholarship on type that we could find. Our goal was to criticize a paradigm, as seen in an exemplary instance: the Cartesian paradigm of infinite gradations in place of discrete gambits, and the universalist pretension that context-free investigations of stimuli provide the most generalizable findings.[15]

A FRESH START

We have spent half the chapter on a critique because the psychological approach so dominates investigations into the elements that make up visual branding. The arguments made here apply broadly, so that it made sense to lay them out once, here at the beginning of Part III.

A rhetorical account of how type may be used to brand begins with evidence from the field: the typefaces now used in the marks of leading brands. This field study becomes more valuable when augmented by a historical examination of how type for branding has evolved over the past century. Although we will give that history its own section at the end of the chapter, the story can be briefly told: type design for branding evolves from almost nothing, in the 1890s, to a great deal of something by the 1980s and after.[16] That's important. Words plus illustration were part of the magazine advertising formula from the beginning. Type for branding was not. Type is like color, and color photography: a new resource, assiduously applied once available, but a later arrival nonetheless.

When we turn a rhetorical eye onto type in branding, we look first at brand marks. Here the opportunity to craft a new typeface is greatest. The name portion of a mark will consist of a dozen letters, more or less. These letters may be printed larger than the 10- or 12-point type that makes up the bulk of magazine editorial or advertising body copy, and these letters may be in color. The name, and the mark, will be propagated billions of times, in ads and on packages, so that the type designer can hope that the consumer might at some point linger on the brand mark, soaking it up, enabling intelligently crafted type to enjoy all the impact which type may have. The designer, and the brand manager, can justify lavishing attention on the typeface used in the mark.

But type for branding may also appear elsewhere in the ad, most notably in the headline. David Ogilvy, the famous advertising copywriter, opined that the headline was the one portion of the ad most likely to be read.[17] Whether read or not, the headline will draw a glance, if in large type and prominently placed; and a glance is sufficient for inferences to be drawn from the typeface used. These inferences are most likely to be secured for the brand if the same typeface is used for ad headlines, month after month, year after year; and these inferences are further leveraged if the type used for the headline is integrated with the type used for the brand mark, and with the type used on the packaging. We say integrated, because these do not need to be identical, although identity is a high form of integration, and one that became more frequent with time as advertisers began to harness type. Integration, in the sense of consistent, is enough.

In short, type can be harnessed for branding in the mark, and in the advertising, and in the packaging. We don't have a collection of old packages, so for our rhetorical analysis of type in branding must proceed along two fronts: type in marks, and type in ads, especially the headlines of ads.

A TYPOLOGY OF TYPE

The first choice is whether to infuse semantic meaning directly into the typeface. This can be done by constructing letter shapes or textures to metaphorically resemble, or metonymically connect to, an object or idea that is relevant to the product category.[18] For example, the letters in the Toys R Us brand mark recall the plastic pieces of which children's toys are made; the childlike character is reinforced by the backwards "R," a mistake a young child learning to write might make, and by the irregular alignment of the letters, consistent with a shaky young hand (Table 6.1). The chosen typeface infuses semantic meaning: Toys R Us is by and for children.

Here are four more examples (Table 6.1). The Corona beer mark uses a medieval typeface; in conjunction with the crown image, it suggests a classic beer, one of great antiquity, originally brewed for the lord and his hidalgos, perhaps on a royal estate. The Oracle mark uses a typeface associated with computer printing, cueing appropriate associations for this

Table 6.1   Examples of figurative typefaces in brand marks

database software firm; the Xbox logo likewise recalls electronic displays. More metaphorically, the type used in the 20th Century Fox logo is made sculptural and three-dimensional, and shaped to resemble a movie theater marquee.

Next, the typeface in the Disney mark harvests a circle of meaning: first, and decades earlier, Disney creates Mickey Mouse and his brood as cartoon characters. Mickey and Minnie are cute little critters, who write in a cutesy way within the comic strips and animated films where they appear. Elsewhere at Disney, dwarves and elves and talking deer, aimed at children, also acquire cute, childlike lettering, as their films are titled on the opening screen, and as the characters walk past signage in their world, or have occasion to write notes. Later, Disney composes its mark in cutesy lettering that calls to mind the world of Bambi, Snow White, and Mickey Mouse. The circle closes: Disney made Mickey and gave him an appropriate typeface, and now Mickey's typeface makes Disney.

Finally, an old example, rare for its era, is the mark of Indian Head, a textile and clothing company that formed the letters of its name from Indian beads. However old its origin, we find this figurative strategy, whether metaphorical or metonymical, to be rare among leading brand marks today; but it is not absent. It is more common among contemporary headlines, where the greater amount of control over type design conferred by modern computer graphics software promotes its occurrence. Two examples, one frozen, and one melting, can be found in Figures 6.1 and 6.2. Likewise, if a Polynesian or East Asian ambience is desired for a brand, easy enough today to construct the letters of the headline from bamboo tubes; or if a South Asian ambience, use elephant tusks. Or one can advertise a frozen treat from letters formed by ice floes.

Such examples are easily spotted, and make great teaching stories. You have to look at hundreds and hundreds of ads to realize that headlines set in figurative type are the exception, not the rule.[19]

Staying at the topmost level of the typology, the second option, if semantic infusions are eschewed, is whether to deviate. Because typeface design is art, an aesthetic operation, when the choice is made to deviate, the result will be artful deviation. This property played an important role in our early studies of advertising rhetoric, which were based on still earlier work by Daniel Berlyne.[20] In the present context, artful deviation fuels the engine of semantic inference from non-linguistic elements. True, such inferences can be triggered on the slightest pretext; the action of drawing inferences is a species-wide human facility, nearly effortless, and ongoing minute by minute when awake.[21] But when the goal is branding – where, after careful deliberation, you decide which inferences to force and how to corral inference-making – it helps to be able to gun the engine by injecting fuel. Artful deviation drives consumer inference-making in response to type, and steers it along desired paths.

Deviation, in our usage, is deviation from expectation. To apply the concept to type presumes that there is an expected typeface, a typeface or set of typeface styles which the magazine reader is used to encountering, a typeface which is familiar and, therefore, one which may not trigger inferences, so that the effect of type is submerged under text comprehension. Expected typefaces consists of those used in the body of printed editorial matter and the body of most printed advertisements. These faces consist of a few serif and sans serif typefaces which are widely used among mass-circulation media, along with script typefaces (see Box 6.1). Although to our knowledge no major publication uses either the Times New Roman typeface which is the default on many Windows computers, or the Arial typeface seen in Powerpoint slides, many publications do use serif and sans serif typefaces that will feel familiar to those regularly exposed to Microsoft's iteration of Times New Roman or Arial. By familiar, we mean

Figure 6.1   Example of a figurative typeface

that most ordinary consumers could not distinguish the typeface actually used by the publication, from the Century Schoolbook or Times New Roman or Arial or MS Gothic available on their Windows computer, if backed up against the wall and forced to decide after only a brief glance.

Therefore, brand managers need not deviate in choosing type; it's easy enough to resort to an expected and familiar typeface in the brand mark. Table 6.2 gives two examples: Morgan Stanley and Neutrogena.

Suppose we put an image of the actual typeface used by these two brands next to a rendition in the Arial and Century typefaces supplied with Microsoft Windows. Put side by side, and with time to peruse the two, even ordinary consumers will probably be able to detect, at levels greater than chance, that those two typefaces are not identical (look at the 'g' in the two iterations of Morgan Stanley, or the 'e' in the two iterations of Neutrogena). But perusing two iterations side by side is a forgiving test.

Let's linger on this question: how sensitive are ordinary consumers to small variations in type, of the sort that separate the sans serif typeface custom-designed for Morgan Stanley, from the Arial typeface on a Windows

Figure 6.2   Another example of a figurative typeface

computer? Suppose that in a laboratory experiment we present multiple pairs
of renditions, some of which are real–real, some of which are Windows–
Windows, and some of which are real–Windows mixes. We'd expect consumers to detect match versus no match, at rates better than chance. The Morgan
Stanley and Neutrogena marks are set in a unique, custom typeface. But this
is still a forgiving test, because the two typefaces are put side by side.

BOX 6.1   ARE SCRIPT TYPEFACES AUTOMATICALLY DEVIANT?

This issue first arose while we were constructing the typology of brand marks for Chapter 3: if the name was in script, should it be placed higher up the *eidos* gradient, relative to other text-only marks? We decided that a script typeface was not inherently more visual than any other text-only typeface.

In this chapter, the question is slightly different. Script typefaces are not the norm in print; should script therefore be considered as per se deviant, with the powers of signification that we have attributed to deviation? Again, we think not. Most brand marks that use cursive do so for the name of a person: Ford, Johnson & Johnson, Coors, Kellogg's, Walgreens, Cartier. There is nothing deviant about using cursive to sign your name.

There were two exceptions: Budweiser and Kleenex. (Coca-Cola is calligraphy, rather than script.) Budweis is a place name and the Budweiser mark is heraldic in design; nothing deviant in seeing cursive in that context.

That leaves only Kleenex, and its use of script probably does rise to the level of deviation, especially in conjunction with its curvature. This curvaceous script typeface promotes inferences about softness that would be advantageous for a brand of facial tissue.

We conclude that script typefaces may sometimes be instances of deviation-up, but not because script is per se deviant. It depends on how the script is executed, as in Kleenex; the execution produces the deviation.

Table 6.2   Two examples of ordinary typeface treatments in brand marks

Real logo typeface	Logo in Microsoft windows font
Morgan Stanley	Morgan Stanley
Neutrogena	Neutrogena

Suppose we change the experimental design. Now we'll show real marks and their Microsoft Windows renditions, not in side-by-side pairs, but one at a time. We'll do this many times in many ways, here presenting the name in a different point size, here with different light–dark contrasts; sometimes presenting the name alone and sometimes in a brand block following text. The question demanded of the experimental subject in each case will be: did we show the real, or the imitation mark? (And we won't give them time to study the real marks first.) Among ordinary consumers, we predict that successes would not exceed chance. Once we mix things up, and make the detection task more difficult (and more real), consumers can't reliably tell that this trial had the real Morgan Stanley typeface, and this trial presented Morgan Stanley in the generic Windows typeface.[22] Such a finding would suggest that the unique, custom Morgan Stanley typeface does not influence consumer judgment; because consumers can't reliably tell it apart from a generic sans serif typeface.[23] It does not deviate.

Conversely, suppose we ran the experiment with graphic design professionals as subjects. We'd predict that professionals would dramatically outperform consumers in this detection task; they might even obtain a perfect score. If you are an expert on type, you know what to look for: the longer extender here, the rounder belly there, the tighter kerning, and so forth. The Morgan Stanley typeface has been customized; it looks different, to those in the know.[24]

It is no accident that the typeface-specific design characteristics in Henderson et al. (2004) had such small effect sizes, or that prior research was equivocal about whether an effect was present at all for some design characteristics (see their citations to prior literature). The thought experiment suggests that lots of the variation in type – alternative typefaces that are distinct in the eyes of professional designers – will pass unnoticed by ordinary consumers. We can still acknowledge that any difference may make some difference; that any difference a professional can see may have some measurable impact when exposed to millions of ordinary consumers. But when deviation is minimal, that effect may be nearly undetectable. The rhetorician asserts once more the primacy of practical demands: the goal is branding, and it's a difficult goal, one that requires brute force to achieve under competitive pressure, even with massive repetition, or the strongest effort. Choice among non-deviant typefaces will seldom make a difference to consumer response in the field. It's enough for a face to look professionally designed and sharply printed, while being sufficiently distinct to satisfy the criteria of trademark law.

In short, in most branding attempts the goal in typeface selection will be to satisfice, rather than optimize. "Do no harm" will be the mantra. A professional art director, charged with marketing a brand positioned as bold, hearty and rugged, will know not to present it in a slender, elfin typeface, or to apply a fancy face, ornamented with swirls. There are hundreds of bold, strong faces out there; the art director will select one according to taste, but all will be serviceable.[25] That selection will do no harm; and it will look good on the brand, because successful art directors got that way by having good taste, sound aesthetic sense. But because typefaces are selected according to taste, the fashion pattern holds: at a macro level, we would expect to see fads and fashions in typeface design. Like fashion in clothing, many faces are serviceable; but what looks exactly right, at any period, will fluctuate.[26]

POSSIBILITIES FOR DEVIATION

With the role and importance of deviation explained, we can examine the possibilities for deviation. We find two, corresponding to the root split in typeface families between sans serif and serif styles. A designer can deviate by adding more, what we will call deviation-up, or by sculpting away material, what we will call deviation-down. The elements added or subtracted correspond to the typeface design factors gathered by Henderson et al. (2004).

In Table 6.3, we show examples of four avenues for deviation, drawn from the collection of brand marks compiled earlier. For weight, deviation-up means bold, thick, even fat letters, as in the 3M mark; deviation-down implies thin, sparse, skeletal letters, as in the Avon mark. The corresponding semantic inferences for the brand might be strong and steady on the one hand, and graceful and airy on the other. For flourishes, deviation-up takes the form of super-serifs: accentuated ascenders and descenders and elaborate serifs, as in the Brooks Brothers mark; deviation-down implies a nadir of plain, sparse representation, where only a few shapes, arcs, and angles are used to construct letters, as in the Philips mark. The corresponding semantic inferences, for the brand, are fancy, aristocratic, and flowing on the one hand, and modern, business-like and unfussy, on the other.

Weight and flourish appear to be the most common routes for deviation, but a few others can be identified. These less common routes, but also weight and flourish themselves, should be thought of as oblique or correlated, rather than orthogonal. Although weighty typefaces may have few flourishes, thin and narrow typefaces are likely to be sparse and plain as well. Other correspondences are noted below; we call out these correspondences to remind the reader that we are not going to replace the Cartesian model of Henderson et al. (2004) with another such. Deviation up or down proceeds by means of choices, which have internal dependences, rather than being orthogonal dimensions in Cartesian space.

Less common options for deviation, but worthy of note, include: (1) soft and rounded versus sharp and pointed; and (2) tightly bunched versus open and spread out (see examples in Table 6.3). Soft, rounded typefaces may suggest a comfortable, soothing brand; sharp, pointed typefaces may suggest an edgy, sharp-looking brand. A tightly bunched typeface may suggest a brand similar to a coiled spring or tensed muscle, a potent and forceful brand; an open typeface may suggest a receptive and welcoming brand, a brand that offers a comprehensive, wide-ranging solution.

Table 6.3 A typology of typefaces

Top-level categories	2nd-level categories	3rd-level categories	Definitions	Examples
Deviant	→Figurative		The typeface resembles or connects to some meaningful and relevant item	See examples in Figures 6.1 and 6.2
	→Not figurative	→By weight	Deviation-up: much heavier letter strokes than usual	3M
			Deviation-down: much thinner, more narrow strokes	AVON
		→By flourish	Deviation-up: more flourishes than customary[a]	Brooks Brothers
			Deviation-down: fewer flourishes	PHILIPS

		TUMS	CLEAR ANTI-DANDRUFF SHAMPOO	bloomingdales	THE LIMITED	See text for discussion
→ Whether curved or angular		Notably soft and curved forms	Notably sharp and angular forms[b]			
→ Whether tight or open		Notably tight, bunched arrangements	Notable open or spaced arrangements			
Not deviant	–	–				The name is rendered in some version of a customary, familiar, expected typeface, one difficult for the layperson to distinguish from the Times New Roman, Century, Arial, or Gothic typefaces in wide use outside of advertising and branding contexts

Notes:
a   Most of the deviation-up instances on the flourishes dimension use a script or brush-stroke typeface.
b   Particularly angular faces – setting aside those letters such as the capitals A, M, or W, which are formed from angles in most faces – were much less common than faces which had been altered to be more soft-edged and curvaceous than normal.

163

In terms of correspondences, soft matches up with loose, open can go together with the absence of flourishes, and thin and narrow can match up with sharp and pointed.

We inserted the qualifier "may" not to be mealy-mouthed, but to emphasize that the impact of typeface alone on branding may be minimal, and that typeface choices, taken in isolation, do little to constrain the inferences a consumer might draw. If a brand wants to be perceived as maternal and welcoming, a soft rounded typeface probably has to be leveraged by the semantics of the name, plus the choice of pictorial content and style, plus also color and layout, all pointing in that same direction, before that choice of typeface can materially contribute to the desired effect. Most of the time in visual branding, typeface plays a supporting role, and is given only a bit part.

A BRIEF HISTORY OF TYPEFACE IN MAGAZINE ADVERTISING

From the launch of mass circulation magazines in the 1890s, brand managers had many typefaces available to them.[27] After all, this time period postdates Gutenberg by four centuries, and type designers – professionals who create or redesign typefaces – go back about that far. But the career of graphic designer – a dedicated commercial artist employed full-time by ad agencies, publishers, and other organs of mass communication – was still nascent. Type could be selected from the bountiful collections offered in specimen books from type foundries. But in this period type was still a hard thing to design from scratch, if only because it was based on the engraving of metal or wood, except for rare cases where it was executed as calligraphy or an otherwise one-off illustration. Brands existed, but brands were still young; and branding, as a coherent activity, scarcely existed.

If this description of the 1890s is apt, then straightforward predictions follow as to how type might be used in the branding of that era. We would expect: (1) fitful, spotty use of deviation and figuration, with many ads using only a generic typeface common throughout that magazine; (2) no special or custom typefaces in the brand mark, or even no brand mark at all, but just the name appearing in the body text as does any other word; (3) inconsistent use of typeface across appearances of the brand, including multiple typefaces to render the name within an ad, and constantly shifting typeface selections over time. And this is what we found in ads from that era (see Chapter 2).

To sum up, at the outset of branded magazine advertising in the 1890s, and for some time thereafter, type was employed primarily to gain attention for the message, rather than to brand. Advertisers might use a big or unusual type, but only to shout, rather than to corral and direct inferences about who was doing the shouting. And in the early years, advertisers might not even shout. Recall the Ivory soap ad from 1898 (Figure 2.6). Up to that point, the four ads on the inside front cover – Ivory's regular position – were the only ads that appeared in front of the editorial matter in the *Ladies Home Journal* (*LHJ*). Hence, this quarter page was a prime spot purchased by a leading brand. Nonetheless, there is no large type anywhere in the ad. Not even the Ivory name is made prominent or called out by a distinctive typeface; it appears in the same face and size as the copy in which it is embedded.

We could show other soap ads from the 1890s and early 1900s that do shout with large type in their headlines, and that do display the brand name prominently, in either a distinctive type face, or placed in an actual brand block with graphic support. But what would then emerge is the inconstancy of usage, the variations from ad to ad as to whether the brand used a large typeface, and which one. Brands did not yet own type. Brands strove only to rise above the fray, to shout, to get noticed, using type and whatever other resources might be to hand.

By the 1920s, few ads are any longer as demure and understated as the Ivory soap ad. First, full page ads in color have proliferated. There is space for large type, both for headlines, and when identifying the brand sponsor. Second, separate brand blocks become more common. These present the brand name in large type, or may show a large image of the package, which also bears the name in large type. Third, distinctive typefaces become more common for representing the brand name, but these typefaces are distinctive all in the same way: this is the era of fancy type, elaborated capital letters at the beginning, and an underlining flourish at the end, as still seen in the surviving Coca-Cola mark.

The 1920s remain a primitive, early era: on the one hand, diverse brands still use the same large display faces, and the same fancy distinctive faces; on the other, brands are still proliferating typefaces, within a single ad and over time. Type is still a matter of shouting and gesticulating: look over here! Look at me!

But the beginnings of a more sophisticated approach are evident here and there. A Campbell's ad for tomato soup may present its headline in the exact same shade of red as its package, and depict a tomato as that same shade of red, claiming that color for the brand; but the headline remains in a generic display face, which is not the same as the typefaces used on the prominent package, much less for the name.

In the 1950s, sophistication continues to develop and spread. Large type headlines, and distinct, set apart brand blocks, become the norm. More and more brands present their name in a custom typeface that does not appear in the ads of any other brand, nor in the magazine's editorial copy. Deviation becomes more common: the distinct typeface used for the name is not only bold, it is extra-bold-bold. Or the fancy typeface is fancy in its own unique way, rather than a generic instance of flowing cursive script.

But, as noted earlier in Chapter 2, there remains a lack of consistency. The distinctive typeface may only appear in the brand block; if the name is mentioned in the headline or a subhead, it will revert to the more generic typeface used there. Or the custom typeface used in the brand block won't be the same as the also custom typeface inscribed on the package beside it. It appears that even as late as the 1950s, no one designer had yet been put in charge of all the visual expressions of the brand. The idea of owning a typeface had arrived, and some brands thought it important to have their own custom typeface; but brands weren't consistent about it. Management had not yet decided that branding must be insistent and unvarying across all visual manifestations. Type had become a recognized resource for brand promotion, but the era of visual branding, as a conscious and deliberate process, had not yet dawned.

Outside the brand name, brand block and package shot, in the 1950s type continues to be normal rather than figurative or deviant. For headlines, the point size gets bigger, and bolder, and may be accentuated with color. A beauty product may use a more elegant face in its headline than a detergent. But custom-designed typefaces are limited to the brand mark and package; most headlines use an ordinary typeface from among the growing inventory available. Prominence of the message, and not visual support for the brand's positioning, remains primary.

In the 1980s, deviation and customization come to headlines. Headlines may be super-extra-mega-bold, shouting as loud as they can; this degree of boldface is not seen in the editorial matter, making it deviant. As the picture bleeds out and across the page, headlines are increasingly printed in reverse type. As such, they aren't type any more, but stencils cut out of the image, and necessarily customized. As such, they can be slanted, curved, or given other deviant treatments. Type becomes a photographic impression, and no longer a piece of lead.

The transition away from mechanical type had come a long way by the 1980s; as offset printing became more common, what the advertiser sent to the magazine was one entire page image, and no longer a mixture of type and image pieces. The gigantic size of some headlines, in itself, forces customization to insure legibility (visual perception doesn't uniformly scale, and typefaces that deviate small or large, relative to their expected use, have to be adjusted to maintain legibility). Plenty of headlines still use an ordinary typeface printed in a large size; but more and more customization occurs.

Although still not common in the 1980s, figurative typefaces begin to appear in headlines. The brand's name, if it appears in the headline, may use its own custom typeface there as well as in the brand block; and if there is a package shot, the typeface is more likely to be the same as the typeface used in the brand block. Brands are coalescing, and becoming vigilant about identification. Branding consultants have set up shop, and now push integration. Graphic designers have begun to wrap their arms around all the tools for visual branding. Type is recognized as a design resource, one tool among others, to be pulled out of the toolbox as needed.

Use of type during the 2010s reflects the diffusion of computer graphics software after 1985: not so much Photoshop, but less prominent programs such as Postscript, Illustrator, and page set-up programs. Two examples may be viewed in Figures 6.1 and 6.2. As typewriters gave way to laser printers and inkjets, and as the web diffused after 2000, type became a pattern of pixels, completing its transition from the old days of engraving on metal or wood. As such, type became digital, each letter a string of 1s and 0s, specifying which pixels to turn on or off, or which apertures in the ink jet nozzle to open or close. A task that once required a highly trained and rare specialist – the design of a complete new typeface – could now be accomplished relatively quickly by a much larger cadre of people. It would still be an error to say "by anyone." Type is hard. Graphics software isn't that much easier to learn than engraving, and the knack for it isn't any more widely distributed. Nonetheless, for a skilled graphic designer – a population that had increased considerably by this point, in the fifth generation of brand advertising – it had become possible to create one-off typefaces feasibly and economically. Accordingly, these proliferate in ads from the 2000s.

7.   Spokes-characters

This term is like logo: it provides the accepted label for a range of phenomena, not all of which, once differentiated, jibe well with the umbrella label. Just as brand mark was the more encompassing term, of which logos (emblazoned and emblematic marks) were but one example, so also spokes-characters, properly speaking (the Green Giant) are but one instance of a larger category, comprised of all attempts to personify the brand.[1] These include, on the one hand, efforts to link the brand with a creature or person; and on the other, efforts to animate the brand, to make it a living being and more than a cultural thing.

As a rule, all animation leads to personification; but to animate, it is not necessary to portray a person or creature alongside of or in place of the brand. The brand can be animated, given life, made to move on its own, by other means. At some cognitive level, animate beings are necessarily approached as persons, much as a young child treats the family pet as a person, and expects any animal encountered in a story to speak and to have personality. Humans anthropomorphize, automatically and without effort. Whatever can move, lives; and whatever lives, can think, feel, and speak. That is scientifically false, but mentally true.

If we were writing 50 or 100 years ago, we might insert something here about how anthropomorphism is characteristic of the primitive mind. We might even talk about spokes-characters as brand totems, or describe personification as totemic thinking. But no knowledgeable scholar can cast such aspersions today. By knowledgeable, we mean "up to date with anthropological thinking since Levi-Strauss," and "familiar with Franz Boas' work." To avoid references to the primitive mind is not merely a matter of political correctness; it's analogous to not explaining combustion by reference to phlogiston, or light with reference to the ether. To speak seriously of brand totems is to lapse back into nineteenth-century levels of scientific understanding.[2] Creatures are good to think with; but that's because metaphor is good to think with, and there's nothing primitive about metaphor.[3]

To avoid such solecisms as "primitive thought," modern thinking on these matters is cast more neutrally, as in Kahneman's (2011) references to System 1 versus System 2 thought, or the distinction between heuristic and systematic processing. For children and other persons not educated to think like scientists, anthropomorphism is a reasonable heuristic. People, such as parents, are only one kind of creature with more mobility and more options than the young child. If parents have thoughts and feelings, manifest as purposeful motion, and experience pleasure or pain, manifest facially, then why not the family pet, who so obviously moves of his own will, and also exhibits pleasure and pain? And if the family pet is a kind of person, why not the bird seen through the window, or the tree moving in the breeze, or the wind itself? That mental process of anthropomorphizing – ugly word – is not primitive thinking; it's a readily available heuristic not yet brought to heel by education.

Personification, in branding, is one of many ways of capitalizing on heuristics widespread among human beings, mental shortcuts and extrapolations which can be exploited for commercial advantage. Or more neutrally, which the rhetorically knowledgeable can deploy in order to promote a brand. Remember, Plato had a reason for casting out advertisers, er, rhetoricians. We do strive to take advantage of human frailty.

Personification is one among the means of persuasion available for visual branding. Consistent with our rhetorical approach, the goal of this chapter is to subdivide concrete instances of this device in a meaningful and useful way, and place visual personification on a firm conceptual footing.

However, our treatment of this element of visual branding will be severely limited, relative to some other elements discussed earlier, such as the brand mark. We are limited by having restricted our inquiry to print, to the visual branding that can be accomplished on a silent, two-dimensional surface. By far the easiest way to animate a brand is to advertise it on television. In a TV ad, there will be voice and movement, plot, character, and drama; all tools difficult to apply in a print ad or on packaging.[4] The brand, when enacted in a moving picture with sound, is animated in fact. On the printed page, its animation can only be suggested. Hence, this element of visual branding will always be more powerfully pursued on television or with web animations and video.

There is a second, derivative limitation. Consider Flo, the spokesperson for Progressive Insurance. If we had not seen Flo on television, where she is almost unavoidable, we would not know her, appearing in an ad, to be the spokesperson for Progressive; she would simply be a female person, a nice-looking actress tapped for this ad execution and, for all we know, not appearing again in any other ad for Progressive.[5] Our knowledge that she is the pitch woman for Progressive, with a character developed over the years, across dozens of TV ads, and millions if not billions of cumulative exposures, comes from outside the print ad. We know from watching television that Flo is a rhetorical device used to animate and personify the brand promise made by Progressive Insurance: a better deal. But that knowledge is not found on the ad page, nor is it part of the general cultural toolkit brought to the page.

Now consider what happens when, as historians, we examine ads from the early 1950s, before either of us was born. Suppose we see a female person in a 1951 ad. If she is labelled Elizabeth Taylor, we will grasp immediately that this is a celebrity testimonial: we are old enough to know who Elizabeth Taylor is. But if the ad shows an unnamed female person, how could we know whether she had been a long-serving pitchwoman during that era? How could we know she was a Flo? We cannot. In this respect, a history of visual branding poses different challenges than a history of advertising language. Absent an intense and prolonged immersion in all media productions from the 1950s – which would make it impossible to do the same for the 1920s and the 1900s – the historian cannot be confident of drawing the same visual inferences from ads as those native to the era in which the ad appeared. The problem dogs all visual elements in ads, but grows acute in the case of spokespersons.

A TYPOLOGY OF PERSONIFICATION IN VISUAL BRANDING

At the top level, animation can be directly shown or only inferred (see Table 7.1). The indirect, inferred branch is short and straightforward. An automobile grille might show an upward-facing shallow curve, and be read as a smiling face. A jar of skin moisturizer might have a straw inserted into water nearby. These can be thought of as liminal cases of anthropomorphism. Here animation is at the boundary of detectability. But when an ad will be viewed millions of times, such borderline instances of personification may nonetheless achieve a desired effect.

Less liminal, but still indirect personification occurs when a package is given appendages that are grasped as arms and legs; even less liminal, but still on the indirect branch, is to sketch facial features onto the package or product. Only when the facial features become a face that is carried over from ad to ad, a familiar and recognized face, do we switch from the indirect to the direct branch, from animation to direct personification.

These borderline instances represent a pictorial invitation to think figuratively: to take the contours on the page as a metaphor for a smile, or the placement of a straw as a metonym for obtaining and retaining moisture. In classical rhetoric, personification – then pursued only verbally – was always classed as a rhetorical figure. Its use in advertising only makes

Table 7.1   A typology of personification

Top level categories	2nd-level categories	3rd-level categories	4th-level categories	Definitions	Examples
Indirect				Without showing a person or creature, traits or elements of an animated being are present	An automobile grill with upturned corners suggests a smile
Direct	→Person	→Real	→Celebrity	A celebrity has a known name and a reputation established outside of the ad	Ann Sheridan in Figure 2.31 or Natalie Wood in Figure WA.16
			→Ordinary	An unnamed and unknown person, who may be selected to suggest characteristics of a typical user of the category	The baby and mother in Figure 2.36
		→Fictive	→Custom	A person who does not exist, but who acquires a name and reputation via the brand's advertising and promotion	Betty Crocker or Flo for Progressive
			→Stock	A type of personage, rather than an individual human being	The king who appears in Burger King ads, or the cowboys who appear in Marlboro ads
	→Creature	→Natural		A photorealistic depiction of a biologically real animal or insect	A photorealistic tiger or bear
		→Fantastic	→Custom	An illustrated portrayal, an image, of a creature who may or may not have a real biological analogue	Tony the Tiger, but also Mr Peanut and the Michelin Man
			→Stock	A named type of fantastic creature	A dragon, elf, or leprechaun

Note: If some of the named characters do not ring a bell, perhaps because you are reading this book a decade or two hence, simply search by name using an image search engine, and you'll be presented with copious images.

sense if consumers have a propensity to respond to the pictorial invitation to think figuratively, a willingness to approach each picture as a metaphor or as a trace of things not shown.[6] This invitation may work better for modern consumers, and modern consumers may be more skilled in taking it up; that would be consistent with our contention that visual branding emerges in history.

On the direct branch, a more complex set of options appears. The first decision is whether to show a human person or to show a creature of some kind. Betty Crocker provides an example of the first, and the Green Giant the second. Each of these options can be further subdivided.

On the human branch, the person shown can be real or fictive. Betty Crocker is a fiction, but Elizabeth Taylor, and all celebrities, are real persons. In turn, celebrity spokespeople represent only one twig on the real person branch. Ads in which a putative ordinary consumer gives a testimonial for the brand also fall here. If that person only appears in a single execution, they are not a spokesperson; but a single appearance is enough to permit the process of metaphorical transfer to take place, even if with only slight effect. Brands are their associations; to be endorsed by an ordinary consumer cast as a staid Midwestern housewife, or instead, by an edgy city girl, positions the brand toward or away from one region or another in semantic space. We'll return to these issues of meaning transfer after laying out the typology.

Stepping back up the typology, the fictive branch also splits. Betty Crocker is a custom character, as is Flo. By custom, we mean her personality and all her traits have been built up from scratch, over the decades for Betty Crocker, and over quite a few years now for Flo. As a custom fictive character, Betty Crocker has only the meanings, for each consumer, that have been experienced by that consumer. If the consumer has read lots of magazines where Betty Crocker ads have appeared, she may develop a rich schema for Betty Crocker, fleshed out with a personality, an inferred family situation, an age, even an education level. A younger woman less exposed to Betty Crocker advertising may have a sparse schema that consists of not much more than associations to the name and to the category of baking products. Because Betty Crocker is custom-built, her meanings can be made to migrate in semantic space over time, if the brand desires either to reposition, or to update its positioning.

The other twig on this branch holds stock or type characters. A type character comes with ready-made associations set by the surrounding cultural discourse, and not easily altered by the brand. The cowboy is a common instance of a type character, as in Marlboro ads. Other examples include the princess, the knight in shining armor, witches, and any other character who appears often enough in the stock of stories told widely within the culture to be recognizable at a glance. The advantage for the brand of using a type character is that the desired associations are automatically triggered upon recognition, from the first use. A cowboy cues a wagon load of connotations, and these come to mind effortlessly. The brand does not have to invest millions in making cowboy to mean something.

Conversely, no matter how often a brand advertises a type character, in no matter what context, the character's associations remain constant, subject only to drift in the larger cultural discourse. Marlboro advertising has induced billions of exposures to cowboys; yet, if a free association task were to be performed with a sample of Americans, it seems unlikely to us that "die of lung cancer" would now be a frequent association to the prompt "cowboy." One brand's advertising is never more than one trickle within the vast river of cultural discourse. The Marlboro man is a whisper in a roaring stadium. Cowboy transforms the brand, but Marlboro does not transform the cowboy.

Interestingly, this one-way transfer of meaning probably does not hold for the celebrity branch. If Elizabeth Taylor appears often enough in ads for cosmetics brands positioned as bold and sassy, then over time that category and those brand meanings will alter her meaning in the eyes of film audiences. Two-way transfer of meaning is possible, but not for type characters.[7] No celebrity – whether the Kardashians, Taylor Swift, or Justin Bieber[8] – has a cultural meaning so well established, or a media footprint so large, as to escape modification when that celebrity regularly appears in paid media for a brand.

Although we have thus far presented the typology as branches spreading over one plane, any of the twigs described can vary over a third or vertical dimension. The third dimension distinguishes alternative ways in which a brand can use the person or creature who has been incorporated into its advertising. At one extreme, the living being can simply accompany the brand. It just sits there. Mere association is the goal. Because this makes thin gruel, more commonly a brand will move its spokes-character up this dimension, to at least make an endorsement. The spokes-character speaks for the brand, endorses it, vouches for it, presents it to the consumer. The brand is given to the consumer by and through the spokes-character. At the highest level, the spokes-character embodies the brand, enacts it. To smoke Marlboro cigarettes is to be a cowboy, to live that rugged and courageous life.[9]

Next, let's look at the creature branch, where brands are promoted by living beings who are not human persons. The first split here distinguishes between natural and fantastic creatures. Tigers and bears and tuna fish and bumble bees all exist in the natural world, and each animal has the traits assigned to it in the surrounding cultural discourse. That ambient cultural discourse trumps scientific knowledge, when it comes to how the animal contributes to branding. It doesn't matter if real bears, the species studied by zoologists, are shy and retiring, and more prone to dumpster dive than rear up in attack; for advertising purposes, bears are fierce and domineering. Scientific fact is drowned out by cultural discourse; why else would we speak of a bear hug, of how that test was a bear, or that fierce bear of a man? Because animals are good to think with, and part of our childhood world from the beginning, all animals that regularly appear in stories carry a vast amount of baggage wherever they go, loads of meaning that can be leveraged by a brand.

But brands can also make use of fantastic creatures, such as giants made of green vegetable matter, little green aliens, dragons, elves, fairies, and any other imaginary creature recognizable from the myths, folklore, and fables that circulate within the local culture. Fantastic creatures, like fictive persons, can also be custom-built or type-characters. Dragons and giants are type-characters, but an artist can also create what is recognizably a fictive character, an unreal animated being, that is *de novo*, and not a type drawn from the existing cultural stock. Examples include the Michelin Man, Chiquita banana, Mr Peanut, Mr Bubble.

Interestingly, fictive type characters are probably more plastic in meaning than human type-characters. Although Marlboro's advertising seems unlikely to affect the meaning of cowboys very much, after a few tens of millions of exposures to the Keebler elves it seems more plausible to us that in a free-association task, "elves" might generate a response of "likes cookies."[10] The meaning of any type character can be more or less tightly bound, more or less multiply reinforced within the larger cultural discourse that brands do not control. Cowboys are mythic within American culture, with a tight bound on meaning; elves are not, and have looser implications. The consumer sees and hears of cowboys in countless discourses; but, except at Christmas time, an adult will rarely encounter references to elves, leaving their meanings more plastic and more available to be appropriated and altered by a brand.

The vertical dimension we introduced earlier, which distinguishes accompaniment, endorsement, or enactment as roles that a human person can take relative to a brand, applies to creatures as well. There is a second vertical dimension that mostly applies to creatures, although it may also apply to persons. This second dimension distinguishes photorealistic treatments of creatures from illustrations; at the extreme, illustrations may be better described as cartoon treatments. In our judgment, a realistic photo of a tiger cues a more restricted range of meanings, limited by those assigned to that real creature within their native habitat. Conversely, when

Kellogg's employs an illustrator to draw Tony the Tiger, meanings become less tightly bound. Tony is a tiger – he draws on the cultural stock of meanings for tiger – but he is also a cartoon version of a tiger, whose meanings stem in part from how he is drawn. Tony can be drawn as grinning, and as a result can take on upbeat, enthusiastic meanings. Real tigers cannot be photographed as grinning; they don't have the face for it. As a rule, cartoon representations are more customizable in meaning, and their meanings more fluid over time, so that *ceteris paribus*, cartoon creatures are more useful to brands. This generates a testable proposition: that most spokes-creatures will be illustrated rather than photographed. This is almost inevitable with fictive creatures, who do not exist to be photographed; so that the test is most interesting in the case of spokes-animals, Charlie the Tuna, Tony the Tiger, and the rest.

DESIRED OUTCOMES OF USING SPOKES-CHARACTERS

A reminder: rhetoricians are not interested in neat lists of possibilities for their own sake; the goal is to identify the available means of persuasion – what works. We are interested in spokes-characters, not only as a logical possibility within the toolkit of ways to communicate about the brand, but as a means of moving the brand forward – promoting it, advancing it. And as soon as we focus on the effect, upon the consumer, of viewing a brand in association with a spokes-character, we enter the territory of psychology. We want to know what happens in the mind, the events that occur within the internal psychic economy, consequent to exposure to Betty Crocker or Tony the Tiger. This requires a theory of meaning, and of meaning change. At this juncture, rhetoricians have no choice but to draw on cognitive psychology. Scientific psychologists are good at what they do, when operating within their proper sphere. It would be foolish for a modern rhetorician to draw on Greek theories of meaning, or Lockean ideas about perception, when a modern scientific account is available.

Unfortunately, cognitive psychology, insofar as it involves theories of meaning, is a vast and turbulent sphere, riven with controversies over epistemological conundrums, idealist versus materialist accounts, whether thinking has a fundamental linguistic character, and on and on. A version of Keynes's epigram applies: "The most hard-boiled advertising man, and the mathematically trained marketing scientist alike, who will have nothing to do with academic controversy, and despise philosophical nitpicking, will often be found the slave of some defunct theory of meaning, already hoary by the Middle Ages, if not discarded earlier in Greece." It isn't easy to navigate contemporary cognitive psychology, and all too tempting to revert to gussied-up versions of ancient ideas.

Mindful of the peril, we will take a straightforward Euclidean approach, and conceive of semantic meaning as comprising a vast space, in which distance corresponds to similarity or dissimilarity in meaning, and in which clustering occurs, so that we can talk of regions of meaning (see Box 7.1 for more on Euclidean models). Dead versus alive would be two examples of clusters located at a distance from one another in semantic space: old, stale, dry, and dull are located in the same region as "dead,"

BOX 7.1   EUCLIDEAN VERSUS CARTESIAN MODELS

In Chapter 6 on typeface, we criticized Henderson et al. (2004) for constructing a Cartesian model of the space of typeface possibilities. Here in the spokes-character chapter, we rely on another spatial model for understanding meaning change. We call it Euclidean rather than Cartesian, but really, what's the difference? Both are spatial models. How can the one model come in for censure, even as the other is praised?

There are two points of difference. First, we critiqued Henderson et al. for applying a Cartesian model to the rhetorical space of typeface possibilities, which exist physically. Here we apply a Euclidean model to meanings: to incorporeal entities that exist in mental space, wherever that resides. We're agnostic as to whether meanings reside in culture – a shared mental space that exists outside the skull – or in mind, understood as activities anchored in individual skulls. But meanings are certainly neither physical things, nor rhetorical gambits.

Second, in a Cartesian model, the dimensions are fundamental. Dimensions such as more (less) harmonious or more (less) organic are what structure the space. These dimensions are taken as real, and locations of typefaces in the space are measures of this reality. By contrast, in a Euclidean model, distances are fundamental. Dimensions can be supplied, but these are derivative. A Euclidean model of the meaning space is built on one metric only: similarity. Meaning is measured as distance from other meanings.* Also, given heterogeneity of distance – some meanings are more similar, others less so – we expect clustering in a Euclidean space.

The Euclidean model is optimized for understanding meaning change, as in our discussion of the effect on the brand of using one spokes-character versus another. Meaning change is defined as movement toward one meaning, a shortening of the distance between them, which will always imply movement away from some other meanings.

The gap that separates Cartesian and Euclidean models of space is as great as the gap that separates physical things from mental things. Application of the one model to physical things can be censured, and application of the other to mental things can be praised, without contradiction.

Note: * Some readers may recognize the connection between Euclidean models and multidimensional scaling (MDS). See Phillips and McQuarrie (2009) for an application of MDS to meaning spaces.

while such ideas as young, fresh, moist, and vivid are located near "alive."[11]

Under this model, meaning refers to position in semantic space, and specific meanings can be captured as a set of distances from other meanings. Meaning change, in turn, can be represented as movement of the brand within semantic space, as movement toward or away from relevant clusters of meanings. These clusters are like stars in the cosmos, where clustering occurs at multiple levels, as super-clusters of galaxy groups, as groups of galaxies, as groupings of stars within a galaxy, as star clusters within one spiral arm, down to the grouping of planets within a solar system.

Under this simple Euclidean model of meaning, the purpose of any attempt to animate or personify a brand is to move the brand toward the "alive" region, and toward meanings that cluster in that region (for example, young, vivid, active), which is also to move the brand away from the "dead" cluster, which simultaneously moves it away from other negative meanings in that region (for example, dull, old, thing). All efforts to animate hold the potential to accomplish this semantic shift for the brand. Consumers, like other humans, often prefer live to dead, vivid to dull, and youthful to decrepit.

This Euclidean model, which conceives of semantics as a space comprised of distances, is enormously flexible. For instance, we can imagine clusters at multiple levels of resolution – very broad ones like live versus dead, but also much more specific ones – all occurring within the live region. For example, here are some descriptors that only apply to living beings, especially persons, but which are far from identical pairs: bold versus cautious, perky versus calm, expressive versus controlled, aggressive versus easy-going, enthusiastic versus phlegmatic, and many, many more. Neither term in these contrasts applies to dead things, which call for a different set of descriptors (for example, hard versus soft). On this model, "live" is a cluster, when semantic space is viewed at the lowest level of resolution. Viewed up close, it is a region that contains yet more clusters located close or distant; in this case, all the subdescriptors that apply to persons, and that distinguish one personality from another.

In personifying a brand, rather than merely suggesting its animation, one has to give it a personality: the personality of the Green Giant, rather than that of Betty Crocker, the personality exhibited by Tony the Tiger, rather than that of Charlie the Tuna. You cannot personify a brand by showing a generic person or creature; one has to show Elsie the Cow, or Sue Bee, and let them speak and act, whereupon each gradually acquires a distinct personality. Each such choice shifts the meaning of the brand in one direction or another, within this more micro-region of semantic space, according to the personality traits than an Elsie or a Tony has accumulated over the years. A properly constructed character, aptly deployed, promotes the brand by moving its meanings in the desired direction: by shifting it within the semantic region that pertains to persons, even as all personifications, regardless of personality, shift the brand toward the region of the living and away from the place of dull, dead things.

Personification as Metaphor

In rhetorical terms, and consistent with a long tradition dating back to the Greeks, to personify a brand is to invoke a metaphor for it. More exactly, personification initiates a metaphorical transfer of meaning. When Kellogg's, the brand, introduces Tony the Tiger, that act of personification invites the consumer to transfer meanings from tiger, and from this very enthusiastic and youthful cartoon tiger to the brand and product, this dull, lifeless bowl of cereal, and the dreary and Sisyphean quest for proper child nutrition.

Now, although to classify personification as metaphor is ancient, keep in mind that we deal here with visual metaphor. There is no verbal assertion that Kellogg's is a tiger among brands; there is only the picture of Tony, and his remembered antics on television, and his attributed testimony. In assessing visual branding via personification, it helps to remember this rule: visual metaphors never assert, but only invite. Metaphorical transfer via pictures is loosely bound, fallible, and mutable. That's what makes visual branding conceptually interesting and a challenge to existing theories of persuasion, forged hundreds or thousands of years ago and anchored on speech.

We can give a precise meaning to metaphorical transfer by referring back to the Euclidean model of semantic space. Recall that under this model all meaning change can be represented as movement in semantic space. Metaphorical transfer occurs when two objects, drawn from distant regions, are juxtaposed, substituted, opposed, or compared. Frosted flakes are nothing like tigers. Brands are dull, dead pieces of property; but tigers, especially irrepressible young tigers, are vivid and fun. Tony moves Kellogg's toward those desirable meanings, and away from others eschewed.

Here is a second rule to keep in mind when dealing with practical applications of metaphor, both visual and verbal: the more unlike are the two objects that make up the metaphor, the more potentially powerful is the impetus to meaning change.[12] Branding is a practical task: it's about causing a specific, desired movement in meaning to occur. Success in branding is not automatic or guaranteed. Branding is conducted against resistance, high up on a crumbling ledge, buffeted by wind, over hidden patches of ice. It's a treacherous affair.

We might say that meaning space is viscous: inertia is strong there. Movement in meaning space – especially controlled movement toward a set of coordinates, as in making a cereal seem Gr-e-e-a-t! – is difficult. Brands inevitably seek the most potent means of persuasion available. Huge financial awards beckon to brand managers who can crack this puzzle. Similarly, if you want a playground swing to move far forward and high up when released, you have to pull back real hard on the backswing. It takes force to succeed, and deviant and distant metaphors apply more force to meaning.

And that introduces a third rule: for branding purposes, visual metaphor, *ceteris paribus*, is more powerful than verbal metaphor. The reason goes back to the second rule: the more deviant the metaphor, or the greater the discrepancy between the unlike things being equated, the more powerful it can be in changing meaning. Verbal metaphor suffers by comparison, especially when it rests on a single word: put a tiger in your tank, as the Esso gasoline ads used to urge. All words are alike, no matter how distant the concepts they invoke: an arbitrary arrangement of phonemes, similar in length, with tens of thousands constructed from the same few dozen available phonemes. The field of pictures is vastly larger and more varied, hence the unlikeness of two objects pictorially juxtaposed can be far greater.

Why have brands resorted more and more to visual branding, adopting spokes-characters and other rhetorical devices? Answer: the difficulty of the branding task has forced them to brand visually. In highly competitive categories where functional differences are minimal – so-called parity products – brand managers seek the most powerful means of promotional differentiation they can find. The strength of their need drives managers to visual branding, and to spokes-characters. Automobile brands never made much use of spokes-characters, nor have computer brands; packaged convenience goods have always been the citadel, the redoubt from which this visual branding strategy has sallied. With a machine, functional superiority, however fleeting, is always possible. But brands of cereal and soap are oh so vulnerable to all seem the same.

Additional Benefits of Personification

In this book we laud brands as cultural things occupying their own unique category. But a cultural thing remains a thing. You can like a thing, or want to be associated with it, but you cannot have a personal relationship with an it. The second great benefit of personification is that it encourages the consumer to relate to the brand as a sentient being. In the case of mere animation, this benefit is correspondingly minimal. The benefit remains rudimentary when small creatures exhibiting little sentience are used in a tangential way, or when there is only a one-off appearance of an unnamed person. But as soon as we have a creature that speaks (Tony the Tiger) or a named person who appears regularly (Flo, Betty Crocker, any celebrity) it becomes possible to relate to the brand using the full repertoire that any of us brings to interpersonal relationships. Most important: personal relationships can get emotional.

Use of a spokes-character permits and encourages a greater range of emotional response to the brand. Out of an emotional response an emotional bond may emerge. Once an emotional bond has been forged, brand switching becomes as wrenching as cheating on a loved one. Loyalty is more likely to be sustained because more deeply felt. All kinds of emotional responses become more likely once the brand becomes a person. The more child-like the consumer – or, in Kahneman's (2011) terms, the greater the dominance of System 1 thinking for that consumer – the greater the impact of personifying the brand by means of a spokes-character.

Another moderating factor is the degree and intensity of personification. An emotional response becomes more likely when the spokes-character is presented as the embodiment of a brand, and when the spokes-character appears over and over for years and years. And the more fully developed the character, by dint of the number and complexity of the plots, interactions, and narratives in which that character has appeared, the greater the variety of emotions that might be invoked by the brand.

To summarize, personification positions the brand as living, not dead, and as an emotional partner rather than an inert thing. This positioning makes it easier to attribute a personality to the brand and to elaborate upon and associate personal characteristics with the brand. If Tony the Tiger is perceived as perky and energetic and trustworthy, then the Kellogg's brand can take on these characteristics as well, and the consumer can relate to the brand as it would relate to such a person.

A final caveat: because brands are cultural things, and present as social actors with the power to communicate, it is always possible for a consumer to attribute a personality to a brand, and experience an emotional response to it, and treat the brand as sentient in any number of ways, without the brand resorting to personification.[13] Humans actively infer about their world, all the time and everywhere and about everything, using the quick and easy heuristics that make up Kahneman's System 1 thinking. A spokes-character is an option, not a necessity. It is one among the available means for branding. A spokes-character is a rhetorical device that may be useful in fueling and directing the inference-making in which consumers are always engaged. Persons provide rich metaphorical fodder; but the impulse to metaphorical thinking does not need persons to be charged up and put in gear.

HISTORICAL SKETCH OF SPOKES-CHARACTER USE IN BRANDING

Personification appears to be as old as brand advertising in magazines. In this book we date the onset of modern brand advertising to the 1890s, when national magazines first built circulations of many hundreds of thousands, and when nationally distributed brands first flourished. Spokes-characters and fictional spokespersons can be found in magazine ads from the 1890s. The Gold Dust twins, the old lady with the broom for Old Dutch cleanser, Aunt Jemima, and Rastus, the African-American butler for Cream of Wheat, can all be seen in ads from this era. New brands introduced new spokes-characters, and not necessarily at launch. Betty Crocker and the Green Giant can be seen by the 1930s, but the products with which they became associated, flour and canned vegetables, acquired their predecessor brand names at launch many years before their spokes-characters were introduced.

Although spokes-characters were in use from the beginning of our period, scholars have argued that the number of characters in use expanded after 1925, with Betty Crocker introduced in magazines in the 1930s and Elsie the Cow in the 1940s (Dotz and Husain 2003). The Depression, on the one hand, and the availability of animation via TV commercials, on the other, have been cited as factors stimulating the use of spokes-characters. The heyday of new character introductions spanned the 1950s and 1960s (Dotz and Husain 2015).

For some time, conventional wisdom has held that the rate of introduction of new, named spokes-characters to be featured in advertising – excepting the one-time appearance of some unnamed cartoon character or illustrated figure – has declined since about 1975 (Dotz and Husain 2003). Whether this levelling off in the creation of new spokes-characters is a temporary lull or the beginning of a permanent decline remains to be seen (Brown 2010). After all, the introduction of entirely new brands has also diminished; less risky brand extensions have become the norm. And the introduction of new characters has not ceased: Flo for Progressive, the AFLAC duck, and the gecko for GEICO, are relatively recent examples from the United States that flourish on magazine pages. Perhaps the rate of "spokes-characters per brand" has not declined; it may be that the store shelves are so full that there are few new brands available to which new spokes-characters could be attached.

On the other hand, a recent content analysis suggests that by 2015, the use of spokes-characters in magazine advertising had ticked up, after a long steady period.[14] Best to conclude that the spokes-character continues to be one among the available means for visual branding, no less powerful today, when used adroitly, than it ever was.

Finally, we also discovered that spokes-characters are mortal. Not only are they born, appearing after launch for an existing brand, but they also die off. Sometimes the spokes-character goes to its grave with the brand, as did the Gold Dust twins, and Sunny Jim, when their brands succumbed to competing products in the 1950s. At other times, the brand continues, but the spokes-character disappears (for example, Kellogg's Sweetheart of the Corn).[15] Most American readers in 2015 will recognize that Betty Crocker is not only a brand, but a fictional spokesperson; but how many readers today can recognize, and assign to their brands, such characters as Anne Marshall, or Dione Lucas, or Mary Blake, or Marie Gifford, who have disappeared, even as the sponsoring brands have continued to thrive?[16] Betty Crocker was once part of a troop. Now she's the last one left on the island.

Brands create and discard spokes-characters, and are not to be identified with them. Spokes-characters are a device, one among many, for positioning a brand in meaning space, and not unique in accomplishing this positioning via metaphorical transfer.

8.   Color

Color poses challenges for a rhetorical account. Here the shortlist of types, the Holy Grail of any rhetorical inquiry, already exists: the colors of the rainbow, the hues any fifth-grader can name – red, blue, green, and so on. The first task of rhetorical analysis – to identify the available means of persuasion – appears to have been completed at the outset.

A second challenge: when it comes to color, does the rhetorician have anything to offer, beyond what psychological science can show? Perception is among the oldest branches of psychology. The legitimacy of a physiological approach to color is patent: retina properties and brain activity are key. Is there any need or occasion for rhetorical analysis of color in branding? Why not leave color to psychology?

To press the point: color lends itself to a stimulus–response account. Brand managers want to know how emotional response might differ if they make a logo red, not blue. Managers also want to know whether color affects more than emotional response; but all such questions concern an economy internal to the psyche: what triggers what, and by what path, inside the head, upon color exposure. These internal psychological matters fall outside the rhetorician's ken.[1]

Color also presents challenges to the historian. First there was only black and white engraving, and then there was color lithography and black and white photographs. Later black and white photography was replaced by color photography, as technology drove the cost of color printing down toward the cost of black and white. Given a near-equivalent cost, color ads took over, because . . . these are more colorful! It is all too simple and straightforward. The historian has nothing to chew. The history of how color entered visual branding takes only a sentence or two.

With these challenges in view, the rhetorical opportunity, such as it is, must be founded on absence and disproportion. Most magazine ads are now in color, but in a few categories brands have kept their marks black. The move toward color is easy to explain; the stubborn rearguard resistance, favoring black in some brand marks, is more interesting. Once it became feasible and cost-effective, why would color ever be absent from visual branding? Here a rhetorician might contribute insight.

Likewise, the use of color to differentiate brands is easy to understand, as is the idea that a color may confer positive associations on a brand. But all colors have positive connotations: we have the green of life, the blue of heaven, imperial purple, passionate red, golden yellow, fertile brown soil. And any color differentiates at a glance. For consumers who are not color-blind, it is impossible to mistake red for green, or blue for yellow. What a powerful means to visual branding, were identification to be the primary goal!

In visual branding with color, the baseline prediction must be: proportionate use of all hues. Once color becomes the norm in branding, we would expect dispersion among colors across competing brands. If the market leader has gone for blue, I go for red; if the two leaders have selected blue and red, I go for green; and if blue, red, and green have been taken up by my competitors, then I look to yellow, purple, orange, or some other less common hue. Apart from a deliberate imitation or brand confusion strategy, there would be no point in being the second, third, or fourth brand to choose blue for its color.

But this baseline prediction is not supported: most colors are uncommon among the marks of American and developed world brands. Red and blue rule. Many brands choose red or blue, but few choose orange or purple or brown. This disproportion points to a second opportunity for rhetorical analysis.

First, we give a brief introduction to psychological research on color. The rhetorician, focused on absence and disproportion in the use of color to brand, needs first to clamber up onto the shoulders of work already performed in psychology.

THE PSYCHOLOGY OF COLOR

Color, in the psychological laboratory, proves to be more complex than color in the marketplace. Hue, which is what ordinary people have in mind when they refer to color, is only one of three dimensions that have to be controlled in laboratory work on color perception, along with darkness and saturation. However, in the marketplace, the brand manager has no control over these other dimensions: field lighting conditions vary and fluctuate, materials age or print haphazardly, and a host of other environmental factors prevent control of perceived darkness and saturation. The brand manager doesn't even have that much control over hue. Magazine printers can be told to print "Pantone #357," and they will try; but each LED screen, whether computer, phone, or tablet, will render that hue a little differently. Randomly select any two field displays of the brand's chosen hue, across different paper coatings or screens, and the variation will be more than sufficient to confound a carefully calibrated laboratory experiment. Psychologists found this out the hard way, by attempting to replicate experiments performed in another laboratory. The equipment needed, and the degree of calibration required to do laboratory science in the field of color perception, is extraordinary.[2]

Paradoxically, the extreme calibration required for laboratory studies of color, and the fruits of success in implementing this calibration, makes these studies irrelevant to the brand manager. Effects that are specific to microscopically controlled color stimuli are effects that a brand manager cannot master. In the field, the brand manager has only a blunt instrument: the hues a fifth-grader can name. Any more subtle variation won't be robust under the field conditions in which brands are viewed, sold, and used. The brand manager can opt for dark red, and this color will, under many conditions, look different from the red of another brand that opted for a light red; but that manager won't achieve an exact degree of darkness, only a darker range.

Hence, much of the psychology of color perception holds no relevance for the brand manager, because it can't be applied in the field. But not all. A version of the nature–nurture controversy rages within color psychology. That's the piece of psychological research that a brand manager needs to grasp.

ARE COLOR INFERENCES NATURAL OR CULTURAL?

Color, like type, belongs to the large set of non-linguistic elements that carry semantic meaning. Red can mean arousal or passion, based on the association with blushing: blood reddening the appearance of the skin. The question of interest: does red mean arousal for everyone? Is this excess semantic meaning pan-cultural, automatic, universal? Or is that meaning culturally local, learned rather than inborn, an inference to which pale-skinned Westerners are prone, but scarce on the ground among darker-skinned residents in, say, sub-Saharan Africa? For a second instance, "red, white, and blue" means something specific to citizens of the USA, but carries no reliable meaning for tribesmen in Borneo. The cultural institution of the American flag, for those who have been exposed to it in laudatory contexts all their lives, will inevitably govern the interpretation of a blue field juxtaposed with red and white stripes, no matter the context where these are encountered. These culturally shaped expectations may be semi-automatic, and near universal among people residing in the middle of the North American continent; but the inferences and associations that attach to "red, white, and blue" are cultural, not natural.

Returning to the marketplace: in the middle latitudes of North America, a brand can reliably evoke desired semantic associations by combining red, white, and blue in its packaging and its brand mark. But when it comes time to market the brand globally, across Saudi Arabia, and Nigeria, and Chile, and Thailand, these colors may reliably cue favorable associations – or not; but the meanings cued won't be the same as in the USA.

Whereas if red had a natural meaning, automatically evoked upon encounter, then a manager could brand with red and count on this branding to have the desired impact across the globe. In 2015, inasmuch as most brands must market globally, it would be nice to discover that colors had robust natural meanings which could be readily attached to a brand in a product category. Except, if a competitor had already grabbed the one right color for that product, and you were left with second-best, well, that would not be so nice.

At present, tentatively, psychological science has concluded that some colors, certainly red, may on average, under the right conditions, reliably evoke not entirely random semantic inferences. In other words: hedge, hedge, hedge that finding. The short version: under laboratory conditions and using North American college students, red, as opposed to blue, will produce semantic associations that differ, under standard statistical hypothesis testing, at $p < 0.05$.

This finding is less than the brand manager might have hoped. Our point: color is not a language. Use of color in branding does not allow fine-tuned control of the meanings evoked in consumers. Rather, a particular color may be appropriate or inappropriate to the product category. For instance, brands of feminine hygiene products never render their marks in blood red, nor their packaging. Neither do brands for hemorrhoid relief. The brand is not sold by evoking the problem it makes to go away. Conversely, brands of food products, to convey ripeness and freshness, may choose red, or gold, or green. Brands in these categories are sold by evoking the pleasures they promise (see Chapter 4 for more on category differences).

Lest we mislead the reader: such clear examples of how a color can be right or wrong for a category are rare. Most colors are compatible with a range of product categories. For instance, in the West, blue is to branding what beige is to apartment carpets: few will find it offensive, and not a few will find it, if not altogether pleasing, completely acceptable.

We conclude that the primary reason to brand with color is to give pleasure rather than to convey specific meanings. Colors are pleasing to view. In most product categories, several colors will be appropriate, and many hues will yield pleasure. Hence, any of several colors will do, as long as it is used consistently, to associate it with the brand, and as long as it prints in a pleasing manner.

Why will most brands choose to deliver pleasure through color branding? The brand must be seen millions, billions of times, on packages, in ads, and wherever promotion occurs. A simple rule can be adduced: these encounters, for most brands, ought to be made more pleasurable than not; hence, anything that gives pleasure is fair game. Because most colors, in most categories, yield pleasure, the color chosen is not so important as consistency in its use. Any color that is favorably regarded in the local culture, or approved by many of the local cultures where a global brand promotes, will be serviceable. And color does perform a service, adding with each exposure one more quantum of pleasure to the ongoing brand encounter.

It follows that identification is not the primary purpose of color branding. Among the set of colors a fifth grader can name, there's not enough variety to go around. Thousands of brands can't use a dozen or two colors to differentiate. Conversely, within any cultural zone – the Euro-North American zone, for instance – there will be favorite colors. Blue is a contender in that zone. But in the Arabic and Muslim countries, green plays that role. By contrast, red is favorably regarded across the major cultural zones (except for a few product categories). With the goal of identification set aside, brands flock to the best colors, with plenty of duplication within any category and cultural zone.

The argument that brands do not use color primarily to identify and differentiate, but to please, can be tested. However, it is desirable to test the argument outside of the brand context first. As yet, brand ownership is concentrated in the Euro-American cultural zone. The point about favorite colors, and the cultural typing that determines which colors are preferred, needs to be tested cross-culturally. Yet it cannot be done with brands, because most global brands today have a Western origin.[3] How to do it?

If we may play the game of Jeopardy, the answer is: flags of nations. The question behind the answer is harder to state. Try this: among all cultural things, what is the closest non-commercial analogue to brand? Or this: what other symbolic device most resembles the brand mark? The answers: nations, and their flags. Nations and flags predate brands and their marks, and are more widespread in origin. Brand loyalty is an analogue of patriotism, and loyalty to kin, clan, tribe, and ethnos. The brand's mark functions like a nation's flag. The brand's mark is meant to be recognized, and invested with positive associations; likewise, the nation's flag. The advantage of studying color in nations' flags: every nation, across all cultural zones, has its flag. None of the nations in this sample used a black and white flag. Flags are the original colored symbol, just as heraldic devices preceded, and laid out a path for, emblematic brand marks.

Flags, in addition to being produced across all major cultural zones, have to fulfill several conditions: (1) be easily recognized, with a glimpse or at a distance, even amid the smoke of battle; (2) provide a locus for emotional responses, not least, for the soldiers who will fight and die under that flag; (3) in general, provide a vehicle suitable for attracting and holding positive associations, and for commanding loyalty. Flags are like brand marks, but ever so much more so.

We next examine the distribution of colors for a sample of national flags, do the same for the sample of brand marks gathered for Chapters 3 and 4, and then compare the color distributions seen in flags to those seen in marks.[4] We then dig deeper into select comparisons within groups of marks. Our predictions:

1. A few colors are disproportionately favored in both flags and marks.
2. These favored colors vary by cultural zone (flags) and product category (marks).

FLAG COLORS

In flags, red was the most favored color, present in 82 percent of the 163 flags examined. Blue, green, and yellow/gold were next, present in 52 percent, 49 percent, and 45 percent of flags, respectively. All the other colors counted – orange, brown, silver, violet/purple, and pink – were present in fewer than 8 percent of national flags (see Table 8.1).

The prevalence of red in flags can be explained using the inverse of the argument that explained its absence in marks for feminine hygiene and hemorrhoid relief products. If national flags are at root battle flags, then red is an appropriate color, because soldiers must follow that flag, shed blood, and die. Interestingly, the only two cultural zones where red is not the most common color in flags – Latin America and sub-Saharan Africa – are the zones where national flags are newest, and where many nations have yet to go to war against other surrounding nations.

However, the frequencies that in the aggregate put a few colors into a rough tie for second place are misleading. The impression of a tie overall is an artifact of aggregation. Blue, green, and gold are present at different frequencies across the cultural zones. Each is a clear second, with no nearby third-place color, in one cultural zone. Blue is a strong second-place finisher in Europe (including its Anglo-Saxon outposts) and in Asia. Green is an equally strong second-place choice in Islamic countries. Only in South America and in Africa do we find rough ties in the frequencies of blue, green, or gold.

In summary, national flags deploy a restricted range of colors. Red dominates in most zones. Blue, green, and yellow are favored in some cultural

Table 8.1 Incidence of colors in national flags

	All nations (N = 163)		Europe & Anglo Saxon (N = 46)		Asia (N = 65)		Islamic (N = 37)		South & Central America (N = 21)		Africa (N = 38)	
		%		%		%		%		%		%
Blue	84	51.5	27	58.7	37	56.9	10	27.0	19	90.5	17	44.7
Red	133	81.6	39	84.8	56	86.2	30	81.1	17	81.0	29	76.3
Yellow or gold	74	45.4	16	34.8	24	36.9	10	27.0	15	71.4	25	65.8
Green	80	49.1	10	21.7	13	20.0	22	59.5	12	57.1	32	84.2
Orange	12	7.4	2	4.3	5	7.7	1	2.7	3	14.3	3	7.9

Note: Israel and Lebanon were not assigned to a subgroup. Islamic nations were assigned to their geographical region as well, hence subgroup counts exceed the total count. Violet, brown, pink, and silver were present in seven or fewer flags, and are not shown. Flag images were obtained from flags.net. A color was scored as present, however minor, if the research assistants (RAs) perceived it to be present; we did not attempt Labrecque and Milne's (2013b) distinction between major and minor presence. The coders agreed in 96 percent of cases.

189

zones. Brown and orange and purple, and even more so pink and silver, are never common in flags anywhere.

Inasmuch as most global brands were developed in Europe, its Anglo-Saxon outposts, or Asia, this exploration of national flags generates a straightforward prediction about color distribution in brand marks: red and blue will dominate. It is not that red and blue are naturally the most appealing colors; rather, red and blue dominate within the Euro-Asian cultural zone where most global brands arose. Red is intense and blue is soothing. One or the other will be favored in many product categories, as a sure route to providing the visual pleasure of color.

COLOR IN BRAND MARKS

That prediction was confirmed: within the 529 brand marks in our total sample, blue is the most common color, present in 43 percent of marks; and red is in second place, at 33 percent (see Table 8.2). Yellow and green trail, at 21 percent and 14 percent, respectively. Orange, brown, pink, and purple are all under 8 percent, as with flags. The surprise is silver, which here among marks comes in at 14 percent, vying with green. But these are mostly automobile brands, whose marks may have originated as hood ornaments. Hence, this count is better labeled the frequency of chrome, and stems from the accidental fitness of chrome to the automobile category, which holds, using a financial metric, a disproportionate number of leading brands.

We conclude that pleasure, contingent upon category appropriateness, and not differentiation, is the primary rhetorical purpose guiding the use of color in brand marks. Had differentiation been the primary goal, we would not see so many marks defaulting to blue overall, or to chrome within the automobile category. Purple or brown would provide instant distinction, because currently rare; but brands do not take up this possibility.

A second conclusion derives from the much lower incidence of red among brand marks as compared to national flags. Flags are different from marks, after all. Blood is a special substance.[5] Blood is appropriate for the symbol of a nation, because nations are bloody affairs. Blood may or may not be appropriate in some product categories, and many brands will eschew red for that reason. Red is blood; blood is power. The brand may choose not to be positioned toward power, especially a power that threatens to slip from control. In which case, red will not be made part of its mark.

A third conclusion: although brand managers want to harness the pleasure of color for their brand, safety is paramount; the wrong color

Table 8.2 *Incidence of colors in brand marks*

Colors present	Total sample (N = 539)		Financial services (N =100)		Retailers (N = 120)		Packaged food (N = 71)		Irritating products (N = 54)		B2B manufacturer (N=53)	
	Incidence	%	Incidence	%	Incidence	%	Incidence	%	Incidence	%	Incidence	%
Black & white only	84	15.6	4	4	40	33.3	3	4.2	9	16.7	6	11.3
Blue	231	42.9	57	57	29	24.2	25	35.2	34	63.0	28	52.8
Red	180	33.4	35	35	42	35.0	40	56.3	9	16.7	13	24.5
Yellow or gold	117	21.7	17	17	15	12.5	37	52.1	10	18.5	4	7.5
Green	77	14.3	16	16	12	10.0	10	13.7	4	15.2	7	13.2
Orange	38	7.1										
Brown	23	4.3										
Violet or purple	14	2.6										
Pink	11	2.0										
Silver, chrome, or gray[a]	60	11.1										

Notes: A color was scored as present, however minor, if the RAs perceived it to be present; we did not attempt Labrecque and Milne's (2013b) distinction between major and minor presence. The coders agreed in 96 percent of cases. There was too little variation in the minor colors to be meaningful; these entries have been omitted to make the table more readable. In the category samples, noteworthy departures from the total sample are called out with a border: solid for high-side and dotted line for low-side departures.
a   Many of these were automobile brands; these colors were otherwise rare.

can cause more harm than an okay color can yield pleasure. The beige carpet analogy is again pertinent. Builders of apartment complexes have to appeal to a diffuse mass audience. Most will conclude that it is better to offend no one than to delight a few and repel others with fashion-forward residential design. Using the same logic, brand managers default to blue. Few people in the Euro-Asian cultural zone actively dislike it, and many favor it, to a greater or lesser degree. Blue is the safe color: a reliable source of visual pleasure, with few risks of untoward association. Red is the risky choice: if appropriate, its connotations of power and passion – its sanguine qualities – supplement visual pleasure with positive, on-target associations, offering the brand manager a two-fer. If inappropriate, the choice of red blows up.

We support these conclusions by next presenting product categories where blue is even more common than in marks overall, and other categories where red is notably less common than in the total sample (Table 8.2). First, as intimated earlier in Chapter 4, red is half as common among irritating marks, at 15 percent, and blue is even more common, at 57 percent (as a reminder, in the total sample the overall proportions for red and blue were 33 percent and 43 percent, respectively). The intensity of red may pose difficulties, when the motive for buying the brand is the negative one of removing a problem; but here the soothing quality of blue is even more of a plus. Conversely, for positively motivated food products, red and yellow, the colors of ripeness, and green, the color of living plants, are, as expected, about twice as common as in the overall sample.

We suggested in Chapter 4 that brands in service categories are especially in need of, and may benefit disproportionately from, visual branding. Intangible financial services seek tangible cues to anchor and ground consumer perceptions in a favorable location. In the visual realm, there's nothing more tangible than color. Our first prediction: black and white marks will be extremely uncommon among service brands, as proves to be the case, at 4 percent, relative to 15 percent overall. The second, more tentative prediction: since no color is category-inappropriate in financial services, the favorite color, overall, will be even more the favorite here. And indeed, blue was present in 57 percent of financial services marks. An alternative explanation for the prevalence of blue marks in financial services would be that management, in this industry, attracts risk-averse people, making blue, the beige carpet of colors, a reflexive design choice.

WHY SOME BRANDS ESCHEW COLOR IN THEIR MARKS

We saw earlier that clothing retailers were much more likely to present black and white marks, although in that discussion we emphasized the argument for why retailers gravitate toward text-only marks. Focusing now on the lack of color, we note two arguments for why clothing retailers might eschew colors. First, when your merchandise is very colorful, you don't need color in your mark, and you may fear clashes. A clothing retailer faces the exact opposite situation of a financial services brand. Second, retailers in general must shout in the street: they must have signage that identifies the store at a distance. Some of this shouting must occur at night. Here a black mark is advantageous, because it can be presented as white light against dark night, as easily as black print on a white page; there is no inconsistency, as it remains a black and white mark in either case. This argument applies to clothing retailers. For other retailers, who worry less about clashing colors but who must still shout in the street, red should be an attractive choice. And this is what we find: red is present in 50 percent of the marks of non-clothing retailers.

CORRECTING CONVENTIONAL WISDOM

We once read a blog post that noted, "technology brands seem to prefer red or blue for their logos." That claim is subtly mistaken. It's not technology brands that are prone to use blue or red: about 66 percent of all global brand leaders use blue or red. Red is the most powerful and intense color, and blue is the most soothing and inoffensive. Once it is understood that differentiation is not the goal of applying color in branding, it makes perfect sense that most brands will make use of one or the other, or both, of these two culturally favored colors.

A second piece of conventional wisdom takes the form of a textbook throwaway line. This might occur in a chapter on visual branding or consumer symbolism: "by combining red, white, and blue in its packaging, an American brand can align itself with patriotic feelings, and cue positive associations surrounding the flag." Not so fast. If true, this statement would also be true for French, Russian, British, Dutch, and Czech brands, all of whose flags are comprised of red, white, and blue. In America, only if there are red and white stripes, and a blue field, is the association to the flag secure (see the Bank America mark). Else, a brand that prints red and blue on a white package simply uses the two most popular colors in the Euro-Asian zone.

SUMMARY

Color is pleasing to the eye. Color in brand marks gives pleasure. A brand must always be promoting itself, not least through its brand mark, which must stand up under billions of repeated exposures. Any locally esteemed color will do for this purpose. The important thing is, first, to avoid malaprop colors; and second, to be relentlessly consistent in use of the chosen color.

HISTORICAL SKETCH OF COLOR IN BRANDING

At first glance, the history is straightforward: brands moved toward color at each opportunity, rapidly adopting new technology and riding down the cost curve. At a second glance, progress was more fitful than might be supposed, and there was backsliding, as discussed in Chapter 2 regarding the 1950s, and hesitation, as seen in the less than complete diffusion of color photography prior to the 1980s. But the direction was inexorable, and the distance travelled between the mid-nineteenth century and the beginning of the twenty-first century is vast. It is almost impossible for a fifth-generation consumer, someone still young as of 2010, to understand the gulf that separates the colorful world they live in today from that inhabited by their great-great-grandparents, who were young in the years after the Civil War, at the dawn of branding.

Fish will never discover water. For today's young consumer, color imagery is water: it is everywhere, and it has always been everywhere. Brands have always dazzled with color. Every brand deploys color. Even the rare brand that uses a black and white mark displays a wealth of colorful merchandising or packaging. Go to a supermarket or department store. Pick up a magazine or turn on the TV. Browse the web, or tap to wake your phone. Everywhere brands, and everywhere color.

That wasn't always true in the West, even decades into the Industrial Revolution.[6] In the USA, take the presidency of Andrew Jackson as a benchmark. By this point there were steam engines, and railroads, and factories. The forest was as green, the sea as blue, the rose as red, then as now. But go to a city during the 1830s and step indoors. It's a black, white and drab world. Clothing and furnishings are dark or white. Soldiers might have a colorful uniform and a flag; rich people might have silk dresses and oil paintings; but the ordinary person inhabits a drear, dull environment. There may be no images at all in that ordinary city person's house: the daguerreotype hasn't been invented, and color lithography hasn't diffused. There's brown wood, whitewash, and dark red brick, but that's the palette, indoors.

Can a plump twenty-first-century person, having ample funds and living next to a 24-hour supermarket, understand, even glimpse, how it feels to be a medieval peasant living on a remote holding, months after the harvest failed, as famine threatens? With respect to color, the gap that separates us from our great-great-grandparents looms as large.

From the dawn of branding, consumers have craved color, and clasped images to their hearts. That's why brands moved toward color, sometimes slowly, sometimes begrudging the cost, but inexorably, more and more. Color pleases. And it satisfies a thirst that can't ever be permanently slaked. People hunger after images. Color imagery is deeply pleasurable, and unendingly attractive. Brands must beckon, and please. Therefore brands had no choice but to lavish color on the world, and to fuel an unending explosion of color imagery.

The difficult thing to understand is how thoroughly our world has been transformed, relative to that of our fifth-generation ancestors, and how central brands were to bringing about this transformation, this wealth of color and bounty of imagery. Many past histories of advertising and of consumption have emphasized the persuasive power of imagery. All contemporary accounts of branding nod to the importance of visual branding, and the utility of color. But no prior account of brand advertising has insisted on the human lust for imagery and sheer unadulterated delight in color. Perhaps we go too far in saying "human;" it may only be deracinated moderns, consumers alienated from their labor, cogs in the capitalist machine, whose lust for color and imagery cannot be quenched. Nonetheless, beginning in the middle of the nineteenth century, in the West, consumers' desire for color and imagery has shaped what brands must do, as gravity bends space.

9. Using pictures to brand

Within Part III this was the most difficult chapter to write, because of the vastness of the topic. To keep the task manageable, we applied these rules:

1. Any mechanical factor, anything that can be expressed as a metric – questions of picture size or position or juxtaposition – has been set aside.
   - We also are not concerned here with whether one picture, or two, or more appear on the page; our concern is with the nature of any picture that does appear.
   - Likewise, we don't place much emphasis, in this chapter, on issues of technology, that is, whether a picture is a photograph or an illustration, printed in color or in black and white.
     - However, photography does offer brands a distinct rhetorical possibility, which we will develop.
2. Anything that falls short of being a picture (mere visual elements such as a decorative border) and anything that is more than a picture (charts and diagrams) is given short shrift.
   - For our purposes, a reproduction of the product's package is not a picture. It is a brand. Likewise, however visual, the brand mark is not a picture.
3. Finally, we do little with pictorial content in this chapter. The recalcitrance of content, when pictures are approached rhetorically, is developed in a separate section prior to the main body of the chapter.

There is one other potential source of confusion, as developed next.

RHETORIC OF VISUAL BRANDING VERSUS VISUAL RHETORIC OF ADVERTISING

These two topics are not the same; and to confuse the two in the present volume would gum up the works. The danger of a mix-up is acute in this chapter on pictures.

A visual rhetoric of advertising would examine the specific pictorial devices that appear in an advertising medium, such as print magazines, and assemble these devices into typologies. Such an effort would be incomplete without an accompanying set of typologies for verbal rhetoric, and a bridge between the two, plus a harbor for such other rhetorical devices as escape the Aristotelian dichotomy of visual verses verbal. Such an advertising rhetoric would also have to examine desired outcomes that go beyond branding to include a variety of other marketing goals.[1]

By contrast, a rhetoric of visual branding must be more narrow in its focus. Everything must come back to branding, to the small number of ways that pictures can be used to build a brand, as opposed to the large number of persuasive goals that might potentially be served by ad pictures. Here we must focus not on kinds of pictures, but on the ways that brand managers may deploy pictures to benefit their brand. And in keeping with the structure of this book, that branding through pictures needs to be presented in historical perspective.

DEFINITION

What, then, is a picture? First, a picture is complete in itself. It can stand alone, and be perused for its own sake, without any sense that something is missing. This criterion sets aside decoration and ornament, borders and background. Second, a picture cannot be reduced to numbers. This hurdle rules out charts and diagrams. Third, the rhetorical differences across pictures, the inputs to a rhetorical typology of pictures, cannot be expressed mechanically. The differences among pictures discussed in this chapter require a fully acculturated person to detect. These are differences in what role the picture might play in branding. A human being in possession of all their faculties can readily detect such stylistic differences; a rule-following automaton might not.

As noted in the introduction, most marketing scholarship has been unwilling to deal with this aspect of visual branding. In the realm of marketing science, what cannot be counted does not exist. Only historians and sociologists have taken up the gauntlet of interpreting pictures in ads,[2] of asking what the picture means, and what the advertiser might have hoped to accomplish with it. And only historians with a rhetorical bent would presume to talk about how pictures brand, or the meaning work assigned to pictures within the complex tableau of a print ad page.

This chapter will also be the most tentative and incomplete in the book. We humbly acknowledge to have but scratched the surface of this enormous topic. Although a picture may only be worth a thousand words, it can require thousands more to discuss; Foucault (1970) expends almost

6000 words interpreting a single painting, more than our publisher allotted for this entire chapter. Our discussion will have to stay at a high level, without investigating any micro-operations of pictorial meaning. Here our narrow focus on brand advertising in print comes to the rescue; we have only to lay open the toolkit by which pictures are made to promote brands of ordinary consumer goods, the roles pictures play in this marketing effort. We need not consider the many, many other uses to which pictures may be put. We don't have to say anything about art, or about semiosis.

Unfortunately, we also are not able to contribute much to understanding pictorial content in advertising. That's not because content is irrelevant to visual branding; quite the contrary. Our limitation is self-imposed, and reflects the limits of a classical rhetoric, as developed next.

EXCURSUS: PICTORIAL CONTENT

Here are a few examples of visual branding proceeding through choice of content, with an explanation of why (classical) rhetoric does not apply. In recent years, Corona beer has taken ownership of beach imagery.[3] These images run toward the tropical, showing beaches we suppose do exist somewhere in Mexico (Corona, before it broke out, was one Mexican beer among many). But to anticipate our subsequent discussion of *tertium quid* (see the Epilogue), it is difficult to specify, a priori, which elements allow definitive classification of an image as a "beach picture," or as "a beach picture appropriate to a Corona effort at visual branding." Palm trees will often be present, but need not be; the same for long stretches of sand, or water in a particular shade of blue, or people wearing bathing suits. The problem: pictorial content presents definitional problems of Wittgensteinian proportions.[4]

Skyye vodka is another brand that has taken ownership of a visual vocabulary, no less than Corona has taken ownership of beach imagery. But its imagery, while equally recognizable, is even harder to describe definitively. We might speak of night life and bar scenes, or of women of the night placed in fictive and surreal settings, or of a comic book aesthetic, and get a nod of recognition – if you have a Skyye ad in front of you. But, if you have never seen a Skyye vodka ad, those words are unlikely to sketch a mental image that looks anything like a Skyye ad. Conversely, if you are a liquor drinker who has been exposed to a variety of liquor advertising, including ads for Skyye, you may well recognize a new ad from Skyye as indeed a Skyye ad, and not an ad for Stolichnaya or Bacardi or Gordon's or any other brand of clear spirits. Pictorial content – objects and settings and people – can be put to work for visual branding, because the brand comes to be reliably associated with some pictorial content, and thus, owns it.

Unfortunately, there is no short list of "pictorial content that may be used to brand." Hence, we cannot specify the available means of persuasion with respect to pictorial content. Therefore, there can be no classical rhetoric of the visual branding that proceeds by taking ownership of content. The rhetorician must stand behind this fence, only looking at the vast pasture rolling away on the other side. It's green, it's lush, it would be wonderfully tasty to browse, but we can't go there. This piece of visual branding – and it is a huge chunk – belongs to some other scholarly discipline. Semiotics? Art criticism? It is not for us to say.

With that limit acknowledged, we return to the aspect of pictures in advertising that does lie within the rhetorician's ken: the short list of styles for combining pictures and words in branding efforts, and the small set of options for branding via two-dimensional pictures.

FIRST CUT: PICTURES AND WORDS

Outside of fashion, few ads contain no verbal text at all; and even here, the name of the brand will be stated. Ad pictures play a part within a larger effort; these do not stand alone, as a painting in a museum might. The creator of advertising combines pictures and words in pursuit of the client's goals, expecting and striving to make these to work together. At the highest level, then, we distinguish three roles that the ad picture can play relative to the words in the ad: the picture can be subordinate, coordinate, or superordinate to the words (Table 9.1).

Visual elements that are not pictures – borders, ornaments, backgrounds – anchor the extreme of subordination. We were surprised to find how common decorative borders were during the first period examined, in the earliest years of magazine advertising for national brands (see, for example, the Ivory ad in Figure 2.5 or the Nabisco ad in Figure 2.11). These decorative elements slowly disappear through the second period, in the 1920s, and are almost gone by the 1950s. Like the subordinate use of pictures proper, decorative borders support or adorn the words. The border marks out the words, declaring, "This is my ad, these words bound in this block make up my ad, heed me, stay within these bounds." And the decorative element in borders also adorns the text, providing a quantum of visual pleasure.

This dimension, running from subordinate to superordinate, correlates with size – smaller pictures are more likely to be subordinate – but the association is rough, and grows more imperfect as the picture grows larger. Although small pictures are mostly subordinate, large pictures may also be

Table 9.1   A typology of pictorial gambits in advertising

Role played by picture relative to words	Specific pictorial gambits
Superordinate	Construct a rhetorical figure
	Offer an experience
	Liberate multiple meanings
	Tell a story
	Dramatize
Coordinate	Play on words
	Personify
	Demonstrate
Subordinate	Dangle bait
	Dose with sugar
	Associate
	Illustrate
	Decorate or ornament

subordinate. These pictorial roles also correlate with time – subordinate pictures are more common, and superordinate pictures less common, early in the century – but the association is again approximate. In short, this high-level distinction captures relative importance, which reflects role, which is independent of size, or era, or other correlates.

PICTURES SUBORDINATE TO WORDS

Subordinate pictures either support the words, which carry the selling message, or adorn the words, apart from any substantive contribution to the message. In a supporting role, the picture may illustrate the words ("See, this is what we are talking about"). Here the picture's task is to make visible the topic developed in words. A common example is the picture that shows the product (see Figure 2.18). Different in appearance, but similar in function, is the picture that shows the problem the product aims to solve. In all these examples, the picture documents what the words describe or assert. The picture provides evidence in support of the words. The picture supplies redundancy, in the sense of signal theory, to make errors of reception less likely. The picture provides a second or back-up channel along which to transmit the same message as carried by the text.

Next, a picture may associate the brand with some other valued object or setting by showing the flag, or a tranquil country scene, or a luxurious venue. The association may be hammered home in the words, or so obvious that the words can go about their business without calling out the association. The brand acts as a moon, shining in the valued object's reflected light. Any picture that suggests an association has the potential to change the brand's meaning, along the lines discussed in Chapter 7, the spokescharacter chapter.

We distinguish between associating the brand with objects and settings, versus associating it with a person. Because persons are so complex in the associations they may trigger, association to a person puts the picture in a coordinate rather a subordinate role, as discussed subsequently. We note in passing that the association strategy lies at the root of many cultural critiques of advertising. Critics assume that as the leech weakens its victim by blood loss, so also advertising cheapens the value of those objects and settings that it prostitutes for the benefit of brands.[5]

Next, many ad pictures which take a subordinate role bear only a cursory relationship to the selling message carried by the words. Here the picture serves not so much to support with evidence or association, as to adorn: to dose the words with sugar. The cute puppy may not be meant to associate the brand with soft cuddly things, but rather, to sweeten the brand encounter.

As noted at the end of Chapter 8, people crave imagery. Photography exploded as soon as the daguerreotype was invented. Magazines exploded in circulation once it became possible to mass reproduce imagery. Magazine circulation exploded again when first color and then color photography became feasible to mass reproduce. People like to look at pictures. People love to look at pictures of kittens, puppies, and babies. People willingly gaze long on pictures of beautiful models, elegant homes, elegiac landscapes. This propensity for imagery has received too little emphasis in the history of advertising. Once this propensity is granted, once the essential sweetness of imagery is glimpsed, we see why ads are constructed as they are.

Pictures can serve as bait as well as dose with sugar. Their function need not be to sell in themselves, nor to support or adorn the selling message carried by the words. Pictures may be supplied to grab as well as hold the eye, as the flower offers nectar to pollinator. Although sweetness holds the eye, shock and bewilderment may be required to grab the eye. Whether through sweetness or vividness, here the picture acts mostly as an on-ramp to the words, or as a sticky bit to hold onto the consumer-insect, who is all too ready to buzz off somewhere else.

INTERLUDE: PICTURES IN PSYCHOLOGY

Academic consumer psychology allots only a subordinate role to pictures. Words come first. Study the manipulations used in experiments: these mostly target words.[6] Text is also primary in theoretical accounts of how advertising persuades. For instance, beginning about 1980, consumer psychologists began to dally with all-embracing dualisms. These dualisms fueled a renewed focus on words in ads. Persuasion, it was held, could proceed along a systematic or heuristic, a central or peripheral route. Systematic processing meant verbal claims, an argument from evidence, of the sort that might persuade a rational-choice economist; pictures might provide supporting evidence, but the argument was carried by the words. By contrast, heuristic or peripheral processing meant a casual, hasty act of inference, based on whatever ad elements happened to be noticed in an uninvolved, desultory scan; hence pictures, if pretty, could guide those inferences to favor the brand. No other role for pictures could be imagined in these early consumer psychology theories. The coordinate and superordinate possibilities were ignored.[7]

Note how these formulations, of systematic versus heuristic routes to persuasion, ignore the fifth supporting role of pictures: as bait. Psychologists have good reason to ignore the possibility that pictures exist to dangle bait. In psychological experiments, exposure is forced: diligent, smart student participants are instructed to look over the ad, and, good students that they are, and sitting as they are in a university building where they also take exams, will read those instructions carefully. The experimental booklet may contain nothing other than these verbal instructions plus the ad stimulus, and/or questions about the ad. There may not even be another ad shown; only the one ad that implements the experimental treatment.

This laboratory set-up is the exact opposite of the conditions under which real advertising exposure occurs. For advertisers, the feature that defines their rhetorical situation is the audience's disinclination, and even active avoidance. The consumer did not buy the magazine to peruse sales messages for soap or for breakfast cereal. Therefore, they may well turn the page more quickly if their visual preprocessing indicates, "This page holds an ad full of words." The first priority of any magazine ad must be to engage the consumer, and to prevent them from passing over it or shutting it out. If consumers don't engage with the ad, nothing else good can happen, no matter how brilliant the words.

Again, as we laid out earlier in the Introduction and in Chapter 6, the goal of laboratory work in consumer psychology is to advance theory. By abstracting away from this real-world condition – by forcing exposure – laboratory psychologists gain the ability to generalize across all degrees of voluntary versus forced exposure. Or so they claim. For the pure-bred psychologist, whether exposure is forced or not is only one of countless particulars that might or might not interact with the experimental treatment, all of which can be safely ignored. Or, as once inimitably put by a doctoral candidate: "Real world only special case! Theory – general!"

If a laboratory environment were specially constructed not to force exposure – an unusual design choice in the 1965–2015 period in the USA – then, holds the psychologist, the results might not generalize beyond unforced exposure, that is, to conditions outside of magazine advertising. This leaves both the practitioner and the rhetorician scratching their heads: who cares about studying phenomena outside of advertising? Psychologists' commitment to universality leads them astray, and away from understanding this one phenomenon, the magazine advertising commissioned by familiar national brands, which consumers are so ready to ignore, unless tempted with bait.

As long as the forced exposure paradigm holds, academic psychologists can never discover the bait role of ad pictures. Forced exposure designs can't illuminate the imperative that drives ad design toward the inclusion of, and emphasis on, pictures: to attract and engage, at the outset and as a prerequisite for the remainder of the persuasive attempt. But the rhetorician, keyed to one persuasive situation, easily absorbs the importance of offering bait, and how this imperative might shape ad design.

In partial defense of psychologists: their dismissal of the requirement for ecological validity – their avoidance of the imperative not to force exposure – may be outdated, more than blind. There may once have been a time when magazine advertisements held as much interest, for the ordinary reader, as any piece of fiction or service column. As a case in point, Richard Ohmann (1996) offers this sketch of how magazines might have been read in 1895, by an upwardly mobile middle-class homemaker. He describes a fictive Mrs Johnson, at home in Cleveland on a muggy autumn day, when a copy of *Munsey's* arrives by mail:

> She must get back to her sewing, but not quite yet – there's time to skim the ads first . . . she lingers a bit longer over the ad for Charter Oak ladies' bicycle . . . Eventually she will study the ads for clothing, wallpaper, parquet floors; but the only ad she reads thoroughly now, and with something like the intent to purchase, is for the Autoharp. (p. 2)

Ohmann describes an era, near the beginning of national brand advertising in magazines, where consumers did peruse each page of ads, same as they would peruse any other page of a magazine to which they had decided to subscribe. And if Ohmann is to be believed, this willing perusal occurred in the case of small, fractional-page ads located way, way in the back of the magazine. In our June 1895 copy of *Munsey's* (Ohmann bases his reconstruction on the October issue), most of the ads are placed after page 320. The first bicycle ad in this issue occurs six pages further: it is 1 inch high, spans the bottom of the page (about 5 inches wide), and is mostly text. The next bicycle ad is a dozen pages further, a quarter-page in size. Altogether, there are more than 60 pages of ads, most fractions of a page, so that four to eight ads appear on each page, at least 250 in all.

If Ohmann's reconstruction is accurate, then consumers of this era were willing to peruse small, text-heavy magazine ads, for brands, there at the beginning. This commitment to perusing ads as well as editorial would validate the psychologist's assumption that it doesn't matter whether ad exposure in the lab is forced or not; there must be plenty of both kinds of ad encounters, out there in the world. Or so the psychologist needs to claim.

We don't know whether Ohmann sketches a true picture of how mass market magazines were read in 1895; but we are certain that now, a century later, consumers do not willingly peruse large numbers of ads in today's descendants of *Munsey's* magazine.[8] Brand advertisers today are lucky if they can get the consumer to pause for a moment on even a full-page, full-color ad replete with clever and seductive imagery.

PICTURES COORDINATE WITH WORDS

When coordinate with words, pictures go beyond supplying supporting evidence, or dosing with sugar, to more actively supplement or leverage brand claims made in words. The before-and-after picture provides one example of how pictures can be coordinate with words. Here the picture demonstrates the truth of what the words assert: we see that she is prettier now than before she got hold of that cosmetic; we see how much cleaner that sink is now, with this brand, than it had ever been with that other brand. In most cases of visual demonstration, the picture plays a coordinate role. The picture itself offers a claim and even an argument.

Here we must acknowledge a technological constraint on what can be done with pictures. An illustration is no less a picture than a photograph; but that hackneyed nostrum, that seeing is believing, only holds for photographs. A consumer can readily dismiss an illustration as fiction, or as naught but a wish. A hand-drawn illustration may have been biased by the artist's intent to deceive.[9] Later in this chapter we will discuss circumstances where this intrinsic weakness of hand-made illustrations flips to a strength; but here, when the goal is a pictorial argument coordinate with that of the verbal text, illustrations are universally incompetent. Only a photograph can credibly claim: this is real. And that claim becomes more credible, the better the caliber of the magazine's printing technology, the more advanced the camera lens and the film, the more sophisticated the lighting, and the more skillful the staging. Put bluntly, better and better technology for faking is required to support photographic claims to show the real. And, after enough technological innovation, color photographs can more credibly claim to be real than can black and white photos.

The technological hurdle for photorealism is substantial. That's why we spent considerable time in Part I calibrating the technological capabilities achieved in each era. Poorly focused, muddily lit, clumsily staged, and indifferently printed photos do not shout "Real!" Pictorial argument is less likely the further back one goes in the history of brand advertising, in part because mounting a visual argument depends on a technological substrate that took decades to jell. Turning this observation on its head: one explanation for why ads in the 1980s and after contain so many so big pictures is that technology had finally advanced to the point of making pictorial argument possible, and even easy to accomplish. A further implication: pictures are powerfully persuasive, perhaps intrinsically more so than words can be, however cunningly selected and arranged. Once photographic technology had advanced enough for pictures to realize their persuasive potential, brands jumped on that bandwagon.

This line of reasoning matures into a three-part explanation for the phenomenon that Pollay (1985) was among the first to observe: that pictures in magazine ads have grown in size, decade after decade, at the expense of words. The three parts are: (1) photographic and printing technologies were advancing throughout the period; (2) advertising clutter worsened year by year, requiring advertisers to dangle bait ever more energetically; (3) photorealistic pictures are inherently more persuasive than words. Reversing the sequence: the picture-superiority effect, while intrinsic, had initially been checked by technological limitations, which slowly gave way, even as the baleful effects of ad clutter and the need for pictorial bait grew more pressing. Net of these three developments, pictures took up more and more of the magazine ad, and the space allotted to words shrank and shrank.

Next, when the picture includes a person, and makes that person a protagonist, the picture will likely play a coordinate role, or even be superordinate.[10] All protagonists, human or creature, potentially assume the role of endorser when they appear in an ad. It is not necessary that a user, expert, or celebrity be portrayed as giving an explicit testimonial. Mere presence may be seen as endorsement of this product by that kind of person. Therefore, when a person appears as protagonist, the viewer, in however truncated form, draws inferences that move from visible personal characteristics to attributed product features and benefits. Psychology teaches that humans have entire cognitive modules devoted to person perception. As evolved primates, making inferences about the people we encounter is a big part of how we use our brains. People like to look at pictures, we have argued throughout; but people find pictures of other people especially absorbing, and remarkably rich in inferential possibility.

In rhetorical terms, every person who appears in an ad as a protagonist is approached by the viewer as metaphor,[11] and interpreted for what they might reveal about what this product offers, the lifestyle constellation in which it fits, and the life projects it might serve.[12] Any and all aspects of the person may serve as a vehicle for the metaphor: if the cowboy has pitted, wrinkled, weathered skin, then he is strong not pretty, true not fancy, like the flavor of this cigarette, and like me, my aspirational self. Because persons serve as such rich metaphors, and provide such a feedstock for inferences, when ads show pictures of people the picture plays at least a coordinate role. And if the words are few, the picture may be superordinate.

We introduced the idea of metaphorical transfer in Chapter 7 on spokes-characters. Our point: a brand doesn't have to have a spokes-character – a creature or person that appears regularly – to benefit from the proclivity to see people as metaphors. Each person or creature who appears in an ad as a protagonist will be approached as a metaphor for the brand. On the other hand, we should not overestimate the power of any single portrayal. The metaphorical impact on the brand, of a person who appears once in one ad, will be small. If a brand really wants to harness the metaphorical transfer that flows from putting a person in an ad, a spokes-character should be constructed and hammered home. But the metaphorical impact of a person-protagonist is never zero.

In conceptual terms, brand advertising, and visual branding, are akin to a mechanical dishwasher which hurls millions of little drops, each carrying a tiny amount of a powerful chemical reagent, against the dirty dishes, over and over. It is the sustained mass bombardment, plus the reagent, that makes the dishes clean enough for the consumer to see their reflection. Take the same tray of dirty dishes outside, and throw one full bucket of plain water against them. Not much cleaning will result, even though a bucket contains millions of drops, and a greater quantity of water than used by the dishwasher. It takes mass advertising, sustained over time, and charged with the reagent of metaphorical transfer, for the brand to emerge cleanly in the eye of the consumer.

Next, a different example of how pictures play a coordinate role occurs when a picture twists the meaning of plain words. Pictures can force words into a pun. This happens when the picture illustrates a second, less likely meaning for the words that appear in a headline or caption. Such a picture destabilizes the meaning of the words. In the best cases, that makes the familiar strange, and sets up a fruitful chain of inferences about the brand, which moves the brand up within the consumer's consideration set. In less successful instances, the verbal–visual pun is naught but arm-waving, a jumping up and down, like those modified wind socks, set up street-side to advertise a store sale, that waver and snap in the breeze, lure and bait.[13]

PICTURES SUPERORDINATE TO WORDS

A style of picture that can play a coordinate role may also play a superordinate role, if the picture is big enough, or made central enough, and the words are few enough. Conversely, subordinate pictures tend to stay in that role, no matter how big. The next few styles of picture can be thought of as spanning coordinate and superordinate roles.

A good example of a style that sits astride this amorphous boundary is the picture that dramatizes the brand's action. A fine line separates vivid demonstrations from drama. When sufficiently intense, a dramatic demonstration may boost the picture into a superordinate role. Drama, rather than demonstration, also becomes an appealing option when the product is positioned less in terms of functional benefits, and more in terms of subjective, emotional, and lifestyle benefits. You can demonstrate that soap gets hands clean; but you can dramatize how a moisturizer brings romance.[14]

Drama is hard to achieve in print, as compared to broadcast; but not impossible to arrange. To instill drama requires more than a still life. A dramatic picture requires character and plot: an agent, typically a person, must be captured in the midst of action; and this action must develop the meaning of that agent, must reveal elements of character and relationships. In short, drama and narrative go hand in hand. If the picture tells a story, there can be drama. If the picture is static, drama is unlikely.

Here again, technological innovation obtrudes. The beginnings of national brand advertising slightly predate the cinema. In 1895, consumers – the mass market – had little experience with narrative or dramatic pictures in print, because they had no experience of moving pictures. True, a painter might depict the battle of Waterloo, and that painting may be approached as drama, as a story in motion, the cavalry about to charge. The possibility of narrative is inherent in two-dimensional representation.[15] But there was not much exposure to such pictures on the part of ordinary people.

Once movies became a regular part of everyday life, large numbers of people became accustomed to photography in motion. Although the 24 stills that pass by each second in a movie are not seen as still photographs but as seamless motion, nonetheless, to watch movies is to become accustomed to drama and narrative composed from photographs. Few film directors set the camera up and let it run uninterrupted. Instead, many, many shots are taken, from different angles using multiple cameras, and varying in length; these individual photographs are craftily edited together so that the viewer experiences a continuously unfolding story. But that is not what the viewer's retina sees: they see a succession of photographs juxtaposed, and have learned to extract a story from these photos, just as directors and producers have learned which photographic sequences can be experienced effortlessly as the unfolding of a story, and not as a bunch of stills jumbled together, or as disconnected strobe flashes.

Once photography and printing had developed enough to achieve photorealism – a point sometime after World War II, we estimate – consumers had simultaneously reached a point where they had become expert movie viewers. Then television was introduced, and consumers spent even more hours per week immersed in narrative and dramatic photography. From that point, it became easier and easier for advertisers to construct a dramatic picture in print, if their rhetorical analysis of the persuasive situation indicated that such an approach might be appropriate. The point: in the beginning, it was not easy to construct dramatic pictures for magazine ads. Neither producers nor consumers knew how. A dramatic picture is a performance, and both producers and consumers have to play their parts to pull it off.[16]

Next, pictures that play a superordinate or at least coordinate role may exploit the multi-vocal character of images. Words can state a single, unitary proposition. Although the theoretical extreme of denotation – a sentence whose words have no connotations and that advances one proposition only – is seldom seen outside of mathematics, nonetheless, verbal text may be tightly constrained in meaning, especially, as in advertising, when the purpose of the words is clear.[17] Pictures can never be so tightly scripted. Pictures don't and can't make statements: "statement," as a descriptor, can only be predicated of verbal text. Pictures permit, encourage, and guide inferences. The guidance may be relatively strong and tight in circumstances where the intent of the communication is clear and the picture plays a subordinate role. But more commonly, encouragement is ample but guidance is loose, and grows increasingly minimal, as one moves from pictures of people, to narrative pictures, to figurative and fantastic pictures.

As we move further along the axis, to pictures that mostly play superordinate roles, we come to the final two categories: the experiential picture and the figurative picture. The experiential picture offers up a consumer good in its own right, separate from what it advertises. These pictures are analogous to artworks, which don't have to have a purpose, or promote anything outside of engagement. Here the advertiser supplies a picture that provides the consumer an opportunity to enjoy an experience. The goal is to have elements of that experience either transfer to, or otherwise promote the brand; but unlike a subordinate picture, which only provides a dose of sugar and intends only a conventional sweetness or prettiness, the experiential picture has more depth and complexity. It may even be grotesque, or transgress in other ways. Such pictures are constructed to engage the consumer. The reasoning: time on the picture is time with the brand.

We first discovered the experiential use of pictures in our work on fashion advertising (Phillips and McQuarrie 2010). By at least the 1980s, magazine advertising for fashion clothing, of the sort that appears in *Vogue* or *Vanity Fair*, had adopted a uniform style across brands. In these fashion ads a photographic picture occupied the entire page, and text other than the brand name never appeared. Plus, there might be well over 100 pages of such ads in a single issue, or 200, or 300 or more. The uniformity and abundance of these fashion ads posed a problem: how could a brand break through the clutter? In response, we observed many brands to resort to what may broadly be described as negativity, and more specifically characterized as grotesque, transgressive, bizarre, and even shocking depictions. Why?

Negativity poses an acute conceptual problem for any simple psychological theory of how pictures work in advertising. The goal of advertising is to promote the brand: to move it in a positive direction. Negativity is acceptable insofar as it shows the problem the brand solves: you may promote a brand of aspirin by showing the headache the brand will make to go away. Negativity is also acceptable if attributed to competitive brands: you may portray their failure. And mild negativity is acceptable as a rhetorical maneuver, in the trope known as epanorthosis (McQuarrie and Mick 1996): you may self-deprecate, or understate, as an opening line, the better to promote yourself in the closing. But from a psychological stance, you dare not show your brand as ugly, despoiled, or disarrayed. Yet, many fashion advertisements appeared designed to present exactly that impression. How can a grotesque picture promote the brand, when the role of the picture is limited to heuristic or peripheral cue, to a subordinate dose of sugar?

The answer: pictures can do much more for a brand than bait the eye, dose with sugar, or provide an illustration to support the words. In Phillips and McQuarrie (2010) we drew on a famous quote of Tolstoy to argue that grotesque pictures could break through the clutter and differentiate a fashion brand within a sea of pretty faces.[18] We argued further that the grotesque – artful negativity – could be powerfully engaging to consumers, encouraging either immersion in the picture, as in art, or storytelling about the picture. Either leads to time on brand, and potentially to differentiation.

To pick up the thread we traced earlier, in discussing drama: some pictures can be grasped as narratives. The consumer approaches these as stills from a movie, a movie they are led to reconstruct or unreel forward. Narratives provide even more fertile ground for inference than photographs of people. If the advertised brand has been properly integrated into the suggested narrative, the ad powerfully supports the desired positioning. There is no way to untell a story that the consumer has told himself. Narrative pictures supercharge the fundamental semiotic characteristic of pictures: their loosely bounded, and hence protean meaning. The inferences that may be drawn from a narrative picture are only loosely scripted. That gives the consumer control, which engages them, which works in favor of the brand.

What fashion ad pictures taught us was that it might not be so easy to construct an effective narrative picture, a picture that the target consumer will willingly embroider into a story. Pretty people posed with pretty things amidst pretty scenery might not suffice, as but a tale told too many times already. The picture might have to be grotesque, fantastic, fictive in the mildly pejorative sense. And not every product category will permit use of that style of picture. This rhetorical possibility, the picture designed to be experienced as art or story, may not always be available.

The final category is the figurative picture, the representation which is not realistic, but artfully deviant along precise lines. These pictures are not so much taken by the consumer to be metaphorical, as deliberately constructed to inject metaphor into the mind stream, to fizz the brain like Alka-Seltzer.

We've been investigating visual metaphors, or to use a broader term, figurative pictures, for more than 20 years. There is not space in this chapter to recapitulate the several sub-typologies we've developed for figurative pictures (Box 9.1 presents one of these typologies); and this would in any case violate our pledge to focus on visual branding rather than visual rhetoric in advertising. Better to profile that research stream, so that you may follow up with any paper of interest:

1. Initially, McQuarrie and Mick (1999) attempted to port their typology for verbal rhetorical figures (McQuarrie and Mick 1996) to the visual sphere. Additional empirical findings for that differentiation of visual figures appear in McQuarrie and Mick (2003) and McQuarrie and Mick (2009). McQuarrie subsequently concluded that visual figures

---

BOX 9.1   A TYPOLOGY OF VISUAL RHETORICAL FIGURES

Judging the earlier effort in McQuarrie and Mick (1999) unsatisfactory, in Phillips and McQuarrie (2004) we made a second attempt to identify the available means for making a picture artfully deviant. The concept of artful deviation draws on Berlyne's (1971) idea that some visual designs, such as incongruous combinations, are more likely to trigger engagement and arousal.

We identified nine different ways an image can be artfully deviant. These are generated by crossing two dimensions: visual structure and meaning operation. Three kinds of deviant visual structure were identified: juxtaposition, fusion, and replacement. Each of these can be arranged to trigger one of three meaning operations: assertions that the juxtaposed, fused, or replaced objects are connected, similar, or opposite. Examples of each type of visual figure are given in Phillips and McQuarrie (2004).

In the context of visual branding, the distinctions among the nine types of visual figure pale before the property that unites them all: artful, clever deviation. When a brand inserts a visual figure into its ad, it is made to seem more interesting and engaging. If adding a puppy, baby, or pretty face is analogous to dosing with sugar, inserting a visual figure is like shaking salt and pepper on the brand, or sprinkling a few flakes of chili. Sugar gives pleasure, but so does spice.

Visual figures are stimulating; they spice things up. In a world cluttered with ads, with consumers working as hard as they can to ignore the thousands of ads raining down on them, a visual figure offers a promise of reward, something to engage the viewer, while also inviting and guiding inferences down the desired path. Sugar and spice: a two-fer.

---

deserved their own *sui generis* typology, rather than one carried over from the verbal realm.

2. Phillips and McQuarrie (2004) proposed such a typology. As shown in Box 9.1, it took the form of a matrix created by crossing visual structure (juxtaposition, fusion, replacement) with meaning operation (connection, similarity, opposition). They gave examples of each of the nine types of figure so distinguished, and developed propositions about the expected impact of each on consumer response.

3. Subsequently McQuarrie (2008b) suggested a larger set of more rigorously derived possibilities for visual structure, without expanding the set of meaning relations.

Both approaches to differentiating visual figures have been taken up by other authors, who have variously suggested alternatives or challenges or supplements to the typologies, and/or collected empirical data to test each framework.[19]

BRIEF HISTORICAL SKETCH

Previous chapters have captured most of the evolution in the use of pictures. Here we'll touch briefly on the categories introduced in this chapter.
A century ago most pictures played a subordinate role relative to words.
The type case for ads prior to the 1920s was a black and white picture of
the product sitting there doing nothing: a still life, indicating only "See,
this is what we are talking about."[20] On the other hand, all the rhetorical
categories make an appearance early on, especially in the case of larger
ads, such as appeared on the back cover, which often contained a single
ad, even a century ago when full-page ads were rare. On the back cover, it
was not rare to see a huge picture offered primarily as a dose of sugar, or
less commonly as a picture to be experienced. Pictures of people were used
from the beginning, mostly in portrait mode, but sometimes in a more narrative or dramatic way. Demonstrations also appear early.

The pictorial styles that become less and less common, the farther back
one goes, are the dramatic, narrative, and figurative styles, including in
the latter those pictures designed to twist the meaning of words.[21] These
perhaps required a degree of visual sophistication on the part of the consumer that was slow to emerge. Even the figurative style was never totally
absent from ads a century ago; but its bloom came late.

Epilogue: conceptual puzzles

The four main sections of this chapter each conclude with discussion questions. The introductory material in each section is designed to set up those questions. We offer no answers in this epilogue. Raising questions is the whole point of it.

HOW DO PICTURES MEAN?

The ad for Gillette "Just Whistle" razors in Figure E.1 provides an opportunity to contrast historical and rhetorical approaches against other approaches to the analysis of visual imagery, such as the cultural, aesthetic, or psychoanalytic. We begin with a rhetorical analysis.

The entire ad consists of a picture bled to the edge of the page. It shows an uncluttered scene of a young woman in a bathing suit, reclining on a towel laid on beach sand. It is a dynamic picture with narrative elements. She is about to take off – or has just put on – her sunglasses for a better look. She looks at the figure whose shadow falls on her; a man, we presume, who has walked over to her side. The overall layout is more characteristic of the 1980s than the 2000s because the copy, although inscribed on the picture, is too voluminous. On the other hand, the layout is more characteristic of the 1980s than the 1950s because the picture takes up the whole of the ad, and the headline is in a custom script typeface, which is consistent with the face used in the brand block, itself made up of the package. The picture also shows a fidelity to skin tones, and an overall richness of color, that was not obtainable in the 1950s.

A complete rhetorical analysis requires that we attend to the headline, which states the brand name, in addition to discussing the visual elements and their arrangement. The first author is too old, now, to know if young men still respond to attractive young women, encountered on the beach or in other public spaces, by whistling; such an act today, on an American college campus, might get you hauled up on charges of sexual harassment.[1] But 34 years ago, and in the decades prior, in movies or on television in the 1950s, 1960s, or 1970s, such whistling was a common trope in North American culture. Whistles were positive feedback, testimony that sexual

Figure E.1   Gillette ad showing the uncertainty of pictorial interpretation

attractiveness had been demonstrated, or even an involuntary and compelled response to female beauty, albeit of bodily form more than visage.

Rhetorically, then, the brand promise is, "If you want to attract the sexual attention and esteem of males, shave your legs using this razor. You will look as beautiful and desirable as this woman here." And this aging heterosexual male rhetorician has to agree that yes, that is one gorgeous, shapely young woman lying there. Her right nipple is subtly suggested, and its visibility suggests a translucency to the garment that does not so much attract the eye as rivet it. Her golden skin tones are more fantasy than reality, seldom seen outside an airbrushed centerfold.

And here we come to the first conundrum of visual interpretation: I don't subscribe to *Good Housekeeping* (*GH*), and I don't buy razors designed for women. I'm not the target. *GH* has few male readers, now or then, and it is difficult to imagine that Gillette intends to sell many of its women-targeted razors to men, when Gillette has so many other razors designed for male shaving. Therefore, it doesn't matter how I respond to the young lady shown in the ad. I'm not the audience.

Keep in mind Plato's slam on rhetoricians: that we only care what works. From a rhetorical standpoint, this ad will fail, unless the female reader of *GH*, who may be 5 to 15 years older, and as many pounds heavier, as compared to the young model in the ad, responds to this image as aspirational, as worthy of emulation, as a desirable image of who she might be, or once was. If so, the rhetorical analysis is largely finished: the strategy used falls under the heading of "sold like soap," one of countless examples in advertising of how a mundane personal care item can be connected to deeply held dreams of life success. The reader dreams that she can compel the attention of prospective mates, fetch them the way a whistle brings a dog running. The picture begs to be experienced; the viewer is invited to weave a fantasy about what will happen next between the young woman on the beach and the man drawn to her.

With the rhetorical analysis made visible, we next set out and compare other perspectives on the imagery in the ad. From a feminist cultural studies perspective, this ad is enraging: it's a piece of sexist trash. For Gawd's sake, the male literally overshadows her. The woman is totally objectified; she strives only to be subjected to his gaze. She's pinned there like a butterfly, with as much freedom. The real brand promise, or threat: "Here's how to subjugate yourself to male dominion."

The psychoanalyst will see things still differently. His eye will be drawn to the huge phallus stretching up from the shadow's crotch to nestle in the girl's armpit (wait, you thought that was the shadow of the male's arm, hand in pocket? But 1980s bathing suits didn't have side pockets, did they?). The theme of taking off clothes, of preparing for sexual congress, is also cued by the removal of her sunglasses. The (Freudian) psychoanalyst will go on to note how the shadow's crotch is right next to her rump, and conclude that this is a picture of imminent sexual activity, constructed to lure the eye by an appeal to repressed desire.

If we have written the preceding two paragraphs correctly, the (female) reader will have been nodding vigorously at the first, while shaking her head at the second. But both interpretations are problematic, and for the same reason. The underlying problem will emerge if we first introduce a fourth perspective on the image, from aesthetics.

By aesthetics we mean the psychology-based aesthetics of Berlyne (1971). For a practitioner of this school, the salient features of the Gillette image are to be found in what is visible on the page. First he will note how the woman's figure forms a cross with the man's shadow, a cross that is elaborated into an asymmetric star by means of the towel which also crosses the shadow, light to its dark. Next, the aesthetician will note the repetition of angles, the way her cocked elbow echoes her bent knee, and the zigzag contours that link them. He will go on to note the sheer number of corners, triangles, and trapezoids created by the crossed figures, and the way these sharp points play up and set off the young woman's curves. The aesthetician will conclude that what the advertiser has done here is create a dynamic image that sizzles with formal energy from the interplay of sharp points and soft curves. Yes, she's a beautiful girl in a revealing bathing suit lying open to our gaze; but you have no idea how boring such a photo could be, that showed no more. This magazine is full of beautiful women, as are all women's magazines by this decade. An ad picture, no matter what its content, has to be artfully constructed if it is to succeed in its rhetorical purpose, which is to draw the eye, and mayhap hold it a bit, so that the advertisement can deliver its message. The formal structure of this photo is artful. Its arrangement of shapes has been carefully designed.

The aesthetic interpretation is the only one that approaches the picture as comprised of lines and shapes and contours and colors. It anchors discussion on what is visible, there on the page. All the other perspectives introduce ideas from outside the picture. We tarted up the psychoanalytic perspective to make it risible, but the feminist and rhetorical perspectives are as guilty of importing meaning to the picture, of finding meanings that are not in the picture until tied onto it by the mind of the viewer. If Freudian psychoanalysis were to give a correct account of human being – few believe so today, but it was not always thus – then its interpretation of the placement of the man's shadow, and its phallic form, may also be correct. But if Freudian psychoanalysis is not correct about repressed desire, and how pictures can harness the energy that goes into that repression, then the interpretation is laughable. Ah, but if the discipline of feminist culture studies is not correct about the objectifying effect of the male gaze, and how patriarchy is sustained by subjugating women's bodies to the desires and wants of men, then the feminist interpretation of the picture is also untenable.

The rhetorical interpretation is equally vulnerable, pulling in the cultural meme of heterosexual whistling, and making assumptions about the demographics of who reads *GH*, the female desire to appear attractive, and more. Rhetoricians are more shameless, of course; they never cared about visual semiotics, nor had any investment in a theory of how pictures mean. For a rhetorician, this picture was constructed to promote a brand. The advertiser's intent is clear, and thus the purpose of the picture is clear. Any act of meaning construal by the viewer that would cause the ad to be deemed a success by the advertiser has plausibility; and plausible is as good as it gets, when a rhetorician plays the game of finding the meaning of a picture. Perhaps the brand promise is not that men will whistle at you, but that you can just whistle, whereupon men will appear for your inspection, come to heel like a pet, once you have the beautiful legs obtained through this razor. A fantasy of power.

The impregnability of the aesthetic perspective comes at a cost: it allows for no semantic meaning to be drawn off the non-linguistic elements that make up the picture. But every attempt to construct semantic meaning from elements other than words must be fraught. Semantic meaning is never in the picture; it has to be carried over by the viewer. Pictures don't mean anything, in the way that well-constructed sentences composed of words always do mean something. But pictures do invite the viewer to bring semantic interpretation to bear, and each picture may be said to beckon, from over here, but not over there, so that not any meaning can be imported.

The final piece: the consumer who viewed the Gillette ad in 1981 was a member of the fourth generation of consumers to be exposed to countless ad pictures; today's consumers are members of the fifth generation. Hold that thought. We've argued in this section that picture interpretation is culturally shaped, a learned rather than native capacity. That's not a new idea,[2] however inconvenient it may be to linguists or rational-choice economists. And it's not a point confined to pictures – the notion that the reader plays an essential role is old hat in the literary sphere. But few would argue that today's readers are better at reading Shakespeare than were Matthew Arnold or Samuel Johnson. Few would argue that Thomas Pynchon or Ernest Hemingway are better storytellers than Daniel Defoe or Henry Fielding, or that Pynchon and Hemingway can tell a story that would have gone right over the head of an eighteenth-century reader.

By contrast, we may suppose that the fourth generation of consumers ever to be exposed to mass pictorial persuasion, in all the history of the world, has developed new skills and competencies for responding to pictures, capacities not widely distributed among ordinary people in 1890 or 1920. Consumers would have gotten more skilled only if advertisers kept pushing out the boundaries; and advertisers would have gone down this route only to the extent that they believed consumers had acquired enough skill to respond. The process is iterative and recursive: pictorial persuasion evolved ecologically. As an advertiser, you can do a lot more with pictures now. As a consumer, you can do a lot more with pictures too. It's not clear that scholars have caught up.

Discussion questions: How can we know what a picture means? How can we test the validity of any interpretation of some picture that appears in an advertisement? Or, might this indeterminacy of meaning be inherent in any attempt at communication, verbal or non-verbal? How different are pictures versus sentences, in terms of how we interpret any one instance? See Sperber and Wilson (1986) for a provocative challenge to the idea that either words or pictures form a code.

BRAND AS *TERTIUM QUID*

Legal thinking follows a different track than marketing science. Although seldom remarked, the difference is important when thinking about brands. Branding, as the search for ownable and effective accoutrements, is easily encompassed within the day-to-day legal reasoning found in court decisions. Courts are routinely called upon to decide who owns what, and to rule whether some property right has been infringed. It is a short step from adjudicating disputes about real property to ruling whether a particular graphic design – for instance, adding a red sole to a woman's high-heeled shoe, or making a pill purple in color[3] – is owned by one brand, or freely available to any manufacturer. It doesn't matter how intangible the accoutrement. Legislation plus case law plus common law provides a rich matrix of reasoning upon which legal thinking may draw. And that is all judges have to do: reason their way to a decision about what is and is not owned by the brand. A brand owns whatever can be supported by a line of reasoning tight enough, and anchored well enough in past rulings, to satisfy other judges. It is not necessary to use the scientific analyses seen in physics, or to have a quantitative model of what a brand owns.

Marketing scientists labor under much tighter constraints. They must capture brand in an equation; and theoretical equations are meaningless unless tied to measurements. Betty Crocker must be measured somehow;

and these measurements must be organized into a model sufficiently descriptive to decide about any new visual representation whether it is consistent with the Betty Crocker brand or not; or, in the case of copycat attempts by competitors, whether the overlap is large enough to infringe.

The problem: most models in marketing science, consistent with its physics heritage, take the form of decomposition models. A brand or other theoretical entity is modeled in terms of its parts. Marketing scientists have no problem with theorizing unobservables: it's not the intangibility of brand that causes problems. Unobservable components are addressed probabilistically. A familiar example is the structural equations model that underlies confirmatory factor analysis.[4] Here one connects an unobservable theoretical entity to concrete measurements by applying to each measure a formula of the form $ax + e$, where x is the observed metric. For instance, a relevant metric to determine whether an image belongs to Betty Crocker might be how maternal this image is judged to be. In the model, a is a coefficient that may be high or low, and it indexes how perspicuous the concrete metric of maternal is, relative to grasping the total meaning of Betty Crocker. The third term of the model, e or error, is a random variable intended to capture the fallibility of measurement. The measures themselves might be seven-point scales completed by students in a rating task.

In a typical structural equations account, we'd supplement maternal with several more metrics – perhaps mature, and maybe also sweet-tempered, each with its own $ax + e$ formula. Betty Crocker-ness is then calculated from these metrics as a latent theoretical variable which reflects, but is not a simple sum of, the metrics chosen and the $ax + e$ formulae applied to each.

To complete the picture, in the typical empirical study we wouldn't only measure Betty Crocker, but might obtain measures of the Pillsbury dough-boy too. And we'd probably measure some response to the brand as well, maybe loyalty, or intentions to purchase.[5] Given a measure of consumer response, we could compare the impact of substituting a more versus a less maternal image, if we had to draw a new visage for Betty Crocker; that is, with the model we can measure the impact of changes in visual branding on consumer response.

We could complicate the model further. In divining the total meaning of the Betty Crocker brand, we don't have to limit ourselves to spokes-character traits; we could throw in brand colors, the spoon now featured as part of the Betty Crocker trade dress, and any other accoutrement of the brand. And we could add other brands beyond Betty Crocker and Pillsbury, and include other consumer responses, or even antecedents to brand perceptions, such as gender, ethnicity, baking experience, and many more. But these would at best be enrichments; they wouldn't change the structure of the model.

Do we capture the meaning of the Betty Crocker brand through this procedure? And what would be the test of success in this endeavor? One possible test: the model picks out the visages which have been used by General Mills to instantiate Betty Crocker, and rejects other female visages drawn from a random inventory of Caucasian female faces old enough to be a head of household, and dated to the same eras. If the model could not satisfy this test – if it didn't have low rates of false positives and false negatives in such a task – then how could it be judged to have captured Betty Crocker-ness?

A second test: if we needed to update the Betty Crocker portrait (this updating has occurred more than once) the model should be able to rank order candidate portraits, ginned up by artists, according to which would be the better choice. As a practical matter a spokes-character depiction is updated by having an artist generate multiple candidate sketches. The branding consultancy and the brand management team decide which subset of sketches they like best; then these preliminary sketches go through a further winnowing, perhaps including consumer testing, until one portrait is selected as the best option, to be propagated from that point as the new Betty Crocker.

A good structural equations model of the Betty Crocker brand should be able to assist in selecting among images. Except, how could it? With consumer ratings input, the model could indicate how globally similar each new candidate sketch is to the existing Betty Crocker portrait, or even tap the central tendency among the half-dozen portraits used by General Mills over the past few decades. But what drives the enterprise of updating the Betty Crocker portrait is the belief that the current portrait is no longer right, and must somehow change, without sacrificing the brand equity built up through that portrait and its predecessors. The new portrait can't be too different, it must "look like" Betty Crocker today; but maximizing similarity with the old portrait is not the driving goal.

Brand managers, human beings empowered with all their faculties, know how to solve this problem. Creative artists first immerse themselves in the brand and its past representations, and then generate sketches which they can tell themselves are new and fresh images of Betty Crocker, but are nonetheless images of her, and nobody else. In vetting candidates, managers and consultants negotiate with the artist(s) and each other, in the same way that opposing legal counsel negotiate their dispute with each other and the presiding judge. Eventually a decision gets made. There's no way to know at the time whether it's optimal, good or even correct; but the brand managers and consultants will be able to explain why the decision went down as it did. Time will tell whether the new portrait of Betty Crocker is judged a success, and by what standard, same as court decisions, in hindsight, emerge as sound or flawed, upheld or reversed on appeal.

Legal thinkers benefit from not being tied to decompositional models. In court decisions on trade dress, out on the bleeding edge of what the brand owns and what it does not, legal scholarship falls back on the concept of a *tertium quid*. The original meaning of this Latin phrase was "third thing." In a typical instance, one party to a debate might claim that everything in the world is either living or dead. Their opponent, if unhappy with this maneuver, would hold out for a *tertium quid*: entities that were neither living nor dead (for example, viruses). In its more modern usage, the idea of a *tertium quid* is captured in such phrases as "the whole is more than the sum of its parts."

By extension, the meaning of a brand, and the boundaries on this meaning, can't be built up from component parts. There's always something more to Betty Crocker than can be specified by any weighted assemblage of maternal, mature, and sweet, or any number of such metrics. People embedded in the local culture and experienced in these matters, and exercising the full suite of human faculties, have no difficulty in discerning, "Yes, Betty Crocker is all those things, but she's something more as well, and that sketch on the right better captures her *tertium quid* than any other sketch up on the wall." Another human being in the room may disagree, and the dispute will have to be negotiated;[6] but it will be negotiated, somehow, much as judges will eventually decide for one party or the other.

Brand, as an identity not coextensive with any of its instantiations, nor definable in terms of its parts, is indigestible within a conventional marketing science framework. In this section we've attempted to highlight those aspects of brand that challenge the philosophy of science underlying conventional marketing theory, using legal reasoning as a foil. And the problem does lie there at the root: with the philosophy of science that dominates the leading journals in marketing, advertising, and consumer research.

Scientism is abroad in the land. It infects business schools and the social sciences. One part physics envy, one part physics triumphalism, this scientism demands that everything that can be known, can be known mathematically. Equations *uber alles*. This scientism forgets that courts and judges struggle every day without benefit of equations, but nonetheless consider their decisions to be knowledgeable and reasonable. For that matter, how could legal reasoning ever be scientific, universal, when everything that comes before the courts is particular?

Discussion questions: (1) Are brands more like atoms, or more like court decisions? Explain. (2) If legal reasoning that goes unquantified is fatally flawed, then "historical knowledge" is probably a non sequitur. Explain the connection. (3) Is scientific knowledge defined by equations tied to measures? Or might that be a rhetorically slanted characterization on our part, in which case, what would be a better way to characterize the conditions for scientific knowledge?[7]

INTERTEXTUALITY

This is a fancy word for the idea that the meaning of one ad, or one brand, or one visual element, depends on which other ads, brands, and visual elements compete for consumer response. Meaning depends on context.

Intertextuality can be developed by examining the typefaces that appear in competing brand marks. Recall that typeface is the type case for a non-linguistic element that can carry semantic content. Recall also our discussion a few pages back of the difficulty of providing a secure and incontestable meaning for a picture or any other non-verbal candidate to carry semantic content. The tendency with typeface, as we saw in the Henderson et al. (2004) study, has been to fasten meanings directly onto the typeface. That attribution denies intertextuality.

Consider Pepsi. Once upon a time, it used a calligraphic, flowing script in its mark similar to that used by Coca-Cola today (Table E.1). At that junction, around 1900, a large number of brands applied such calligraphic treatment to the lettering of their marks; it was as common then as boldfaced marks today. Many brands of that era were proper names (Hambleton 1987), so to style the brand's mark as a signature made perfect sense, even when the brand didn't take the surname of the inventor or entrepreneur who introduced it.

Today, Coca-Cola is one of the few leading brands to use such a calligraphic treatment for its mark. As a consequence, the meaning of that calligraphic typeface has changed. In 1900, that face meant "name of something or somebody, especially something or somebody prominent enough to be named repeatedly on signs and displays." Today that script typeface connotes "classic," "heritage," "olden times," "the good old days," and related associations. These descriptors are all highly appropriate to Coca-Cola's current brand positioning. But the Coca-Cola typeface only carries these meanings because it is one of the sole survivors, one of the few marks to continue to use such a typeface 100 years later. The meaning of a calligraphic typeface today thus depends in part on its rarity among the typefaces used by brands: intertextuality.

Consider again Pepsi. By the 1960s, Pepsi had abandoned the script typeface, and moved far in the direction of the other extreme, toward a

Table E.1   Pepsi and Coca-Cola typefaces as examples of intertextuality

	Pepsi	**Coca-Cola**
Early 1900s		
By 1960s (Pepsi) and 1940s (Coca-Cola)		
Coca-Cola after New Coke		
Recent		

Notes: Dates are taken from the Logopedia site, and deemed reliable, but not independently checked. The table shows only snapshots of the evolution of these two brand marks; it is not a complete record of changes over time.

stripped-down and simplified sans serif typeface, and also switched much of its mark from red to blue. The tendency, in the Henderson et al. tradition, is to find some inherent meaning in the presence or absence of serifs, and the use or eschewal of script. The Pepsi and Coca-Cola typefaces from the 1960s get located along two different dimensions in an *n*-dimensional Cartesian model of typeface meanings. But the meaning of Pepsi's typeface depends crucially on not being in the same typeface as Coca-Cola. A sans serif typeface, taken in isolation, might be construed as bare, stark, stripped down; or more positively, as pure, clean, and simple. Placed next to Coca-Cola's typeface, the Pepsi typeface pushes to redefine the Coca-Cola mark as fussy, aging, and outdated. In that comparison, Pepsi emerges as youthful, modern, and streamlined; exactly where Pepsi, as the challenger, needs to be positioned. But those meanings are only cued by juxtaposing Pepsi's typeface choice against that of Coca-Cola: intertextuality.

The one point where Coca-Cola dropped the use of a script typeface is notable: it coincides with one of the great branding pratfalls, the introduction of New Coke. This rebranding was intended as a response to the growing competitive threat posed by Pepsi. It was accompanied by a shift to an unadorned and less calligraphic typeface. This departure was rolled back as the New Coke strategy lost favor; and ever since, Coca-Cola has maintained its script typeface, regardless of other changes. This visual element proved too tightly tied to the brand to be replaced, again due to intertextuality, as the Pepsi typeface continued to move even further toward an unadorned and informal modernity (compare the even more streamlined character of recent iterations relative to those of the 1960s).

Intertextuality challenges logical empiricist tenets concerning the proper form of a scientific theory no less than *tertium quid* and family resemblance. To return to the hypothetical structural equations model: to accommodate intertextuality each latent variable, corresponding to each brand's visual identity, would have to be connected by recursive paths to every other latent variable, corresponding to competitor brands' identities. Hence, the meaning of any one visual identity – which is to say, the path coefficients leading from the visual elements that serve as its indicators – becomes a changing function of the other brand identities, whose indicators are also being affected. Such a model is unlikely to be identified in statistical terms; which is another way of saying that brand identity can't be captured by any of the elements used to express it. A theoretical idea that cannot be represented in terms of a latent variable structural equations model is dubious under a logical empiricist framework. But ideas of *tertium quid* and intertextuality are crucial for grasping how visual branding proceeds in the world.

Discussion questions: How might you gather evidence to test the hypothesis of intertextuality? To keep things simple, focus your study design on typefaces. Consider these thought starters: (1) If the hypothesis of intertextuality is correct, what are the implications for laboratory tests of the semantic content carried by broad families of typefaces, that is, clusters of typefaces arrayed in the same region of the n-dimensional space of Henderson et al. (2004)? (2) For your proposed research program, does it matter if the typefaces are generic, publicly available from a type foundry, and currently used by no brand? (3) Does it matter if the typefaces have been customized for an existing brand, but applied by you to fictive brands? (4) Is intertextuality mostly important for typeface, or might it also shape other visual elements used to brand?

DO CONSUMERS EVOLVE?

In past work we've advanced an ecological model of how advertisers interact with consumers.[8] We use the metaphor of the biome: the complete system which embraces brand advertisers, who compete with one another;

consumers, who may be differentiated into subpopulations whose size waxes and wanes; and resources. For brand advertisers, resources include the available means of persuasion, and the agents, including copy-writers, art directors, media publications, and branding consultants, who execute branding. For consumers, resources range from purchasing power to time and attention. As in any biome, all parties must deal with limited resources. Brands compete for consumers' limited purchasing power and limited time. Consumers strive to maximize their utility from the limited resources available to them. And finally, both brands and consumers obey a survival imperative, but not all of either group will thrive.

Next, consider how prey and predator relate in a real biome. Predators develop sharp teeth; prey species develop thick hides. Teeth get sharper; hides get thicker. An uneasy and unstable equilibrium is the normal state of the system. If hides get too thick, the prey population soars, exhausts available grasslands, and then crashes, which undercuts species survival. If teeth get too sharp, the predator population overwhelms the prey population, and both populations crash.

Finally, biomes are not closed systems. At random intervals, new predators arrive, as when humans used endurance running to bring down prey made lumbering by their thick and heavy hides. At which point, the old tooth-and-hide equilibrium collapses. Or, new resources arise to feed new prey species, who may evolve to be more nimble, to reach new food located high up in the tree canopy. Old predators, weighed down by huge teeth, and unable to climb trees, then die out.

Stated as a hypothesis, the ecological perspective suggests that whatever works in advertising at one point – sharp teeth – will cease to work as well at a later point, as consumer hides thicken. Cunning words pushing a guilt appeal might have worked in the 1920s, when these appeared in droves. But consumers developed a resistance, as the body develops immunity to disease. And in time, verbal guilt appeals stopped working.

At a more macro level, verbal appeals requiring any considerable amount of copy have slowly lost their effectiveness, as consumers were bombarded with ever more ads, decade after decade, generation after generation. It's the easiest thing in the world to ignore written copy. Reading an argument pursued over several paragraphs is effortful, in a way that glancing at a picture is not. Once consumers adapt to incessant advertising, they learn not to read ads; and every verbal appeal that used to work, stops working.

It's not that nothing works, but rather, everything that does work, stops working. Alternatively, this hypothesis may only apply locally, to verbal appeals in advertising but not to pictures. If people still want to look at pretty pictures – even though they are now surrounded by thousands more

pictures, every day, than their great grandparents ever saw – then the ecological challenge may not apply. Rhetorically stylized ad pictures may be
like endurance running, against which prey weighed down by thick hides
had no hope, a new predator on the consumer veldt.

The ecological model of ad persuasion offers a temporal challenge to
the universalist pretensions of scientific psychology. Scientific laws are
supposed to be unchanging. Lab experiments are supposed to generalize
to future worlds and past worlds, as well as out in this world. The laws of
physics certainly do.

Surprisingly, literary and art critics may join with scientists, in this one
respect: no literary critic believes that a drama which delighted the Greeks
can no longer excite pleasure in moderns. No art critic believes that a fresco
which delighted a Renaissance prince can no longer please the modern eye.
Beauty, or art, is supposed to be as pan-temporal and pan-cultural as scientific psychology proposes to be. To argue that a style of advertising that
was successful at one point will subsequently cease to work, and that this is
the norm among ad appeals, threatens to offend both scientists and literary
and art critics, leaving the rhetorician without any ally.

How might this proposition be tested? Well there you have the problem
with history: one can't go back in time and run experiments on consumers
who are now dead. Is it enough to show that an appeal was common once,
but rare today? In any such test, the ecological hypothesis has to be distinguished from two rivals:

1. If advertising is like fashion, then types of appeals will flourish and
    then recede; with, on occasion, a renewed surge in popularity at
    some later point. It's not that appeals cease to work, but that fashion
    changes incessantly.
2. A different rival would propose not continual obsolescence, but a
    learning process, in which early advertisers cast about widely for
    appeals that might work, and gradually winnowed the list down to a
    smaller number that did work. We moderns are perceptually biased
    when we look back at old advertising: we tend to notice appeals
    that are no longer used, because these stand out. Under this rival
    hypothesis, it's not that verbal guilt appeals stopped working, and thus
    disappeared; rather, these never worked, but it took a generation or
    two for advertisers to discover that truth.

The larger question here is whether history has a direction, or is only
"one damned thing after another." In answering this question, historians
must find a way through Scylla and Charybdis. The twin dangers: seeing
a direction that isn't there, versus failing to find the pattern, trend, or line

of development that is present. Consider, for instance, descriptions of historical progress that culminate in the present day. These get derided in the faculty club as Whig history. On the other hand, technology does progress over time, even if we can't know whether there is a culmination point, or if it has been reached. Automobiles are better today, as compared to 1900, or even 1950; and don't get McQuarrie started on personal computers now, versus those he used in graduate school. If advertising is a social and cultural technology, then it makes sense that it may have progressed, and that old ad appeals, the ones no longer seen, are like 5¼ inch floppy disks, which are an inferior form of portable storage, rightly discarded. But if advertising is more like poetry than technology, then we would expect to see fashion cycles, as genres wax and wane. Few people believe that poetry progresses.

Discussion questions: Can these disparate positions on advertising's time course be tested? How do you test two alternative characterizations of how the history of something unfolded?

CONCLUSION

Two themes are woven through these puzzles. Each puzzle stems from the uncertainty that bedevils the human sciences, an uncertainty that extends to whether that phrase might be an oxymoron. The second embracing theme is the indivisibility of key concepts in branding. The path to success in the physical sciences has been one long story of decomposition, from elements to atoms to electrons to quarks. But Betty Crocker does not decompose.

Much intellectual work remains for today's graduate students in marketing, advertising, and consumer behavior. Perhaps some way may be found to break up Betty Crocker into meaningful pieces; or perhaps Wittgenstein must step ahead of physics, and take his rightful place as a staple of graduate education within the disciplines that grapple with branding.

Notes

INTRODUCTION

1. If you are not already familiar with the psychological perspectives named and applied in this paragraph, helpful resources include Rodgers and Thorson (2012) and Solomon (2016).
2. We've had several occasions to introduce the topic of rhetoric in advertising, adopting a slightly different perspective in each. For further reading, see the introduction to McQuarrie and Phillips (2008b), or the chapter by McQuarrie and Phillips (2012), where rhetoric is compared to other approaches to advertising, or see McQuarrie and Mick (1996), which represented an initial attempt to develop a rhetorical typology for use in advertising. For a more general introduction to classical rhetoric, not limited to advertising, see Corbett (1990).
3. For an excellent example of this style of work, see the papers by Henderson and Cote (1998) and Henderson et al. (2004), which we treat in detail in Chapters 3 and 6.
4. For examples of such work, see Janiszewski and Meyvis (2001), Jiang et al. (2015), and Nordhielm (2002).
5. There are exceptions. See Low and Fullerton (1994), and a forward citation search of that paper for more recent examples. Of late, the *Journal of Macromarketing*, and its newer sibling the *Journal of Historical Research in Marketing*, have expanded the opportunities for publishing historical work. The claim in-text applies to older and more prominent outlets, such as the *Journal of Marketing Research, Journal of Advertising*, and *Journal of Consumer Research*.
6. The debate on these matters stretches back over three decades in consumer research, with roots in the earlier "crisis in social psychology" of the 1970s. Mook (1983) and Sears (1986) are good on the roots of the dispute. In consumer research and marketing the debate was launched by Calder et al. (1981), who were partially opposed by Lynch (1982), opposed from another angle by Wells (1993), and then supported by Petty and Cacioppo (1996) and Sternthal et al. (1994). Hunt (2003) is good on the larger issues in philosophy of science invoked by the disputants, if a bit too sympathetic to logical empiricism. Recently, the parent field of social psychology has entered a new crisis, arising from exposure of fabricated experimental data and the difficulty of replicating even honest experimental findings. The philosophical debate may soon be joined anew. See McQuarrie (2014) and Open Science Collaboration (2015) for entry points to the more recent crisis.
7. Gergen (1973) was among the first to call out the pan-cultural and pan-temporal pretensions of laboratory psychology. A forward citation search of that paper, and browsing scholar.google.com for other papers by Gergen, will bring you up to date on the challenges posed by history to psychology. From outside psychology, Sewell (2005) is informative on how historical knowledge differs from the theoretical knowledge espoused elsewhere in the social sciences.
8. The catchphrase that appears at this juncture runs: "It's not the data that generalize, but the theory." See Mook (1983) for an able exponent of this view. The catchphrase deserves extended reflection; ultimately we found it to be the intellectual inverse of being introduced to a boy and girl, and upon being told they are twins, asking, "Are they identical?"

9. Some of these exceptions are organized in McQuarrie and Mick (1999). See also the collections edited by Scott and Batra (2003) and Wedel and Pieters (2008).
10. For documentation, see Pollay (1985), who first called out this trend, and the updated sample in McQuarrie and Phillips (2008a), which showed the trend still in motion, 30 years after the terminus of Pollay's data.
11. For instance, works that examine pictorial content may focus on gender, ethnicity, and class.
12. If you have access to a trove of food or soap packages, from across the past century, analogous to the copious number of ads that may be obtained by purchasing old magazines, please write to us; we don't know of any such archive.
13. We eschew the idea that anything can be a brand. Although we believe that politicians, for instance, are marketed, and do advertise, we do not think a person or non-profit organization can be a brand (celebrities might be an exception). Or if you prefer, the brands we aim to study – attached to goods sold for money to consumers – are distinct. We acknowledge that this viewpoint on brand is an outlier, in a world where books and courses promise to help you with your personal brand, or show you how to brand your small department of clerks buried deep in a bureaucracy. But we abhor the mix of imperialism and intellectual sloppiness that slaps this label everywhere, blurring distinctions that matter.
14. For a more mainstream account of brands, see Aaker (2009), Jones and Slater (2003), Keller (2003, 2012), and Keller and Lehman (2006); for an alternative culturally informed account, see Holt (2004).
15. Paleontologists continue to argue about whether Neanderthals engaged in symbolic thought.
16. It is not always thus; General Mills has recently agreed to sell the Green Giant, a brand and spokes-character almost as old as Betty Crocker. Corporate names change too; the predecessor of General Mills was Washburn-Crosby, a name you will frequently see in ads from around the end of the nineteenth century.
17. A search for Betty Crocker images will unearth several compilations of how her depiction has changed over time.
18. These were wide-ranging in-person interviews with individuals holding titles such as art director or creative director. We hoped to get a zero-based view of visual branding by talking to professionals whose job it is. See Phillips et al. (2014a, 2014b) for a description of the findings.
19. However, quality did vary: some of the early copy was noisome in its effulgence, or convoluted so as unreadable nearly to be.
20. For consumer researchers, Linda M. Scott, notably in Scott (1994a), provides an excellent entry point to the large literature on art criticism, and she writes knowledgeably about rhetorical aspects of painting and other fine art.
21. In this paragraph we draw on the history of rhetoric offered in Bender and Welberry (1990). Lanham (2006) is helpful both on medieval rhetoricians and on contemporary visual rhetoric.
22. See also Belk and Pollay (1985) and Leiss et al. (2005 [1986]). However, we take issue with the Leiss et al. treatment on multiple counts. For instance, we do not accept their periodization of magazine advertising (see their pp. 168–224).
23. Ohmann (1996) proceeds likewise, but wears his politics on his sleeve in a way that Marchand does not.
24. See McQuarrie and Statman (2015) for an attempt to combine rhetorical and content analysis, to the mutual benefit of both.
25. The first paper in this stream was Phillips and McQuarrie (2002), which looked at how the verbal and visual rhetoric in magazine ads evolved between the early 1950s and the 1980s. Next came McQuarrie and Phillips (2008b), which tracked changes in advertising layout from the 1960s to the 2000s. Most recently, McQuarrie and Statman (2015) looked at ads for investment products from 1960 to 2010, and charted a trend toward increasingly visual appeals.

26. We enjoy the biographical approach as much as anyone, and colorful characters abound in the development of modern advertising. Best on this score is Fox (1984); equally good on prominent players, but lacking an overall narrative structure, is Hambleton (1987). Tedlow (1990) goes in-depth on the biography of select enterprises; not only the founders, but also the organizations that they built. Wood (1958) and Presbrey (1929) also offer biographical detail, especially of early English predecessors in the advertising trade in the case of Wood, and of his contemporaries at the turn of the century in the case of Presbrey, who had founded an ad agency.

27. But to construct this account, we had to read more widely in the history of advertising, and this note provides a guide to selected sources that may be useful to subsequent scholars. The first prerequisite is to understand the business environment in which magazine advertising arose, and here there is no substitute for Chandler (1977). Next, Norris (1990), Pope (1983), and Porter (2006) variously confirm, support, or extend the story told by Chandler. All contemporary writers on brands and advertising must draw on, respectively, Hotchkiss and Franken (1923) and Presbrey (1929), as these authors collected contemporaneous data that would not otherwise be retrievable today. Strasser (1989) provides a good all-round account of the evolution of marketing activities, not just advertising, around the turn of the twentieth century. Next, for narrative histories of print advertising, with supporting illustrations, we enjoyed Goodrum and Dalrymple (1990) and Rowsome (1959). Heavier going, but useful for the prehistory of magazine advertising, are Wood (1958) and Presbrey (1929). For illustrated compendia of visual elements, we looked at Dotz and Husain (2015), Morgan (1986), Hornung (1956a, 1956b), and Hornung and Johnson (1976). The larger terrain, concerning the evolution of consumer culture, is vast; examples include Ewen (1988), Leach (1993), Lears (1994), and Ohmann (1996).

28. The contemporary rhetorical tradition begins with the more semiotic and psychoanalytic accounts of Baker (1961), Leymore (1975), and Williamson (1981), and later, Mick (1986) and Umiker-Sebeok (1987). More specifically rhetorical treatments were introduced by McQuarrie and Mick (1996, 1999), Phillips and McQuarrie (2004), and Scott (1994a, 1994b). If you are reading this note some years after publication, forward citation searches on these latter five papers will provide an efficient means to get up to date on subsequent rhetorical work in marketing, advertising, and consumer scholarship.

29. Mott (1957, Vol. 5), is the authoritative source on the history of American magazines in the initial period. Marchand (1985) draws on the *Ladies Home Journal* (*LHJ*), but sampled more widely, with the *Saturday Evening Post* the anchor. Authors in the gender and cultural studies traditions, especially feminists, also focus on the *LHJ*, but typically on the fiction and the articles more than the ads; Scanlon (1995) is representative.

30. In addition, we try to limit the number of endnotes. Most notes also contain some gloss or commentary.

31. There are plenty of books on branding that aim to do exactly that; Wheeler (2013) is representative.

CHAPTER 1

1. If you do care, Presbrey (1929) has one of the more extended accounts of the prehistory of brand advertising (see also Wood 1958). Ownership marks – for example, cattle brands – are very old. But are these brands as we know them today, that is, the consumer goods that surround us, after centuries of the mass media, and over a century of mass markets? If you have a taste for the ontology of cultural things, a nice essay could be constructed on this topic.

2. To our knowledge, no cross-national historical timeline has been constructed for advertising. Our history will focus on the United States, which is not a bad focus, given the

centrality of commercial being in the evolution of American society; but we acknowledge up front that the timeline, and even the pattern of change, may have been different in Britain, on the Continent, or even in Canada. This note is to remind you that each historical assertion in the book has the tacit preface, "in the United States . . . "

3. Goodrum and Dalrymple (1990), Presbrey (1929), and Rowsome (1959) provide useful insight into these early days. For many years illustrations were forbidden in newspaper ads, and type was limited to agate size. Likewise, branded goods were rare before about 1880, with many goods sold from unlabeled bulk containers; for example, the cracker barrel.

4. Mott (1957) is the authoritative source; Fox (1984) and Rowsome (1959) add color to the story. The magazines that launched the new regime included the old *Cosmopolitan*, *Munsey's*, and *McClure's*, as well as the *Ladies Home Journal*. The dominance of the *Saturday Evening Post* came later.

5. Cohen (1986) and more recently Petty (2011) trace the evolution of trademarks and their legal protection. Morgan (1986) exhibits hundreds of early trademark designs.

6. Here Chandler (1977) is the crucial source, although a little knowledge of business cycle history helps too. Most Americans emerge from their high school history class regarding the late nineteenth century as a booming era of wealth creation: the Gilded Age of Robber Barons, when the United States first grew to be one of the largest economies on the planet. Mostly forgotten today are the crash of 1873, the depression of the 1890s, and the 20 years of deflation between, worse than anything seen by Japan in the years since 1989. Also not top of mind is how quickly the large national corporation coalesced, in the decade after 1893 (Porter 2006). The modern corporate and branding scene was not yet in place before 1890; but it was all there by 1905.

7. When McQuarrie first began teaching marketing in the 1980s, received wisdom was that once a brand became a market leader, with a substantial share, it was rarely dislodged: to own such a brand was like owning an annuity that would throw off cash indefinitely. Golder and colleagues put the hammer to this old chestnut, showing how mortal brands were, and how finite the dominance of even a multi-decade leader (Golder 2000; Golder and Tellis 1993). Those interested in pursuing this issue should consult Hotchkiss and Franken (1923) and Presbrey (1929) for data on early brand leaders.

8. Fox (1984) offers a briskly paced narrative of this prehistory. Rowsome (1959) adds insight from the field.

9. See Hornung (1956b) for an illuminating history of nineteenth-century ad design.

10. As always, finding the true point of beginning is elusive. Was P.T. Barnum, active well before the Civil War, one of these business owners with flair, or is he better regarded as the first publicity agent, or the first professional promoter, or one of the earliest makers and stewards of brands?

11. Fox (1984) notes: "As late as 1892, no general agency had a regular employee spending all his time writing copy" (p. 35). We found the older histories – Rowsome (1959), Presbrey (1929), and Wood (1958) – to give the most insight into nineteenth-century developments. Presbrey, who was an advertising man, experienced first hand how the advertising of that era was produced.

12. Fox (1984, pp. 40ff) locates the rise of the art director toward the end of the decade of the 1890s.

13. Morgan (1986) has a good discussion of how Uneeda was launched. It was some years later before the first complete market planning effort, one where a new product was deliberately invented to meet an identified market need, with full attention to the design of the brand as well as the product. Strasser (1989) locates this point of beginning with the development of Crisco shortening in 1912 by Procter & Gamble.

14. It could be argued that most forms of mass-media advertising don't seek a direct response, so that television advertising could serve the purpose as well as magazine advertising. But television advertising would only yield a 60-year history. Besides, consider the difficulty of sampling old television ads. Sampling is child's play in the case of old magazines – the internet abounds with copies for sale – but much, much more

difficult for television. Where do 1950s television ads reside now? Stored in what format? Viewable on what machine?

15. Most of the book authors we cite, if still alive, would satisfy this age criterion. In our view, much of what is written about advertising, even today, uses a mental model of advertising unduly based on the 1980s or even earlier. The book you hold may be the first historical inquiry to use ads from the 2000s as a conceptual anchor. The heyday for initial efforts at the historiography of advertising had ended by the early 1990s.

16. Ah, but what if there has been differential fading of ink shade, so that however bad the 1980s photo looks now, it was pristine when newly published? This question neatly captures the vast gulf that separates the historian from the psychological scientist. If we were dealing with a year or two, and an aerobic process, we could lock one copy of the magazine in a hermetically sealed and temperature controlled vault, and leave another copy lying around our sunny living room, and experimentally determine whether ordinary magazine storage leads to differential fading of ink shades. Here's the rub: if you locked a bottle of fine wine into the vault as well, but for 30 years, would you be comfortable in assuming that its contents provide an unchanging metric for how that wine tasted when freshly bottled? No; wine changes anaerobically and despite constant temperature. It is not possible to experimentally and directly compare the taste of a 1983 vintage when new, versus that wine's taste when cellared for 30 years. That is the historian's dilemma.

CHAPTER 2

1. Quoted in Pope (1983, p. 4). Wood (1958) adds context to probe what Johnson meant. Presbrey (1929), who was himself an advertising man in the later nineteenth century, has interesting reflections on how each generation supposes that the advertising of its age is [insert any superlative], relative to what came before.

2. On the picture window style of layout, see Chamblee and Sandler (1992) and Feasley and Stuart (1987). Our 1899 and 1900 copies of the *LHJ* show ads in the same format and in the same position on the inside cover, albeit with a different illustration; by 1905, Ivory had taken a whole page, located one or two pages in from the front cover, but again using a similar picture window layout.

3. Although Andrews Heating was prominent in its era, this is one of several durables examples where we were not able to use a surviving brand.

4. Rossiter and Percy (1997), in their pioneering attempt to systematize ad planning, make much of the distinction between two basic branding tasks: whether the consumer must recall the brand from memory, or merely recognize the brand when encountered at the point of purchase. The latter task is important for many packaged goods, hence the eventual ubiquity of the package shot in ads for this category.

5. If we were writing a history of advertising rhetoric, rather than one focused on visual branding, we would call out the alliteration in the headline, and discuss in detail the use of figurative language. Here we can only point you to McQuarrie and Mick (1996) for a sustained treatment of figures of rhetoric in advertising.

6. Figures with the WA prefix can be viewed at the companion website for this book, https://www.e-elgar.com/visual-branding-companion-site.

7. Then again, this illustration may have started life as a photograph, as the copy professes; nonetheless, it has been touched up and otherwise altered to at least give the appearance of an illustration, which supports our point. See Jussim (1974) for side-by-side examples of how the same image could print differently under different treatments.

8. Deconstructing the gender and racial biases of the ads in these old magazines is a common focus when scholars approach advertisements for insights into social and cultural history. Scanlon (1995) and Garvey (1996) provide entry points for the feminist critique, while Kern-Foxworth (1994) and Manring (1998) consider portrayals of racial

minorities. On a personal note, even McQuarrie, a fairly mainstream white heterosexual male baby boomer, found the casual racism and sexism of ads as late as the 1920s to be shocking.

9. This is one of those points where our account departs from received wisdom. Past authors, knowing that photos were reproduced in magazines from the 1890s, and finding a couple of sterling examples of ads that used photos, have sometimes written as if photography quickly became the norm. We did not find that to be true across the 1000 or so ads from the 1920s that we reviewed from the *LHJ* and *Saturday Evening Post* (*SEP*). Photos are present, especially portrait photos in the editorial; but photos were not the dominant visual element in ads.

10. Marchand (1985) writes at length about the use of modern art and the associated aesthetic sensibility in ads of the 1920s and 1930s. However, in our judgment Marchand makes the appearance of modern art too central to the advertisers' project; we are struck more by its absence in ads from the 1950s, which suggests that what Marchand saw as fundamental was but a phase, or a passing vagary of fashion. Scott (1994a) adds a valuable rhetorical perspective on the use of art in ads, and what it reveals about consumers' sophisticated powers of interpretation.

11. For access to this literature, start with Finn (1988) and Hendon (1973), examine their references, and then look for subsequent citations of them.

12. Fox (1984) has a nice discussion of endorsements, which adds value by including stories of the notable female copywriters of the day. McCracken (1986) is a classic analysis of the rationale for using celebrities to promote brands.

13. Although its attribution to Chekhov has been contested, the maxim runs something like this: if a gun is placed over the mantel in the first act of a play, then someone must pick it up and fire it before the play ends; else, what was the point of showing that gun? Every detail of staging must support the drama, or be excised.

14. Lest the reader think we are cherry-picking the efforts of obscure brands, amateur ad agencies, or junior designers, Rinso was a product of Lever Brothers, a predecessor of Unilever, now a major rival of Procter & Gamble and among the titans in the consumer packaged goods arena.

15. We had to go outside our core set of magazines, and to a less sophisticated advertiser, to get a pure example of the picture window layout, which suggests that this style may have peaked even before the 1980s. Alternatively, branded convenience goods may never have been as prone to the picture window layout as durables.

16. An interesting conundrum, which combines elements of historical consciousness and epistemology, is whether consumers of 30 years ago, who had not experienced the advanced technology of image reproduction that was to come, would have been as critical of the Shake 'n Bake imagery. Were they less likely to see and be put off by red paint? Did they instead see a rich tomato sauce, and have the hoped-for Pavlovian response? And what is the meaning of such assertions which, like so much else in history, cannot be tested?

17. For an introduction to the rhetorical uses of white space in print advertising, see Pracejus et al. (2006). That paper, revised under severe space constraints, was part of a larger stream, and a search of O'Guinn and "white space" on scholar.google.com will reveal additional publications expanding on the authors' findings.

18. However, we acknowledge that there is no way to distinguish a linear trend from an S-shaped process, during the period when both are in the middle of their time course. We can't know, at present, whether the trend toward the visual in brand advertising will top out, and if so, whether it might have already done so. We can only show how far the trend toward the visual has come, and how long it has been in motion.

19. This would make a good discussion topic for a seminar. If assigned as a paper topic or exam question, respondents should be pushed for the criteria that separate an illuminating metaphor from a scientific theory. Proponents of the life cycle metaphor should be pressed on the processes it illuminates. Antagonists should be pressed on whether their skepticism is substantive: what alternative explanation, beyond "stuff happens," can

they give for the patterns of growth and decline visible among specific brands, products, and types of appeal?

CHAPTER 3

1. This author team wrote a later paper that considers marks that do not contain a separate visual element (Henderson et al. 2004), and that paper will anchor our discussion of typeface in Chapter 6.
2. Park et al. (2013) graciously made available to us some details on the brands and marks included in their empirical work, and we acknowledge with gratitude their generosity. In the course of those communications, they mentioned that they had begun the research with a third category in mind, where the symbol would stand alone without any name (for example, the Nike swoosh). However, they found too few of these to make up a meaningful category for analysis. Our own experience was similar: we found only a few brands which regularly present a mark that does not contain any text.
3. We've been constructing such typologies for some time now; see McQuarrie and Mick (1996), Phillips and McQuarrie (2004), and the how-to advice in McQuarrie (2008a).
4. These were drawn from among the 77 brand marks classified by Park et al. (2013). We located the visual representations reproduced in the table a few years after Park et al. performed their research; hence, the designs shown here may not be the same as those rated in their research. Brand marks get updated on an irregular schedule.
5. Initially we had approached this project as the basis for a journal paper. Accordingly, we trained two undergraduate coders to apply the categories, and had them independently rate each of the marks as to where it should be placed in the typology. Inter-rater reliability was acceptable (83 percent agreement), and most disagreements involved displacement up or down the typology by only one category, as seen by a correlation of greater than 0.90 between the raters' judgments. Because we disparage content analysis elsewhere in this book, and because we have evolved the typology since then, by collapsing some categories, we saw no point in playing up those content analyses, beyond mentioning that yes, we did some.
6. Artful deviation is a key property of rhetorical figures in McQuarrie and Mick (1996), who drew on Berlyne (1971). It is discussed again in Chapter 6 on typefaces, and in Chapter 9 on pictures, where Phillips and McQuarrie (2004) provides the basis.
7. All these complications are swept aside in Jiang et al. (2015). They create artificial logos: nested circles for the curve condition and nested squares for the angular condition. In a second experiment, the angles created by white space are ignored, since the printed shapes are held to be curved (yet, two ovals tilted to touch at one end create an angle in the white space, do they not?). Plus, no alphabetical letters, with their confounding mix of curves and angles, are included in their logo stimuli. It is an exemplary experiment with respect to the laboratory strategies of isolation and abstraction; as exemplary, among logo studies, as Henderson et al. (2004) among typeface studies (see Chapter 6). We think the generalizability of the Jiang et al. work to logos in the world is dubious; but that question might make for a good seminar discussion.

CHAPTER 4

1. On the importance and value of color for brands, see Labrecque and Milne (2012, 2013a), Park et al. (2013), Schmitt and Simonson (1997), and also Chapter 8 in this book.
2. The services marketing literature is now vast, with its own journals. Foundational papers that support the ideas in this paragraph include Lovelock (1983) and Parasuraman et al. (1985).

3. Her distinction has subsequently appeared in typologies of advertising appeals (Rossiter et al. 1991; Taylor 1999).
4. A key source is Frazer (1922); for an adaptation to contemporary consumer behavior, see St James et al. (2011).

CHAPTER 5

1. Mollerup (1997) has useful material on the influence of heraldry and other non-commercial resources on the development of brand marks.
2. See Van der Vlugt (2012) for examples of these early heraldic brand marks, including Alfa Romeo, Bayer, and Deutsche Bank, among others.
3. Strasser (1989) has a helpful account of the growth of self-service retailing; see the pictures of an early Piggly-Wiggly store on p. 250, and consider the implications of store shelf display for branding in advertising.
4. As noted earlier, Rossiter and Percy (1997) put the distinction between brand recognition and brand recall on a firm theoretical foundation, and explain why ads for some goods must prominently display an exact reproduction of the package.
5. See Golder and Tellis (1993) and Golder (2000) for reflections on these questions.
6. For a good example of how brands were understood at that point, see Gardner and Levy (1955).
7. For instance, what we call the brand mark, Nelson (1981) calls the "sig-cut": a graphic design passed from the client to the ad agency to be pasted up exactly as received.
8. Morgan (1986) and Van der Vlugt (2012) are good sources for perusing the magnitude of change over time (but Van der Vlugt's series tend to be more complete, with Morgan limited to showing one early and one subsequent design). The website logopedia.com is also a helpful source for assembling the history of individual marks although, again, it is of unknown completeness.
9. By primary, we mean that there are many more exposures to the package than to any other visual presentation of the brand. A consumer may go weeks or months without exposure to an advertisement, but they go to the supermarket each week, and once the package is purchased, an exposure occurs every time the cabinet or refrigerator door is opened. Ad exposures are counted in the millions, but package exposures number in the billions.
10. And within service categories, the population of marks does appear to shift uniformly up the *eidos* gradient toward the very top. See McQuarrie and Statman (2015) for a case study.
11. See Chapter 6 on typeface and Chapter 8 on color for more on these latter two developments.

CHAPTER 6

1. This point was made by Childers and Jass (2002). For sound symbolism see Klink (2000), Lowrey and Shrum (2007), and Yorkston and Menon (2004). Although sound symbolism has nothing to do with visual branding per se, sounds, like typeface, can support branding, and both contribute to the sensory experience of brands (Brakus et al. 2009).
2. See van der Lans et al. (2009) and Yorkston and Menon (2004) for supportive evidence, and Chapter 8 on color for more on the theme of nature versus nurture.
3. Linda M. Scott has been eloquent in dismissing this metaphor. See Scott and Vargas (2007) for discussion of a middle ground, which they term a writing system.

4. We thought to say *Homo significans* here, but that term has already been appropriated as "man the symbol-using animal." Sense-making by drawing inferences doesn't require symbols. It doesn't require signs either, unless these are circularly defined as "anything from which meaning can be inferred." We prefer to keep the focus on the activity: that as humans we draw inferences, willy nilly. No point in making a circular reference to signs.

5. As soon as we refer to factor analysis, we narrow our audience considerably. Alas, most of this critique of Henderson et al. will only be accessible to, and of interest to, graduate students in marketing or psychology and their instructors. Here and there in this section, we'll gloss points in a note; but if factor analysis is not a phrase that rolls easily off your tongue, and you are not accustomed to reading scholarly articles like Henderson et al., you might want to skip ahead to the section titled "A Fresh Start."

6. As Henderson et al. acknowledge, three of these factors closely resemble what Osgood et al. (1964) had found to be universal, fundamental factors in responses to stimuli. We count that as a weakness of the research program, when viewed from the practical perspective of a brand manager, who may be interested in more than four consumer responses; but from the standpoint of doing scientific psychology, the convergence with the findings of Osgood et al. is arguably a strength. An illuminating seminar discussion beckons here.

7. In addition to Childers and Jass (2002), studies of note include Doyle and Bottomley (2006, 2011). A forward citation search on Henderson et al., combined with perusal of the reference sections of these four papers, should produce a comprehensive bibliography of marketing-related research on typeface.

8. If the domain were art, this financial assumption would not hold; but in the branding domain we are dealing with commercial art, created by individuals who expect to be compensated for their designs.

9. The rhetorician, as an omnivore, is as interested in harvesting the insights of evolutionary biology as those of psychology.

10. There is a discrepancy between their text (p. 62, left column bottom), which refers to 16 universal and 8 typeface-specific design characteristics, and their Table 1, which shows 12 and 11, respectively.

11. We promised we would minimize the statistical and technical apparatus. But psychological science lives and dies by statistical analysis, and to pursue the critique of its exemplar in Henderson et al., we had no alternative. Here is a plain English account. Psychology strives for statistically significant findings; in this case, associations so strong that they would be unlikely to occur by chance. The psychologist wants to know which typefaces are strongly associated with which consumer responses. When the statistical procedure is regression, R^2, which corresponds to the percentage of variance explained, is the metric of choice for strength of association. But a second rule applies, beyond statistical significance: the size of the effect. Small R^2 values may be significant, if the sample is large; but if the effect size is less than 2 percent, the finding may not be actionable. Bottom line: Henderson et al. had difficulty showing that typeface-specific design characteristics had any practical import with respect to shaping consumer response.

12. See McQuarrie (1998, 2004, 2014) and McQuarrie et al. (2012) for a sustained critique of why this practice is problematic in a marketing context.

13. Again, we are lightly skipping over a prolonged wrangle in the philosophy of science, concerning the connection between theory and observation. See Hunt (2003) and Stove (2001) for a discussion of Karl Popper's position.

14. See Doyle and Bottomley (2006) for an experimental investigation into fit.

15. It should also be apparent that only an apostate could have written this section, or any of the critiques of psychology laid out in this book. McQuarrie received his PhD in social psychology from the University of Cincinnati in 1985, and for some years published experiments that do not escape this critique.

16. The wording here is precise: "type design for branding." There were hundreds of typefaces in circulation by 1890, and from the beginning, advertisers appear to have

pondered which typeface to select. But selecting a generic typeface from a commonly available stock is not the same as designing a custom typeface for a brand.

17. The ongoing replacement of text by picture, and the demotion of headlines to captions, as described in Chapters 1 and 2, inserts a piquant question mark when Ogilvy's statement is read today.

18. "Metaphor" is a term marred by sloppy usage outside of rhetorical scholarship. In strict usage, metaphor rests on similarity, while metonym rests on contiguity. The White House, a typical metonym for the President, in no way resembles the human being who resides there; but because of its contiguity, it can substitute for him or her, and convey additional connotations, the same as a metaphor does. Continuing on the theme of sloppy usage, we decry the proliferation of synonymous terms left over from the early days of rhetoric. For example, McQuarrie has never seen a synecdoche that could not also be described as a metonym. He's on a long-term mission to clean up the mess. See McQuarrie and Mick (1996) for a start.

19. Likewise, Hagtvedt (2011) devoted a study to what he called incomplete typefaces, taken to be a distinct kind (the rastered appearance of the IBM logo provides one example). Unfortunately, besides IBM, we did not find any other incomplete typeface logos anywhere in our total sample of 529 brand marks.

20. Daniel Berlyne, active in the 1960s, founded the discipline of experimental aesthetics, where commonsense hypotheses about aesthetic features, of the sort that abound in the design literature, were submitted to experimental test. Some examples of such hypotheses: do diagonal lines snag viewer attention? Are incongruous combinations arousing? The influence of Berlyne on our thinking can be seen in studies such as McQuarrie and Mick (1992, 1996, 1999, 2009) and Phillips and McQuarrie (2009).

21. Earlier, in note 4 to this chapter, we placed the emphasis squarely on inference-making, and dispensed with its concretization as signs, thus dispensing as well with semiotic theory. For another account that puts the emphasis on inferencing, without reference to signs, see Sperber and Wilson (1986). They make the important point that language comprehension requires as many inferences as does extracting meaning from typeface or pictures; but that in most linguistic contexts, there are many, relatively tight guidelines or channels for these inferences. See McQuarrie and Phillips (2005) for an application of the Sperber and Wilson concept of strong versus weak implicature to pictures in advertising.

22. There is a large methodological literature on signal detection theory, and we'd urge anyone who proposes to conduct such an experiment to first get up to speed on that literature, along with its characteristic statistical procedures.

23. Unless the custom typeface exerts a subliminal effect. We invite you to devise an ironclad design for detecting subliminal effects of typeface, while simultaneously showing that these effects, though truly subliminal, would nonetheless be substantial enough make a difference in the marketplace.

24. There may also be consumers who are more visually skilled than average, on whom typefaces exert a greater effect (Bloch et al. (2003)). McQuarrie, by contrast, suffers from severe myopia, aggravated by astigmatism and prism. Possibly he can't see well enough to be affected by minute differences across typefaces, leading him to misestimate ordinary consumers' sensitivity to type.

25. When we interviewed art directors for Phillips et al. (2014b), we found them to have strongly held judgments about the typefaces used by brands, but also found that their judgments did not agree. That was our clue that the judgments made by professionals, regarding the fitness or failings of a typeface, had a large taste component.

26. On taste and fashion, see McQuarrie (2015), which draws heavily on Campbell (1987), who gives an account of how the modern fashion pattern first developed.

27. For a modern perspective on type, which considers its evolution from the nineteenth century into the twentieth century, and the role played by prominent designers of type, see Blackwell (2004); for examples of nineteenth-century typefaces, which were folk or anonymous designs, see Hornung (1956a, 1956b).

CHAPTER 7

1. The academic literature on spokes-characters is not as large as the phenomenon deserves. Good points of entry include Callcott and Phillips (1996), Garretson and Burton (2005), and Phillips and Gyoerick (1999). There is also a separate literature on anthropomorphic thinking among consumers, which can be entered via Aggarwal and McGill (2012) or Delbaere et al. (2011).

2. Pettman (2013) has an illuminating discussion of what totemic thinking meant to nineteenth-century thinkers, and how the idea was gradually abandoned in scientific anthropology. Brown and Ponsonby-McCabe (2014) take a more embracing and literary approach to the use of creatures for branding. On the other hand, if you are an educated person with a commitment to Kahneman's (2011) System 2 thinking in your professional life, and in the management of your household affairs, you will be horrified if you search amazon.com books for "totem animal." There are literally dozens of books on finding your inner totem, obtaining a spiritual animal companion, listening to your animal spirit, and much more. Oy!

3. See Phillips (1997) for the phrase, and McQuarrie and Phillips (2005) and Phillips and McQuarrie (2004, 2009) for perspectives on the use of metaphor in advertising and visual branding.

4. The late Barbara Stern (1994) did much to bring the thinking of Kenneth Burke, and perspectives for the study of drama generally, to bear on marketing questions. Her papers, with Deighton et al. (1989), are good starting points for a forward citation search.

5. Flo has appeared in so many ads at this juncture that it seemed pointless to reproduce any one; simply search for "Flo Progressive" on an image search engine.

6. The terms in this paragraph are often applied sloppily. Because "metaphor" is the most familiar, it is sometimes applied to every non-literal expression, whereas "figurative" is the proper embracing term for all artful deviations in expression. Figurative derives from "rhetorical figure." Metaphor, which asserts similarity, is one kind of rhetorical figure; but metonym, which relies on a connection or association, is another; and there are a dozen or two more that appear frequently in advertising. See McQuarrie and Mick (1996) for a zero-based attempt to identify and unify the set of rhetorical figures relevant to advertising. That boundary, and the zero base, saved McQuarrie and Mick from having to deal with the hundreds of named rhetorical figures that a literary critic might need to know (see also the body of work by Richard Lanham, for example, Lanham 2006).

7. The foundational work here is McCracken (1986), who posits a circulation of meaning between advertising and other cultural expressions.

8. We chuckle to think of how obscure these names will someday seem, should this book achieve any longevity.

9. Embodiment brings us back around to ideas of totemism and group identification with the totem animal. But then what are we to make of Catholic liturgy, and its invocation of the body and blood of Christ during the Eucharist; is that "primitive thinking" too? Better to stick to embodiment as a neutral trope.

10. Excepting, of course, those consumers who have spent more time watching *Lord of the Rings* than viewing cookie commercials.

11. Note how carefully and assiduously we avoid any mention of bipolar opposites. Down that path lies the quicksand of a foolish structuralism, of no greater intellectual heft than "left brain–right brain thinking." Treating live and dead as two ends of a continuum would also throw us back into the Cartesian formulations critiqued in Chapter 6. See Box 7.1 for more on the issues at stake in choosing to eschew polarities.

12. McQuarrie and Mick (1996) and Phillips and McQuarrie (2004) introduce and develop the idea of artful deviation as the feature that unifies all figurative expressions, and distinguishes figurative from literal expression. On the importance of making a metaphor deviant, see Phillips and McQuarrie (2009).

13. Jennifer Aaker (1997) and Susan Fournier (1998) made pioneering contributions to the study of brand personality and brand relationships. A forward citation search on these two papers will bring you up to speed on what has become a large literature.
14. See Phillips et al. (2016), "Spokes-Characters in Print Advertising: An Update and Extension," working paper. The content analysis compared spokes-character use in a sample of ads from *Sports Illustrated* and *Good Housekeeping* in 2015 with a sample taken from 1953 to 1997.
15. See Hill (2002) for more examples.
16. Anne Marshall appeared in Campbell's ads, Dione Lucas appeared in Cut-Rite ads, Mary Blake appeared in Carnation ads, and Marie Gifford appeared in Armour ads. Some may have been real persons; but countless consumers have believed Betty Crocker was real too.

CHAPTER 8

1. In marketing, prominent contributors to psychologically based analyses of color include Bottomley and Doyle (2006) and Labrecque and Milne (2012, 2013a, 2013b).
2. A good source to get up to speed on the exigencies of laboratory work is Elliot and Maier (2014). As an example, researchers in marketing have thought their work to be precise enough if they used Photoshop and similar software to specify the exact hue used. Elliot and Maier rebut this assumption (p. 100). Only a spectrophotometer, a specialized device costing some thousands of dollars, will meet the standard for laboratory psychology.
3. Of course this is changing, as economic wealth spreads across the planet. But even after several decades of wealth diffusion, a major non-Western brand is far more likely to have originated in East Asia than sub-Saharan Africa.
4. As described in notes to Chapter 3, research assistants independently counted whether a color was present in a flag. The flag sample contained all flags of non-colonies and non-city states as of 2014. As most flags are multicolored, the counts that follow are counts of any appearance of the color in a flag.
5. From the song "Swamp" by Talking Heads.
6. Whether it was different in China or India, where colorful silk had long been widely used, would be an interesting cross-cultural comparison. But perhaps there, too, it was only in the royal court and the palaces of nobles that color was present; before modern days, peasants may have worn drab rags in Asia, as in Europe.

CHAPTER 9

1. We hope to write this book someday. Until then, interested readers may consult McQuarrie and Mick (1996) for a typology of verbal rhetoric, Phillips and McQuarrie (2004) for a typology of visual rhetoric, and McQuarrie and Mick (1992) and McQuarrie and Phillips (2005) for some preliminary thoughts on the intersection of visual and verbal rhetorical devices in advertising.
2. To get a sense of the range of work outside of marketing and psychology, Marchand (1985) might be juxtaposed with Leiss et al. (2005 [1986]) and Messaris (1997).
3. Phillips et al. (2014a, 2014b) reproduces examples of Corona ads and also the Skyye ads discussed next.
4. The philosopher Ludwig Wittgenstein, across more works than we care to cite, challenged the conventional philosophical view that all members of a category must have some features, some divisible elements, in common. See the Epilogue for an application of his insight to assessing historical change in spokes-character appearance.

5. For examples of such cultural criticism, see Ewen (1988), Leach (1993), Lears (1994), and Ohmann (1996). From time to time, Leiss et al. (2005) also veer in this direction.
6. See McQuarrie et al. (2012) and the introductory portion of McQuarrie and Mick (1999).
7. See McQuarrie and Phillips (2012) for an expansion of this argument, and other chapters in that collection for a more positive exposition of the psychological perspectives that we criticize here.
8. Unfortunately, nobody knows, then or now; the field study of media consumption, although sometimes attempted for television, has to our knowledge never been performed for magazines, or at least not written up as scholarship. We're all guessing what real consumers do, whether we talk about magazine reading in 1895 or in 1995. Neglecting to observe consumers in their native habitat is an example of collateral damage caused by an obsession with Theory (Wells 1993).
9. Or as Marchand (1985, p. 152) put it, attempting to capture the professional wisdom of the day: "The viewer of a pen or brush illustration was unlikely to forget the deliberate artifice employed by the creator of the illustration. But the photograph . . . encouraged the viewer to remain unconscious of any intervening, manipulative creator and to experience the voyeur's sense of directly glimpsing the world's reality."
10. Whether or not an ad portrayal makes that person a protagonist is one of those judgments that acculturated persons can readily make, but are challenging for rule-following automatons to handle.
11. Technically we should say "metaphor or metonym" throughout what follows, but that would make for clumsy prose; and if we substituted the more general "figure," drawing on McQuarrie and Mick (1996), we'd bewilder those who haven't read that paper. Sorry.
12. Chapter 7, on spokes-characters, develops this model of meaning change.
13. The early paper by McQuarrie and Mick (1992) developed this idea of the pun-making potential of pictures under the heading of resonance. It was written before McQuarrie had fully adopted the rhetorical mindset laid out in McQuarrie and Mick (1996) and subsequent papers.
14. Deighton et al. (1989), focusing on television advertising, suggest an all-embracing dichotomy: all ads proceed as either lecture or drama. It is not necessary to accept the dichotomy to appreciate their insight that drama persuades differently than lecture. On drama in ads, see also papers by the late Barbara Stern.
15. Gerrig (1993), who laid the foundation for the narrative transportation theory of Green and Brock (2000), was careful to include a pictorial example of narrative, a painting by J.L. David. See Phillips and McQuarrie (2010) for more on narrative pictures.
16. This paragraph is but a fragment of a larger account of the impact of moving pictures on culture and society (Messaris 1997), an account which we lack the expertise to advance. We wish only to make the point that the advent and subsequent explosion of moving pictures changed what could be done with still pictures in advertising.
17. In Sperber and Wilson's (1986) terms, strong implicature, or univocality, is easier to achieve with words, but not a baseline. Weak implicature, which goes along with multivocality, occurs with words as well as pictures. We recommend a study of Sperber and Wilson as a corrective to the sloppy application of the word code to pictures or even language, a failing of too many semiotic accounts.
18. In one translation of Tolstoy's *Anna Karenina*, the line runs: "All happy families are alike; each unhappy family is unhappy in its own way." In an advertising context, the brands making use of grotesque appeals may stand out, relative to the happy-face ads, all alike, that throng the magazine. See Phillips and McQuarrie (2010) for reproductions of this category of fashion ads.
19. A convenient way to take stock of this follow-on research is to do a forward citation search on McQuarrie and Mick (1999) or Philips and McQuarrie (2004), with the former running about 500 citations at the time of writing in May 2016, and the latter about 200.
20. Based on Marchand (1985, pp. 150ff) and Fox (1984), by the 1920s the advertising

profession contained partisans for pictures, people who advocated for more use of pictures and less reliance on words, using varied arguments already more sophisticated than anything found in the psychological literature on heuristic or peripheral cues. But while the arguments for pictures were in place, delivery in the marketplace was not. We believe most readers, shown a statistically representative sample of ads from magazines in the 1920s, 1950s, and 1980s, and told to arrange these ads from more pictorial and visually intense to more wordy and verbose, would unerringly place ads from the 1920s on the "wordy, less pictorial" side of the scale. As we've insisted throughout, when making judgments about historical trend lines in advertising, there is no substitute for looking at copious examples of actual ads from each era. Whatever partisans of the era might have written, ads from the 1920s were still not that visual, in comparison with what was to come.

21. See Phillips and McQuarrie (2002) for the development of this trend in the last half of the twentieth century.

EPILOGUE

1. As will emerge, McQuarrie drafted this section, and first-person references are to him.
2. Scott (1994a, 1994b) is eloquent on this score.
3. The disposition of the court cases associated with these two instances may be searched by means of the brands: Louboutin, a designer of fashion items; and Nexium, a pill for gastric distress.
4. This next portion, up until the paragraph that begins "Brand managers, human beings . . ." will only make sense for readers with some training in structural equation models. That's probably a small subset of our total audience, but likely to be a large subset of our core audience: graduate students in the business disciplines.
5. It shouldn't matter, if half the student raters are 20-year-old males who have never baked anything in their lives – should it? Such issues seldom concern marketing scientists. It excites no comment when Park et al. (2013) had students respond to rating scales such as "makes my life richer and more meaningful," and "expresses who I am as a person," for brands such as AFLAC, Caterpillar, Goldman Sachs, and John Deere. If you have not been initiated into the brotherhood, it might strike you as odd to have college students rate the brand of an investment bank or manufacturer of mining equipment; but within the profession, it's a non-issue.
6. And not necessarily by the HPPR algorithm (highest-paid person in the room).
7. In answering, as noted earlier, be careful not to confuse scientific knowledge with techno-logical prowess, lest you be accused by philosophers of holding to a fallacious theory of pragmatic truth (Hunt 2003).
8. We touched on this theme in Phillips and McQuarrie (2002), and developed it at more length in McQuarrie and Phillips (2008a). In a similar vein, McQuarrie (2014) applies a Darwinian perspective to journal publication in the marketing, advertising, and consumer behavior disciplines.

Source of advertisements

GH = Good Housekeeping, LHJ = Ladies Home Journal, SEP = Saturday Evening Post

Figure 0.1	*GH*, 11/2014
Figure 2.1	end matter, Henry V. Poor, *History of the Railroads*, original 1859
Figure 2.2	end matter, Poor 1859
Figure 2.3	end matter, *Poor's Manual of 1888*
Figure 2.4	*Cosmopolitan*, 7/1895
Figure 2.5	*LHJ*, 8/1894
Figure 2.6	*LHJ*, 7/1898
Figure 2.7	*LHJ*, 12/1907
Figure 2.8	*LHJ*, 12/1907
Figure 2.9	*SEP*, 9/9/1905
Figure 2.10	*SEP*, 12/17/1910
Figure 2.11	*LHJ*, 12/1907
Figure 2.12	*LHJ*, 9/1908
Figure 2.13	*SEP*, 12/17/1910
Figure 2.14	*LHJ*, 12/1907
Figure 2.15	*LHJ* 12/1907
Figure 2.16	*LHJ*, 12/1907
Figure 2.17	*LHJ*, 7/1921
Figure 2.18	*LHJ*, 2/1923
Figure 2.19	*LHJ*, 7/1921
Figure 2.20	*LHJ*, 7/1921
Figure 2.21	*LHJ*, 7/1921
Figure 2.22	*LHJ*, 7/1921
Figure 2.23	*LHJ*, 7/1927
Figure 2.24	*LHJ*, 6/1926
Figure 2.25	*GH*, 8/1954
Figure 2.26	*GH*, 5/1951
Figure 2.27	*LHJ*, 4/1956
Figure 2.28	*LHJ*, 5/1954
Figure 2.29	*GH*, 5/1951

Figure 2.30   *GH*, 2/1952
Figure 2.31   *LHJ*, 5/1952
Figure 2.32   *LHJ*, 5/1954
Figure 2.33   *LHJ*, 4/1956
Figure 2.34   *GH*, 2/1952
Figure 2.35   *LHJ*, 5/1952
Figure 2.36   *LHJ*, 4/1956
Figure 2.37   *LHJ*, 5/1954
Figure 2.38   *LHJ*, 4/1956
Figure 2.39   *Money*, 6/1980
Figure 2.40   *GH*, 10/1987
Figure 2.41   *GH*, 10/1987
Figure 2.42   *GH*, 4/1981
Figure 2.43   *GH*, 4/1981
Figure 2.44   *GH*, 11/1984
Figure 6.1   *Cooking Light*, 7/2015
Figure 6.2   *GH*, 7/2015
Figure E.1   *GH*, 4/1981

Companion Website Figures

Figure WA.1   *LHJ*, 9/1908
Figure WA.2   *LHJ*, 2/1923
Figure WA.3   *LHJ*, 2/1923
Figure WA.4   *LHJ*, 2/1923
Figure WA.5   *LHJ*, 6/1926
Figure WA.6   *GH*, 2/1952
Figure WA.7   *LHJ*, 4/1956
Figure WA.8   *LHJ*, 5/1954
Figure WA.9   *LHJ*, 4/1956
Figure WA10   *LHJ*, 5/1954
Figure WA.11   *LHJ*, 5/1952
Figure WA.12   *LHJ*, 4/1956
Figure WA.13   *GH*, 8/1954
Figure WA.14   *GH*, 10/1987
Figure WA.15   *GH*, 4/1981
Figure WA.16   *GH*, 4/1981
Figure WA.17   *GH*, 10/1987
Figure WA.18   *GH*, 11/1984
Figure WA.19   *GH*, 4/1981
Figure WA.20   *GH*, 10/1987

References

Aaker, David A. (2009), *Managing Brand Equity*, New York: Simon & Schuster.

Aaker, David A. and Donald E. Bruzzone (1985), "Causes of Irritation in Advertising," *Journal of Marketing*, 49 (2), 47–57.

Aaker, Jennifer L. (1997), "Dimensions of Brand Personality," *Journal of Marketing Research*, 34 (August), 347–356.

Aggarwal, Pankaj and Ann L. McGill (2012), "When Brands Seem Human, Do Humans Act Like Brands? Automatic Behavioral Priming Effects of Brand Anthropomorphism," *Journal of Consumer Research*, 39 (2), 307–323.

Armstrong, J. Scott (2010), *Persuasive Advertising: Evidence-Based Principles*, New York: Palgrave Macmillan.

Baker, Stephen (1961), *Visual Persuasion: The Effect of Pictures on the Subconscious*, New York: McGraw-Hill.

Belk, Russell W. and Richard W. Pollay (1985), "Images of Ourselves: The Good Life in Twentieth Century Advertising," *Journal of Consumer Research*, 11 (March), 887–897.

Bender, John B. and David E. Wellbery (1990), *The Ends of Rhetoric: History, Theory, and Practice*, Stanford, CA: Stanford University Press.

Berlyne, Daniel E. (1971), *Aesthetics and Psychobiology*, East Norwalk, CT: Appleton-Century-Crofts.

Blackwell, Lewis (2004), *20th Century Type*, New Haven, CT: Yale University Press.

Bloch, Peter H., Frederic F. Brunel, and Todd J. Arnold (2003), "Individual Differences in the Centrality of Visual Product Aesthetics: Concept and Measurement," *Journal of Consumer Research*, 29 (March), 551–565.

Bottomley, Paul A. and John R. Doyle (2006), "The Interactive Effects of Colors and Products on Perceptions of Brand Logo Appropriateness," *Marketing Theory*, 6 (1), 63–83.

Brakus, Josko, Bernd H. Schmidt, and Lia Zarantonello (2009), "Brand Experience: What Is It? How Is It Measured? Does It Affect Loyalty?," *Journal of Marketing*, 73 (May), 52–68.

Brown, Stephen (2010), "Where the Wild Brands Are: Some Thoughts on Anthropomorphic Marketing," *Marketing Review*, 10 (3), 209–224.

Brown, Stephen and Sharon Ponsonby-McCabe (2014), *Brand Mascots and Other Marketing Animals*, New York: Routledge.

Calder, Bobby J., Lynn W. Phillips, and Alice M. Tybout (1981), "Designing Research for Application," *Journal of Consumer Research*, 8 (September), 197–207.

Callcott, Margaret and Barbara J. Phillips (1996), "Elves Make Good Cookies: Creating Likable Spokes-Character Advertising," *Journal of Advertising Research*, 36 (5), 73–79.

Campbell, Colin (1987), *The Romantic Ethic and the Spirit of Modern Consumerism*, Oxford: Blackwell.

Cartwright, H.M. and Robert MacKay (1956), *Rotogravure: A Survey of European and American Methods*, Lyndon, KY: MacKay Publishing.

Chamblee, Robert and Dennis M. Sandler (1992), "Business-to-Business Advertising: Which Layout Style Works Best?," *Journal of Advertising Research*, November–December, 39–47.

Chandler, Alfred D. (1977), *The Visible Hand: The Managerial Revolution in American Business*, Cambridge, MA: Belknap Press.

Childers, Terry L. and Jeffrey Jass (2002), "All Dressed Up With Something to Say: Effects of Typeface Semantic Associations on Brand Perceptions and Consumer Memory," *Journal of Consumer Psychology*, 12 (2), 93–106.

Cohen, Dorothy (1986), "Trademark Strategy," *Journal of Marketing*, 50 (January), 61–74.

Cohen, Jacob and Patricia Cohen (1983), *Applied Multiple Regression/ Correlation Analysis For The Behavioral Sciences*, Hillsdale, NJ: Lawrence Erlbaum Associates.

Corbett, Edward P.J. (1990), *Classical Rhetoric for the Modern Student*, 3rd edn, New York: Oxford University Press.

Deighton, John, Daniel Romer, and Josh McQueen (1989), "Using Drama to Persuade," *Journal of Consumer Research*, 16 (December), 335–343.

Delbaere, Marjorie, Edward F. McQuarrie, and Barbara J. Phillips (2011), "Personification in Advertising: Using a Visual Metaphor to Trigger Anthropomorphism," *Journal of Advertising*, 40 (1), 119–129.

Dotz, Warren and Masud Husain (2003), *Meet Mr Product: The Art of the Advertising Character*, San Francisco, CA: Chronicle Books.

Dotz, Warren and Masud Husain (2015), *Meet Mr Product: The Graphic Art of the Advertising Character*, San Rafael, CA: Insight Editions.

Doyle, John R. and Paul A. Bottomley (2006), "Dressed for the Occasion: Font–Product Congruity in the Perception of Logotype," *Journal of Consumer Psychology*, 16 (2), 112.

Doyle, John R. and Paul A. Bottomley (2011), "Mixed Messages in Brand

Names: Separating Impacts of Letter Shape from Sound Symbolism," *Psychology and Marketing*, 28 (7), 749.

Elliot, Andrew J. and Markus A. Maier (2014), "Color Psychology: Effects of Perceiving Color on Psychological Functioning in Humans," *Annual Review of Psychology*, 65, 95–120.

Ewen, Stuart (1988), *All Consuming Images*, New York: Basic Books.

Feasley, Florence G. and Elnora W. Stuart (1987), "Magazine Advertising Layout and Design: 1932–1982," *Journal of Advertising*, 16 (2), 20–25.

Fennell, Geraldine (1978), "Consumers' Perceptions of the Product-Use Situation," *Journal of Marketing*, 42 (2), 38–47.

Finn, Adam (1988), "Print Ad Recognition Readership Scores: An Information Processing Perspective," *Journal of Marketing Research*, 25 (2), 168–177.

Foucault, Michel (1970), *The Order of Things*, New York: Random House.

Fournier, Susan (1998), "Consumers and Their Brands: Developing Relationship Theory in Consumer Research," *Journal of Consumer Research*, 24 (March), 343–373.

Fox, Stephen (1984), *The Mirror Makers: A History of American Advertising and Its Creators*, New York: William Morrow.

Frazer, James G. (1922), *The Golden Bough: A Study in Magic and Religion*, London: Macmillan.

Gardner, Burleigh B. and Sidney J. Levy (1955), "The Product and the Brand," *Harvard Business Review*, 33 (2), 33–39.

Garretson, Judith A. and Scot Burton (2005), "The Role of Spokes-Characters as Advertisement and Package Cues in Integrated Marketing Communications," *Journal of Marketing*, 69 (4), 118–132.

Garvey, Ellen Gruber (1996), *The Adman in the Parlor: Magazines and the Gendering of Consumer Culture, 1880s to 1910s*, New York: Oxford University Press.

Gergen, Kenneth J. (1973), "Social Psychology as History," *Journal of Personality and Social Psychology*, 26 (2), 309.

Gerrig, Richard J. (1993), *Experiencing Narrative Worlds*, New Haven, CT: Yale University Press.

Golder, Peter N. (2000), "Historical Method in Marketing Research with New Evidence on Long-Term Market Share Stability," *Journal of Marketing Research*, 37 (2), 156–172.

Golder, Peter N. and Gerard J. Tellis (1993), "Pioneer Advantage: Marketing Logic or Marketing Legend?," *Journal of Marketing Research*, 30 (2), 158–170.

Goodrum, Charles and Helen Dalrymple (1990), *Advertising in America: The First 200 Years*, New York: Harry N. Abrams.

Green, Melanie C. and Timothy C. Brock (2000), "The Role of

Transportation in the Persuasiveness of Public Narratives," *Journal of Personality and Social Psychology*, 79 (5), 701–721.

Hagtvedt, Henrik (2011), "The Impact of Incomplete Typeface Logos on Perceptions of the Firm," *Journal of Marketing*, 75 (4), 86–93.

Hambleton, Ronald (1987), *The Branding of America*, Dublin, NH: Yankee Publishing.

Henderson, Pamela W. and Joseph A. Cote (1998), "Guidelines for Selecting or Modifying Logos," *Journal of Marketing*, 62 (2), 14–30.

Henderson, Pamela W., Joan L. Geise, and Joseph A. Cote (2004), "Impression Management Using Typeface Design," *Journal of Marketing*, 68 (4), 60–72.

Hendon, D.W. (1973), "How Mechanical Factors Affect Ad Perception," *Journal of Advertising Research*, 13, 39–45.

Hill, Daniel Delis (2002), *Advertising to the American Woman: 1900–1999*, Columbus, OH: Ohio State University Press.

Holt, Douglas B. (2004), *How Brands Become Icons: The Principles of Cultural Branding*, Boston, MA: Harvard Business School Press.

Hornung, Clarence P. (1956a), *Handbook of Early Advertising Art Mainly from American Sources, Typographical Volume*, 3rd edn, New York: Dover Books.

Hornung, Clarence P. (1956b), *Handbook of Early Advertising Art Mainly from American Sources, Pictorial Volume*, 3rd edn, New York: Dover Books.

Hornung, Clarence P. and Fridolf Johnson (1976), *200 Years of American Graphic Art*, New York: George Braziller.

Hotchkiss, George Burton and Richard B. Franken (1923), *The Leadership of Advertised Brands*, Garden City, NJ: Doubleday Page.

Hunt, Shelby D. (2003), *Controversy in Marketing Theory*, Armonk, NY: M.E. Sharpe.

Hunt, Shelby D. and Robert M. Morgan (1995), "The Comparative Advantage Theory of Competition," *Journal of Marketing*, 59 (2), 1–15.

Huss, Richard E. (1973), *The Development of Printers' Mechanical Typesetting Methods, 1822–1925*, Charlottesville, VA: University Press of Virginia.

Janiszewski, Chris and Tom Meyvis (2001), "Effects of Brand Logo Complexity, Repetition, and Spacing on Processing Fluency and Judgment," *Journal of Consumer Research*, 28 (1), 18.

Jiang, Yuwei, Gerald J. Gorn, Maria Galli, and Amitava Chattopadhyay (2015), "Does Your Company Have the Right Logo? How and Why Circular- and Angular-Logo Shapes Influence Brand Attribute Judgments," *Journal of Consumer Research*, 42 (5), 709–726.

Jones, John Phillip and Joan S. Slater (2003), *What's in a Name? Advertising and the Concept of Brands*, Armonk, NY: M.E. Sharpe.

Jussim, Estelle (1974), *Visual Communication and the Graphic Arts: Photographic Technologies in the 19th Century*, New York: R.R. Bowker.

Kahneman, Daniel (2011), *Thinking, Fast and Slow*, New York: Macmillan.

Keller, Kevin Lane (2003), "Brand Synthesis: The Multidimensionality of Brand Knowledge," *Journal of Consumer Research*, 29 (March), 595–600.

Keller, Kevin Lane (2012), *Strategic Brand Management: Building, Measuring, and Managing Brand Equity*, 4th edn, New York: Prentice-Hall.

Keller, Kevin Lane and Donald R. Lehmann (2006), "Brands and Branding: Research Findings and Future Priorities," *Marketing Science*, 25 (6), 740–759.

Kern-Foxworth, Marilyn (1994), *Aunt Jemima, Uncle Ben, and Rastus: Blacks in Advertising, Yesterday, Today, and Tomorrow*, Westport, CT: Greenwood Press.

Klink, Richard R. (2000), "Creating Brand Names with Meaning: The Use of Sound Symbolism," *Marketing Letters*, 11 (1), 5–20.

Labrecque, Lauren I. and George R. Milne (2012), "Exciting Red and Competent Blue: The Importance of Color in Marketing," *Journal of the Academy of Marketing Science*, 40, 711–729.

Labrecque, Lauren I. and George R. Milne (2013a), "The Marketers' Prismatic Palette: A Review of Color Research and Future Directions," *Psychology and Marketing*, 30, 187–202.

Labrecque, Lauren I. and George R. Milne (2013b), "To Be Or Not To Be Different: Exploration of Norms and Benefits of Color Differentiation in the Marketplace," *Marketing Letters*, 24 (2) http://link.springer.com/journal/11002/24/2/page/1, 165–176.

Lanham, Richard A. (2006), *The Economics of Attention*, Chicago, IL: University of Chicago Press.

Leach, William (1993), *Land of Desire: Merchants, Power, and the Rise of a New American Culture*, New York: Vintage Books.

Lears, Jackson (1994), *Fables of Abundance: A Cultural History of Advertising in America*, New York: Basic Books.

Leiss, William, Stephen Kline, Sut Jhally and Jacqueline Botterill (2005 [1986]), *Social Communication in Advertising: Consumption in the Mediated Marketplace*, 3rd edn, New York: Routledge.

Leymore, Varda Langholz (1975), *Hidden Myth: Structure and Symbolism in Advertising*, New York: Harcourt.

Lovelock, Christopher H. (1983), "Classifying Services to Gain Strategic Marketing Insights," *Journal of Marketing*, 47 (3), 9–20.

Low, George S. and Ronald A. Fullerton (1994), "Brands, Brand Management, and the Brand Manager System: A Critical-Historical Evaluation," *Journal of Marketing Research*, 31 (May), 173–190.

Lowrey, Tina M. and Larry J. Shrum (2007), "Phonetic Symbolism and Brand Name Preference," *Journal of Consumer Research*, 34 (3), 406–414.

Lynch, John G. (1982), "On the External Validity of Experiments in Consumer Research," *Journal of Consumer Research*, 9 (December), 225–239.

Manring, Maurice M. (1998), *Slave in a Box: The Strange Career of Aunt Jemima*, Camden, NJ: Rutgers University Press.

Marchand, Roland (1985), *Advertising and the American Dream: Making Way for Modernity, 1920–1940*, Los Angeles, CA: University of California Press.

McCracken, Grant (1986), "Culture and Consumption: A Theoretical Account of the Structure and Movement of the Cultural Meaning of Consumer Goods," *Journal of Consumer Research*, 13 (June), 71–84.

McQuarrie, Edward F. (1998), "Have Laboratory Experiments Become Detached from Advertiser Goals? A Meta-Analysis," *Journal of Advertising Research*, 38 (6), 15–16.

McQuarrie, Edward F. (2004), "Integration of Construct and External Validity by Means of Proximal Similarity: Implications for Laboratory Experiments in Marketing," *Journal of Business Research*, 57 (2), 142–153.

McQuarrie, Edward F. (2008a), "A Visit to the Rhetorician's Workbench: Developing a Toolkit for Differentiating Advertising Style," in Edward F. McQuarrie and Barbara J. Phillips (eds), *Go Figure! New Directions in Advertising Rhetoric*, Armonk, NY: M.E. Sharpe, pp. 257–266.

McQuarrie, Edward F. (2008b), "Differentiating the Pictorial Element in Advertising," in Michel Wiedel and Rik Pieters (eds), *Visual Marketing: From Attention to Action*, Hillsdale, NJ: Lawrence J. Erlbaum, pp. 91–112.

McQuarrie, Edward F. (2014), "Threats to the Scientific Status of Experimental Consumer Psychology: A Darwinian Perspective," *Marketing Theory*, 14 (4), 477–494.

McQuarrie, Edward F. (2015), *The New Consumer Online: A Sociology of Taste, Audience, and Publics*, Cheltenham, UK and Northampton, MA, USA: Edward Elgar Publishing.

McQuarrie, Edward F. and David Glen Mick (1992), "On Resonance: A Critical Pluralistic Inquiry into Advertising Rhetoric," *Journal of Consumer Research*, 19 (3), 180–197.

McQuarrie, Edward F. and David Glen Mick (1996), "Figures of Rhetoric in Advertising Language," *Journal of Consumer Research*, 22 (March), 424–438.

McQuarrie, Edward F. and David Glen Mick (1999), "Visual Rhetoric in Advertising: Text-Interpretive, Experimental, and Reader-Response Analyses," *Journal of Consumer Research*, 26 (June), 37–54.

McQuarrie, Edward F. and David Glen Mick (2003), "Visual and Verbal Rhetorical Figures Under Directed Processing Versus Incidental Exposure to Advertising," *Journal of Consumer Research*, 29 (4), 579–587.

McQuarrie, Edward F. and David Glen Mick (2009), "A Laboratory Study of the Effect of Verbal Rhetoric Versus Repetition When Consumers Are Not Directed to Process Advertising," *International Journal of Advertising*, 28 (2), 287–312.

McQuarrie, Edward F. and Barbara J. Phillips (2005), "Indirect Persuasion in Advertising: How Consumers Process Metaphors Presented in Pictures and Words," *Journal of Advertising*, 34 (Summer), 7–20.

McQuarrie, Edward F. and Barbara J. Phillips (2008a), "It's Not Your Father's Magazine Ad: Magnitude and Direction of Recent Changes in Advertising Style," *Journal of Advertising*, 37 (3), 95–105.

McQuarrie, Edward F. and Barbara J. Phillips (2008b), *Go Figure! New Directions in Advertising Rhetoric*, Armonk, NY: M.E. Sharpe.

McQuarrie, Edward F. and Barbara J. Phillips (2012), "A Rhetorical Theory of the Advertisement," in Shelly Rodgers and Esther Thorson (eds), *Advertising Theory*, New York: Routledge, pp. 227–240.

McQuarrie, Edward F., Barbara J. Phillips, and Steven Andrews (2012), "How Relevant Is Marketing Scholarship? A Case History with a Prediction," *Advances in Consumer Research*, 40, 342–348.

McQuarrie, Edward F. and Meir Statman (2015), "How Investors Became Consumers," *Journal of Macromarketing*, 0276146715595671.

Messaris, Paul (1997), *Visual Persuasion: The Role of Images in Advertising*, Thousand Oaks, CA: Sage Publications.

Mick, David Glen (1986), "Consumer Research and Semiotics: Exploring the Morphology of Signs, Symbols, and Significance," *Journal of Consumer Research*, 13 (2), 196–213.

Mollerup, Per (1997), *Marks of Excellence: History and Taxonomy of Trademarks*. London: Phaidon.

Mook, Douglas G. (1983), "In Defense of External Invalidity," *American Psychologist*, 38 (April), 379–387.

Moran, James (1973), *Printing Presses: History and Development from the 15th Century to Modern Times*, Berkeley, CA: University of California Press.

Morgan, Hal (1986), *Symbols of America*, New York: Penguin Press.

Mott, Frank L. (1957), *A History of American Magazines, Vol. 5: 1885–1905*, Cambridge, MA: Harvard University Press.

Nelson, Roy P. (1981), *The Design of Advertising*, 4th edn, New York: William C. Brown.

Newhall, Beaumont (1982), *The History of Photography*, Boston, MA: Little, Brown.

Nordhielm, Christie L. (2002), "The Influence of Level of Processing on Advertising Repetition Effects," *Journal of Consumer Research*, 29 (3), 371–382.

Norris, James D. (1990), *Advertising and the Transformation of American Society, 1865–1920*, New York: Greenwood Press.

Ohmann, Richard (1996), *Selling Culture: Magazines, Markets, and Class at the Turn of the Century*, New York: Verso.

Open Science Collaboration (2015), "Estimating the Reproducibility of Psychological Science," *Science*, 349 (6251), aac4716.

Orth, Ulrich R. and Keven Malkewitz (2008), "Holistic Package Design and Consumer Brand Impressions," *Journal of Marketing*, 72 (3), 64–81.

Osgood, Charles Egerton, George J. Suci, and Percy H. Tannenbaum (1964), *The Measurement of Meaning*, Champaign, IL: University of Illinois Press.

Parasuraman, Anantharanthan, Valarie A. Zeithaml, and Leonard L. Berry (1985), "A Conceptual Model of Service Quality and Its Implications for Future Research," *Journal of Marketing*, 49 (4), 41–50.

Park, C. Whan, Andreas B. Eisingerich, Gratiana Pol, and Jason Whan Park (2013), "The Role of Brand Logos in Team Performance," *Journal of Business Research*, 66, 180–187.

Pettman, Dominic (2013), *Look at the Bunny: Totem, Taboo, Technology*, London: John Hunt Publishing.

Petty, Richard E. and John T. Cacioppo (1996), "Addressing Disturbing and Disturbed Consumer Behavior: Is It Necessary to Change the Way We Conduct Behavioral Science?," *Journal of Marketing Research*, 33 (February), 1–8.

Petty, Ross D. (2011), "The Co-development of Trademark Law and the Concept of Brand Marketing in the United States before 1946," *Journal of Macromarketing*, 31, 85–100.

Phillips, Barbara J. (1997), "Thinking Into It: Consumer Interpretation of Complex Advertising Images," *Journal of Advertising*, 26 (2), 77–87.

Phillips, Barbara J. and Barbara Gyoerick (1999), "The Cow, the Cook, and the Quaker: Fifty Years of Spokes-Character Advertising," *Journalism and Mass Communication Quarterly*, 76 (4), 713–728.

Phillips, Barbara J. and Edward F. McQuarrie (2002), "The Development,

Change, and Transformation of Rhetorical Style in Magazine Advertisements 1954–1999," *Journal of Advertising*, 31 (4), 1–13.

Phillips, Barbara J. and Edward F. McQuarrie (2004), "Beyond Visual Metaphor: A New Typology of Visual Rhetoric in Advertising," *Marketing Theory*, 4 (1–2), 111–134.

Phillips, Barbara J. and Edward F. McQuarrie (2009), "Impact of Advertising Metaphor on Consumer Belief: Delineating the Contribution of Comparison versus Deviation Factors," *Journal of Advertising*, 38 (1), 49–62.

Phillips, Barbara J. and Edward F. McQuarrie (2010), "Narrative and Persuasion in Fashion Advertising," *Journal of Consumer Research*, 37 (3), 368–392.

Phillips, Barbara J., Edward F. McQuarrie, and W. Glenn Griffin (2014a), "How Visual Brand Identity Shapes Consumer Response," *Psychology and Marketing*, 31 (3), 225–236.

Phillips, Barbara J., Edward F. McQuarrie, and W. Glenn Griffin (2014b), "The Face of the Brand: How Art Directors Understand Visual Brand Identity," *Journal of Advertising*, 43 (4), 318–332.

Phillips, Barbara J., Jennifer Sedgewick, and Adam Slobodzian (2016), "Spokes-Characters in Print Advertising: An Update and Extension," working paper, University of Saskatchewan.

Pollay, Richard W. (1985), "The Subsidizing Sizzle: A Descriptive History of Print Advertising, 1900–1980," *Journal of Marketing*, 48 (Summer), 24–37.

Pope, Daniel (1983), *The Making of Modern Advertising*, New York: Basic Books.

Porter, Glenn (2006), *The Rise of Big Business 1860–1920*, 3rd edn, New York: Wiley-Blackwell.

Pracejus, John W., G. Douglas Olsen, and Thomas C. O'Guinn (2006), "How Nothing Became Something: White Space, Rhetoric, History, and Meaning," *Journal of Consumer Research*, 33 (1), 82–90.

Presbrey, Frank Spencer (1929), *The History and Development of Advertising*, New York: Doubleday.

Rodgers, Shelly and Esther Thorson (2012), *Advertising Theory*, New York: Routledge.

Rossiter, John R. and Larry Percy (1997), *Advertising Communication and Promotion Management*, New York: McGraw-Hill.

Rossiter, John, Larry Percy, and Ron Donovan (1991), "A Better Advertising Planning Grid," *Journal of Advertising Research*, 31 (5), 11–21.

Rowsome, Frank (1959), *They Laughed When I Sat Down: An Informal History of Advertising in Words and Pictures*, New York: Bonanza Books.

Scanlon, Jennifer (1995), *Inarticulate Longings: The Ladies' Home Journal,*

Gender, and the Promises of Consumer Culture, New York: Psychology Press.

Schmitt, Bernd and Alex Simonson (1997), *Marketing Aesthetics: The Strategic Management of Brands, Identity, and Image*, New York: Free Press.

Scott, Linda M. (1994a), "Images in Advertising: The Need for a Theory of Visual Rhetoric," *Journal of Consumer Research*, 21 (September), 252–273.

Scott, Linda M. (1994b), "The Bridge from Text to Mind: Adapting Reader-Response Theory to Consumer Research," *Journal of Consumer Research*, 21 (December), 461–480.

Scott, Linda M. and Rajeev Batra (2003), *Persuasive Imagery: A Consumer Response Perspective*, Mahwah, NJ: Lawrence Erlbaum.

Scott, Linda M. and Patrick Vargas (2007), "Writing with Pictures: Toward a Unifying Theory of Consumer Response to Images," *Journal of Consumer Research*, 34 (3), 341–356.

Sears, David O. (1986), "College Sophomores in the Laboratory: Influences of a Narrow Database on Social Psychology's View of Human Nature," *Journal of Personality and Social Psychology*, 51 (3), 515–530.

Sewell, William H. (2005), *Logics of History: Social Theory and Social Transformation*, Chicago, IL: University of Chicago Press.

Sobieszek, Robert A. (1988), *The Art of Persuasion: A History of Advertising Photography*, New York: Harry N. Abrams.

Solomon, Michael R. (2016), *Consumer Behavior: Buying, Having, and Being*, 12th edn, New York: Pearson.

Sperber, Dan and Deidre Wilson (1986), *Relevance: Communication and Cognition*, Oxford: Blackwell.

St James, Yannik, Jay M. Handelman, and Shirley F. Taylor (2011), "Magical Thinking and Consumer Coping," *Journal of Consumer Research*, 38 (4), 632–649.

Stern, Barbara B. (1994), "Classical and Vignette Television Advertising Dramas: Structural Models, Formal Analysis, and Consumer Effects," *Journal of Consumer Research*, 20 (March), 601–615.

Sternthal, Brian, Alice M. Tybout, and Bobby J. Calder (1994), "Experimental Design: Generalization and Theoretical Explanation," in Richard P. Bagozzi (ed.), *Principles of Marketing Research*, New York: Basil Blackwell, pp. 195–220.

Stove, David (2001), *Scientific Irrationalism*, London: Transaction Publishers.

Strasser, Susan (1989), *Satisfaction Guaranteed: The Making of the American Mass Market*, Washington, DC: Smithsonian Books.

Szarkowski, John (1989), *Photography Until Now*, New York: Museum of Modern Art.

Taylor, Ronald E. (1999), "A Six Segment Message Strategy Wheel," *Journal of Advertising Research*, November–December, 7–18.

Tedlow, Richard S. (1990), *New and Improved: The Story of Mass-Marketing in America*, New York: Basic Books.

Umiker-Sebeok, Jean (1987), *Marketing and Semiotics: New Directions in the Study of Signs for Sale*, New York: Walter de Gruyter.

Van der Lans, Ralf, et al. (2009), "Cross-National Logo Evaluation Analysis: An Individual-Level Approach," *Marketing Science*, 28 (5), 968–985.

Van der Vlugt, Ron (2012), *Life Histories of 100 Famous Logos*, Amsterdam: BIS Publishers.

Wedel, Michel and Rik Pieters (2008), *Visual Marketing: From Attention to Action*, New York: Taylor.

Wells, William D. (1993), "Discovery-Oriented Consumer Research," *Journal of Consumer Research*, 19 (March), 489–504.

Wheeler, Alina (2013), *Designing Brand Identity: An Essential Guide for the Whole Branding Team*, Hoboken, NJ: Wiley.

Williamson, Judith (1981), *Decoding Advertisements: Ideology and Meaning in Advertising*, London: Marion Boyers.

Wood, James Playsted (1958), *The Story of Advertising*, New York: Ronald Press Company.

Yorkston, Eric and Geeta Menon (2004), "A Sound Idea: Phonetic Effects of Brand Names on Consumer Judgments," *Journal of Consumer Research*, 31 (1), 43–51.

Author notes

Edward F. McQuarrie is Professor Emeritus at the Leavey School of Business, Santa Clara University, USA. During his 30 years at Santa Clara, he taught undergraduate and MBA courses in advertising, market research, and marketing strategy. McQuarrie received his PhD in social psychology from the University of Cincinnati in 1985 and his BA in psychology and literature from the Evergreen State College in 1976.

He has published in three broad areas: (1) consumer response to advertising, with a focus on rhetoric and narrative; (2) qualitative research techniques and market research appropriate to technology products; and (3) emergent online consumer behaviors. He has written three books: *Customer Visits: Building a Better Market Focus*, now in its third edition; *The Market Research Toolbox: A Concise Guide for Beginners*, now in its fourth edition; and most recently, *The New Consumer Online: A Sociology of Taste, Audience, and Publics*. His papers have appeared in the *Journal of Consumer Research, Journal of Consumer Psychology, Journal of Advertising, Journal of Advertising Research, Journal of Macromarketing*, and elsewhere. In 2014 he received the Best Article award from *Marketing Insights*.

Barbara J. Phillips is Rawlco Scholar in Advertising and Professor of Marketing at the University of Saskatchewan, Canada, where she teaches courses on integrated marketing communications and branding. She received her MA and PhD in advertising from the University of Texas at Austin, USA; her undergraduate degree in marketing is from the University of Manitoba, Canada.

Her research focuses on visual images in advertising and their influence on consumer response. Her papers have appeared in the *Journal of Consumer Research, Journal of Advertising, Journal of Advertising Research, International Journal of Advertising, Marketing Theory*, and elsewhere. With McQuarrie she edited the book, *Go Figure! New Directions in Advertising Rhetoric*. She has received the Best Article award from the *Journal of Advertising* twice; in addition, she received the Dunn Award from the University of Illinois, USA for excellence in advertising research.

General index

rebranding 129, 138–139, 223–224
resource-advantage (R-A) theory
    125–128
retailer brand marks
    characteristic examples 118
    clothing 193
    comparative distribution 117
    difficulty securing brand
        identification 127
    discussion 115–120
    findings 114
    incidence of colors in 191–192
    proposition 113–114
    rationalization 140–141
rhetoric
    and assumptions made by
        rhetorician 147
    classical
        applied to persuasion 94–95
        applied to visual branding 3–4,
            11–12
        fundamental assumption of 23
        limits of 198–199
        and personification 170–171
        and scientific thinking about
            causation 98–99
    historians of 50
    vs. semiotics 6, 8–9, 217
    of visual branding vs. visual rhetoric
        of advertising 196–197
rhetorical
    analysis
        of brand advertising 11–12
        of brand marks 93–96, 99, 105
        first task of 183
        of Gillette ad 213–218
        pictorial content refractory to
            6–7
        vs. psychological analysis 1–5
    challenges 10, 183
    critique of psychological approaches
        to brand marks 130–131
    devices
        harbor for 197
        migrating to pictures 30
        spokes-characters as 170, 180–181
    figures
        artful deviation as main property
            of 234
        identifying 238

typology of visual 211
    verbal 210
perspective
    and personification 169–171,
        178
    vs. psychological perspective on
        type 145–154
    as ruthlessly pragmatic 145
practice, change in 22–23, 31
strategy, hosiery ad 42, 44–45
structure of brand mark tables 116,
    118, 122, 125
typology of pictures 197, 210–211
rhetoricians
    and ad persuasion 226
    ancient and medieval 13
    approach to Tide ad 1
    as assuming existence of small
        number of discrete choices
        145–146
    on beginning of advertising 21
    contributions to color 183–184
    drawing on cognitive psychology
        175–176
    and evolutionary biology 149,
        236
    as offended by polyglot 98
    perceptions of advertisers and brand
        managers 2–3
    perceptions of consumers 2
    and pictures 203, 217
    problematic predilections for 150
    proceedings as to typeface 148–149,
        151–153, 160
    respecting limits of their discipline
        11
    seeing advantage to studying brands
        11–12, 24
    as seeking available means of
        persuasion 130, 147, 175, 199
    as seldom enthused about yes–no
        distinctions 94
    sole care of 23, 215
    and stand-alone graphic designs 105,
        107
    and technology 30, 50
    universalist assumptions made by
        147
    and visual interpretation 215, 217
Rowsome, F. 87, 230–231

Index of brands, advertisers, and spokes-characters